IBM® Lotus® Symphony For Dummies®

Y0-CCY-811

Lotus Symphony Compared to Other Suites

Suite Name	Word Processor	Spreadsheet	Presentation	Web Browser	E-Mail	Database	Adobe PDF Support	Other	Cost
Lotus Symphony	✔	✔	✔	✔			✔		Free
Microsoft Office	✔	✔	✔		✔	✔	✔	Multiple suites	$499
Microsoft Works	✔	✔						Sometimes included free with new PC purchases	$225
Corel WordPerfect Office	✔	✔	✔		✔	✔	✔	Includes other tools	$149
Google Docs	✔	✔	✔		✔		✔	Online only	Free
Zoho Office Suite	✔	✔	✔		✔		✔	Online only	Free
ThinkFree Desktop	✔	✔	✔				✔		Free
OpenOffice.org	✔	✔	✔		✔	✔	✔		Free

Lotus Symphony Help and Support

- **Lotus Symphony Support Site:** `http://symphony.lotus.com/software/lotus/symphony/index.jspa?search_type=forum`
- **Lotus Symphony Have a Question Site:** `http://symphony.lotus.com/software/lotus/symphony/supportForum.jspa?search_type=forum&forumID=41`
- **Lotus Symphony Documents Forum:** `http://symphony.lotus.com/software/lotus/symphony/supportCategory.jspa?categoryID=2`
- **Lotus Symphony Buzz:** `http://symphony.lotus.com/software/lotus/symphony/buzz.jspa`

For Dummies: Bestselling Book Series for Beginners

IBM® Lotus® Symphony™ For Dummies®

Cheat Sheet

Lotus Symphony Operator Reference

Lotus Symphony includes operators that specify calculation types being performed on items in a formula. For example, the + operator enables you to combine two values or expressions. Two types of operators are available:

- *Comparison operators* enable you to compare two values or expressions and return TRUE or FALSE.
- *Arithmetic operators* enable you to perform some type of arithmetic operation on two values in a formula. The results return as numeric values.

AND Operator (Comparison)

Combines two values or expressions in a formula.

+ Operator (Arithmetic)

Combines two expressions or values in a formula.

Eqv Operator (Comparison)

Enables you to calculate the equivalence of two expressions.

Imp Operator (Comparison)

Enables you to perform a logical implication on two expressions.

− Operator (Arithmetic)

Subtracts two expressions or values in a formula.

/ Operator (Arithmetic)

Divides two expressions or values in a formula.

Mod Operator (Comparison)

Enables you to get a return of the integer remainder of a division calculation.

• Operator (Arithmetic)

Multiplies two expressions or values in a formula.

^ Operator (Arithmetic)

Enables you to raise a value to a specific power.

Not Operator (Comparison)

Enables you to negate an expression by inverting the values.

Or Operator (Comparison)

Enables you to perform a logical OR disjunction on two expressions.

Xor Operator (Comparison)

Enables you to perform a logical Exclusive-Or combination of two expressions.

For Dummies: Bestselling Book Series for Beginners

IBM® Lotus® Symphony™ FOR DUMMIES®

by Rob Tidrow

Foreword by Eric Otchet
Product manager, Lotus Symphony

Wiley Publishing, Inc.

IBM® Lotus® Symphony™ For Dummies®

Published by
Wiley Publishing, Inc.
111 River Street
Hoboken, NJ 07030-5774

www.wiley.com

Copyright © 2008 by Wiley Publishing, Inc., Indianapolis, Indiana

Published by Wiley Publishing, Inc., Indianapolis, Indiana

Published simultaneously in Canada

For general information on our other products and services, please contact our Customer Care Department within the U.S. at 800-762-2974, outside the U.S. at 317-572-3993, or fax 317-572-4002.

For technical support, please visit www.wiley.com/techsupport.

Wiley also publishes its books in a variety of electronic formats. Some content that appears in print may not be available in electronic books.

Library of Congress Control Number: 2008931636

ISBN: 978-0-470-29079-8

Manufactured in the United States of America

10 9 8 7 6 5 4 3 2 1

WILEY

About the Author

Rob Tidrow has worked in the technology industry for the past 15 years. Rob has authored or co-authored over 30 books on a wide variety of computer and technical topics, including Microsoft Windows Vista, Wireless Networking technologies, Microsoft Windows XP, Microsoft Outlook, Windows 2003 Server, and Microsoft Internet Information Server. His most current work is *Teach Yourself Visually Microsoft Vista* (Wiley). He lives in Centerville, Indiana, with his wife, Tammy, and their two sons, Adam and Wesley. You can reach him at robtidrow@yahoo.com.

Author's Acknowledgments

I wish to thank Eric Otchet, Product Manager, WPLC, IBM Software Group for the resources, review of the initial proposal and outline, and expert advice on this book. His guidance was invaluable. I wish also to thank the following people for their outstanding commitment to excellence on this book: Greg Croy, acquisitions editor; Christopher Morris, project editor; Heidi Unger and Jen Riggs, copyeditors; John Head, technical editor; Carole McClendon, literary agent; and the production crew. I would also like to thank my wife, Tammy, and my sons, Adam and Wesley, for continuing to give me encouragement and motivation to finish.

Publisher's Acknowledgments

We're proud of this book; please send us your comments through our online registration form located at www.dummies.com/register/.

Some of the people who helped bring this book to market include the following:

Acquisitions, Editorial, and Media Development

Senior Project Editor: Christopher Morris

Executive Editor: Gregory Croy

Copy Editor: Heidi Unger

Technical Editor: John Head

Editorial Manager: Kevin Kirschner

Media Development Project Manager: Laura Moss-Hollister

Media Development Assistant Producer: Angela Denny

Editorial Assistant: Amanda Foxworth

Sr. Editorial Assistant: Cherie Case

Cartoons: Rich Tennant (www.the5thwave.com)

Composition Services

Project Coordinator: Katherine Key

Layout and Graphics: Reuben W. Davis, Melissa K. Jester, Christine Williams

Proofreader: Melanie Hoffman

Indexer: Sharon Shock

Publishing and Editorial for Technology Dummies

    Richard Swadley, Vice President and Executive Group Publisher

    Andy Cummings, Vice President and Publisher

    Mary Bednarek, Executive Acquisitions Director

    Mary C. Corder, Editorial Director

Publishing for Consumer Dummies

    Diane Graves Steele, Vice President and Publisher

    Joyce Pepple, Acquisitions Director

Composition Services

    Gerry Fahey, Vice President of Production Services

    Debbie Stailey, Director of Composition Services

Contents at a Glance

Foreword ....*xix*

Introduction 1

Part I: Introducing IBM Lotus Symphony 7
Chapter 1: Starting IBM Lotus Symphony 9
Chapter 2: Switching to IBM Lotus Symphony..25
Chapter 3: Getting Help from Lotus Symphony.......................................37

Part II: Using IBM Lotus Symphony Documents — the Word Processor Application 51
Chapter 4: Creating a Document..53
Chapter 5: Formatting for Style 77
Chapter 6: Designing Complex Documents 105
Chapter 7: Working with Other Document Types 129

Part III: Using IBM Lotus Symphony Spreadsheets — the Spreadsheet Application 139
Chapter 8: Creating a Spreadsheet 141
Chapter 9: At Home on the Range...165
Chapter 10: Printing Spreadsheets...175
Chapter 11: Adding Spice to Your Spreadsheets 187
Chapter 12: Making Calculations 211

Part IV: Using IBM Lotus Symphony Presentations — the Presentation Application 229
Chapter 13: Creating a Presentation 231
Chapter 14: Modifying a Presentation..259
Chapter 15: Making Presentations Picture-Perfect....................................273
Chapter 16: Animating for a Purpose 283
Chapter 17: Creating Web Pages 297
Chapter 18: Presenting a Screen Show..313

Part V: The Part of Tens 327
Chapter 19: Ten Reasons To Use IBM Lotus Symphony...................................329
Chapter 20: Ten Places to Look for Support for Lotus Symphony.......................333

Part VI: Appendixes 337

Appendix A: Installing IBM Lotus Symphony 339

Appendix B: Function Reference..347

Appendix C: About the CD 355

Index 359

Table of Contents

Foreword...*xix*

Introduction 1

About This Book 1
Foolish Assumptions...2
Conventions Used in This Book...2
What You Don't Have to Read..2
How This Book Is Organized 2
    Part I: Introducing IBM Lotus Symphony..............................3
    Part II: Using IBM Lotus Symphony Documents —
       the Word Processor Application..................................3
    Part III: Using IBM Lotus Symphony Spreadsheets —
       the Spreadsheet Application 3
    Part IV: Using IBM Lotus Symphony Presentations —
       the Presentation Application....................................3
    Part V: The Part of Tens..4
    Part VI: Appendixes 4
Icons Used in This Book 4
Where to Go from Here...5

Part 1: Introducing IBM Lotus Symphony 7

Chapter 1: Starting IBM Lotus Symphony 9
Starting Lotus Symphony 9
Getting to Know the Lotus Symphony User Interface.................11
    Discovering the Lotus Symphony Documents window 14
    Discovering the Lotus Symphony Presentations window.............16
    Discovering the Lotus Symphony Spreadsheets window.............17
    Discovering the Lotus Web Browser window 19
Using the Symphony Toolbars...20
    Displaying toolbars..21
    Moving toolbars 21
Starting Lotus Symphony When Windows Starts........................22
Shutting Down Lotus Symphony 23

Chapter 2: Switching to IBM Lotus Symphony 25
Understanding Why You Want to Switch 26
    Comparing Lotus Symphony to other suites..........................27
    Understanding the benefits of Lotus Symphony 29
    Understanding Lotus Symphony requirements.......................31

Switching from Microsoft Office Applications 32
    Preparing your computer for Lotus Symphony 32
    Preparing your old documents for Lotus Symphony 33
    Making the switch to Lotus Symphony 36

Chapter 3: Getting Help from Lotus Symphony 37

Browsing the Help Contents 37
Searching for Help Items 42
Using Online Resources for Help 46
Submitting Feedback to IBM 48

Part II: Using IBM Lotus Symphony Documents — the Word Processor Application 51

Chapter 4: Creating a Document 53

Starting Lotus Symphony Documents 53
Creating a Lotus Symphony Documents Document 55
    Creating a blank document 56
    Creating a document using a template 56
    Creating a document from another document 60
Saving Your Documents...61
    Saving in Open Document format 62
    Saving in PDF format 63
    Saving in Word DOC or other formats 64
Entering Content..66
    Typing new text..66
    Embedding graphics and clip art 67
Editing Text 68
    Modifying text manually 68
    Checking your documents for spelling errors 69
Navigating a Document...70
    Using the mouse to move through a document.......................70
    Using the keyboard to move through a document....................71
Viewing Text..72
    Using zoom settings..72
    Turning on/off rulers 72
Outputting Your Documents...73
    Previewing your documents..73
    Printing documents 75
    Saving documents for reuse in other documents....................76

Chapter 5: Formatting for Style 77

Formatting Text 78
    Changing the font..79
    Changing the font size...82
    Changing other text properties...................................84

Lotus Symphony Documents Formatting with Lists..............................87
    Creating a bulleted list...87
    Modifying a bulleted list 88
    Creating a numbered list...89
    Modifying a numbered list 90
Understanding Templates and Styles 90
    Using styles to format documents..91
    Creating new styles..93
    Modifying existing styles 95
    Saving your own templates 95
    Using the Template Organizer 97
Formatting Graphics 99
    Resizing graphics 99
    Positioning graphics...100
    Deleting graphics 102
Using Subscript and Superscript 102
    Making text subscript..103
    Making text superscript 103

Chapter 6: Designing Complex Documents.....................105
Recognizing Complex Documents 105
Creating Tables..106
    Setting up a table 107
    Modifying a table 109
Using Captions for Graphics or Tables.......................................110
    Creating captions..111
    Modifying captions 112
Setting Up Cross-References 113
    Creating cross-references 113
    Updating cross-references...115
    Removing cross-references 115
Inserting Fields...116
Inserting Footnotes 117
    Creating footnotes 117
    Modifying footnotes...119
    Formatting footnotes...119
Inserting Endnotes 121
    Creating endnotes..121
    Modifying endnotes 121
    Formatting endnotes 121
Creating a Table of Contents..122
    Setting up tables of contents..122
    Updating tables of contents 124
    Using tables of contents...124
Creating Indexes 124
    Setting up index entries 125
    Creating indexes 126
    Automating Repetitive Tasks with Macros..................................127

Chapter 7: Working with Other Document Types.................**129**

Understanding the Types of Documents Lotus Symphony
Documents Handles..129
Document files..130
Importing Specific Document Types...131
Working with Microsoft Word files.....................................131
Working with Lotus and IBM word processing files...............134
Working with spreadsheet files in Lotus Symphony
Documents 134

**Part III: Using IBM Lotus Symphony Spreadsheets —
the Spreadsheet Application.. 139**

Chapter 8: Creating a Spreadsheet.............................**141**

Starting Lotus Symphony Spreadsheets......................................141
Starting Lotus Symphony Spreadsheets from a menu..................143
Starting Lotus Symphony Spreadsheets from a
spreadsheet file 143
Starting Lotus Symphony Spreadsheets from a document
attached to an e-mail message 144
Creating a Lotus Symphony Spreadsheets Spreadsheet.......................144
Creating a blank spreadsheet..145
Creating a spreadsheet using a template 145
Creating a spreadsheet from another spreadsheet....................148
Entering Content..150
Cells, rows, and columns 150
Adding data manually...151
Specifying type of data you enter.....................................152
Using fills to enter data 152
Embedding data from other documents..............................154
Navigating the Spreadsheet 156
Moving around with the mouse.......................................157
Moving around with the keyboard....................................157
Selecting Data..158
Selecting a word or number in a cell.................................158
Selecting data in multiple cells 159
Selecting all data 159
Saving Your Spreadsheets..160
Using different file formats 160
Saving in Open Document format......................................160
Working with Files from Other Spreadsheet Applications....................161
Working with Word Processing Files 163

Chapter 9: At Home on the Range **165**

Knowing Your References 165
Using relative references 166
Using absolute references 168
The value of absolute references 169
Understanding Ranges 170
Naming a range 171
Using named ranges in formulas 173

Chapter 10: Printing Spreadsheets **175**

Understanding How Lotus Spreadsheet Prints 175
Using Print Preview 176
Printing an entire spreadsheet 179
Viewing and removing unwanted page breaks 180
Printing non-Lotus Symphony Spreadsheets spreadsheets 181
Setting Up Print Options 181
Configuring page setup options 181
Modifying Lotus Symphony Spreadsheets printer options 185

Chapter 11: Adding Spice to Your Spreadsheets **187**

Adding Charts 188
Creating charts in your spreadsheets 189
Editing charts 192
Modifying the look and feel of charts 193
Changing chart types and styles 197
Adding Backgrounds to Spreadsheets 199
Modifying Border Colors and Sizes 200
Inserting Graphics into Your Spreadsheets 201
Embedding graphics for some pizzazz 201
Modifying position and size of graphics 203
Rotating a graphic 203
Changing a graphic's color and brightness 203
Cropping graphics down to size 205
Creating Spreadsheet Applications 205
Making the application look good 206
Distributing the application 206
Automating repetitive tasks with macros 208

Chapter 12: Making Calculations **211**

Adding Formulas to Spreadsheets 211
Understanding formulas 212
Modifying formulas 214
Working with operators 214

Calculating with dates and times...215
Filtering calculations 216
Working with the Solve Equations tool...................................218
Working with Functions 220
Choosing functions 221
Modifying functions 223
Using nested functions 224
Working with DataPilots 224
Setting up DataPilot tables 224
Filtering DataPilot data 226
Modifying DataPilot tables...227
Outputting DataPilot data...227

Part 1V: Using 1BM Lotus Symphony Presentations — the Presentation Application 229

Chapter 13: Creating a Presentation............................231

Starting Lotus Symphony Presentations 231
Creating a presentation from another presentation 233
Creating a presentation using a template...................................233
Navigating a Presentation..236
Moving around with the mouse 236
Moving around with the keyboard 237
Jumping to a specific page..238
Adding Information to Your Pages 239
Inserting text 239
Adding new pages using Instant Layouts 240
Adding a bulleted or numbered list to a page...........................242
Formatting text with styles...244
Viewing Your Pages..245
Setting zoom options...247
Changing display quality...248
Using Lotus Symphony Presentations Tools 248
Displaying the Guideline Grid 249
Turning on rulers 251
Turning on (or off) snap lines 251
Setting up Instant Corrections..252
Adding Tables to Pages 253
Inserting a table 254
Modifying a table 255
Moving a table 257
Saving Your Presentation 257

Chapter 14: Modifying a Presentation 259

Working with Page Properties 259
Changing page orientation and format 260
Using a different page layout...262

Modifying page margins...262
Selecting a page background...263
Changing Page Order 266
Removing a Page..267
Working with Master Page Designs 268
Viewing the Master Page design 268
Modifying the Master Page design................................268
Creating a New Master Page design 271

Chapter 15: Making Presentations Picture-Perfect..............273

Working with Graphics in Your Presentations 273
Understanding when to use graphics.............................274
Inserting a graphic on a page 275
Moving a graphic 276
Resizing a graphic 277
Removing a graphic 277
Locating new graphics 278
Working with the Eyedropper...278
Creating Drawing Objects...280

Chapter 16: Animating for a Purpose 283

Understanding Lotus Symphony Presentations Animations 283
Using Page Transitions 284
Adding transitions 285
Modifying transitions 287
Removing transitions 288
Inserting Image Animations...289
Creating an image animation...289
Modifying image animation objects 292
Removing image animations...295

Chapter 17: Creating Web Pages................................297

Designing Documents for the Web......................................297
Using appropriate styles for Web pages.......................299
Adding hyperlinks to pages..302
Creating tables for Web pages 303
Adding graphics for Web pages 304
Saving files for the Web..304
Converting Lotus Symphony
Presentations files to Web pages 305
Displaying your Web pages 307
Publishing Your Web Pages 310
Publishing your Web pages to an intranet site................310
Publishing your Web pages to a Web server 311

Chapter 18: Presenting a Screen Show 313

Preparing Your Show for Presentation................................313
Putting the final wraps on a show 314

Knowing what things to look for when finished 314
Rehearsing Your Timings 317
Playing a Screen Show 319
Starting a show from a page 320
Starting a show from the start 321
Zooming while you give a show 322
Ending a show 323
Navigating During a Presentation..323
Moving around with the mouse 324
Moving around with the keyboard 324

Part V: The Part of Tens *327*

Chapter 19: Ten Reasons to Use IBM Lotus Symphony 329

It's Free 329
It Includes an Easy-to-Use Word Processor 329
It Supports Open Source Files and a Wide Range of Others 330
It Supports Microsoft Office Files..330
You Can Use It to Create Powerful Business Analysis Spreadsheets ...330
It Provides Powerful Collaboration Features to Work in Lotus Domino
    Environments 331
It Supports Open Document Format (ODF)....................................331
It Has a Developer's Toolkit 332
It Has a Built-In Web Browser 332
Despite Its Cost, It's Feature-Rich..332

Chapter 20: Ten Places to Look for Support for Lotus Symphony . . .333

Lotus Symphony Home Page 333
Lotus Symphony Support Forums..333
Lotus Symphony Forum: Have a Question 334
Lotus Symphony Forum: General Feedback 334
Lotus Symphony Documents Forum: Issues and Troubleshooting 334
Lotus Symphony Presentations Forum:
    Issues and Troubleshooting 335
Lotus Symphony Spreadsheets Forum:
    Issues and Troubleshooting 335
Lotus Symphony Buzz...336
Lotus Symphony Help...336
Lotus Symphony For Dummies Author Site.....................................336

Part VI: Appendixes 337

Appendix A: Installing IBM Lotus Symphony 339
Understanding System Requirements for IBM Lotus Symphony 339
Acquiring a Copy of the IBM Lotus Symphony Install Program 340
Installing Lotus Symphony 344

Appendix B: Function Reference.............................347
Lotus Symphony Operator Reference...347
Lotus Symphony Function Reference 348

Appendix C: About the CD.................................355
System Requirements 355
Using the CD 356
What You'll Find on the CD 356
    IBM Lotus Symphony.exe 357
    Forum Support Plug-In For IBM Lotus Symphony 357
    Clip Art 357
    Sample Book Files 357
Troubleshooting 358
Customer Care 358

Index 359

Foreword

C hange is always a difficult task. We get used to doing things in the same way and then, when we are asked to use a new tool or to do something different, we tend to resist. Lotus Symphony is an office productivity suite that provides the ability to create documents, spreadsheets, and presentations. I'm sure many of you have used other products that do the same thing, which means you may have to re-learn some things when you switch to Lotus Symphony. This book takes the stress out of learning how to use Symphony. The author takes you through a step-by-step process in each of the three applications, starting with the most basic tasks and then moving into the more complex functions. Each chapter is filled with very useful tips and detailed instructions to help you start using Symphony and minimize your stress. As you get more familiar with Symphony, you will be able to refer to the book for those functions that are seldom used and quickly find the information you need to get your content created. A handy function reference is included, as well as information on how to get support and additional information on Symphony.

I hope you enjoy using this book and Lotus Symphony. I invite you to join our growing user community through our Web site. And don't forget to tell your friends and family about Lotus Symphony.

Eric Otchet

Product Manager, Lotus Symphony, IBM

Introduction

ree!

Okay, now that I have your attention, I can get down to business. Actually, this book shows you how you can get down to business using an extremely powerful, user-friendly, *free* program called IBM Lotus Symphony. That's right. If you're in the market for something reasonably priced, you found the place. Not only do you get a great book to help you understand the program, but you also get a free program while you're at it.

With IBM Lotus Symphony, you get a free word processor, a free spreadsheet program, and a free presentation program. Plus, as an added bonus, you get a Web browser as well, but I'm sure you already have one of those.

Now if only someone would offer me free (or even cheaper) gas. . . .

About This Book

IBM Lotus Symphony For Dummies serves as your no-nonsense guide to using all of the IBM Lotus Symphony applications. I focus on providing the essentials that you need to know to be successful using these applications. In this book, you'll explore the steps for completing many tasks, such as these:

- ✓ Creating IBM Lotus Symphony documents, spreadsheets, and presentations
- ✓ Discovering how to migrate Microsoft Office Word, Microsoft Office Excel, and Microsoft Office PowerPoint files into IBM Lotus Symphony
- ✓ Making sense of Open Document and Open Office applications
- ✓ Creating complex word processing documents, including indexes, tables of contents, and cross-references
- ✓ Tapping into Lotus Symphony Spreadsheets's powerful functions and analytical features
- ✓ Creating image animations for your presentations
- ✓ Designing and saving presentations as Web pages

Foolish Assumptions

In *IBM Lotus Symphony For Dummies,* I don't assume that you have experience with IBM Lotus Symphony applications. However, I do assume that you have some working knowledge of computers and basic experience with Microsoft Windows.

Conventions Used in This Book

Conventions? Well, I can tell you about the conventions at the Javits Center in New York or the Las Vegas Convention Center. But you're probably far more interested in the set of rules that I use in the book. These conventions are as follows:

- ✓ **Italics:** As you read through the book, you'll see that I *italicize* terms that I'm defining.
- ✓ **Bold text** is used to indicate specific commands that you are to perform.
- ✓ **Monospaced font:** Finally, URLs and programming code stand out from normal text with a `monospaced font`.

What You Don't Have to Read

I'm confident that you'll find this book's narrative to be so compelling and thought-provoking that you can't help but digest each and every word. However, you can feel free to avoid a couple of modules in the book, if you like, without missing the information you absolutely need to know:

- ✓ **Text marked with a Technical Stuff icon:** This icon warns you that certain paragraphs provide technical details that are interesting, but not essential.
- ✓ **Sidebars:** You'll discover shaded sidebars popping up here and there throughout the book. These sections provide interesting info, but it isn't directly part of the discussion at hand.

How This Book Is Organized

This book is carved into six parts. The following is a summary of these parts.

Part I: Introducing IBM Lotus Symphony

Before diving into the core applications of IBM Lotus Symphony, you need to learn how to start Lotus Symphony, what to consider when switching from another application suite to Lotus Symphony, and how to get help using IBM Lotus Symphony. You then can jump into the parts that discuss each of the applications.

Part II: Using IBM Lotus Symphony Documents — the Word Processor Application

This part looks at the Lotus Symphony Documents application. It's a word processor. The chapters in this part show how you can create documents, use the Style List to create, use, and modify styles, and design complex documents. If you aren't sure what they are, *complex documents* include tables of contents, indexes, and cross-references.

Part III: Using IBM Lotus Symphony Spreadsheets — the Spreadsheet Application

In Part III, you look at creating and formatting spreadsheets, setting up references and ranges, printing spreadsheets, and more. You also look at setting up your own calculations using formulas you create and using built-in functions provided with Lotus Symphony Spreadsheets.

Part IV: Using IBM Lotus Symphony Presentations — the Presentation Application

Within part IV, you'll look at creating presentations for playing back as slide shows. You can show slide shows on-screen, on a Web site, and via a digital projector. This part describes viewing your pages in different zoom settings, animating page elements, creating image animations, and creating Web pages using Lotus Symphony Presentations.

Part V: The Part of Tens

The part of tens has two chapters. One lists and describes ten (really good) reasons to use IBM Lotus Symphony as opposed to other application suites. The other tells where you can find Lotus Symphony support — for free, even.

Part VI: Appendixes

To finish the book, you can look forward to reading about installing IBM Lotus Symphony (as a matter of fact, you should read this chapter first), using the Function Reference as a reference, and finding out what's on the CD-ROM.

Icons Used in This Book

Just like a legend provides assistance on a road map, so too do icons throughout this book. You'll find these four icons:

The Remember icon indicates a paragraph that's particularly amazing, vital, or significant to the future of the world. Okay, perhaps that's a little overboard, but the icon does show you info that's especially important for your understanding of the Lotus Symphony.

The Tip icon highlights important programming tips that you should take note of.

The Warning icon alerts you to snags and pitfalls that can occur if you aren't careful.

As I mention in the "What You Don't Have to Read" section, the Technical Stuff icon points out technical but nonessential info. These paragraphs are meant to feed that little geek inside everyone.

Where to Go from Here

Now that you've made it this far, you're ready to begin working in IBM Lotus Symphony. Instead of reading the book sequentially, you might find it more helpful to jump to the chapters containing material you need help on first. The following are some suggestions:

✔ To explore IBM Lotus Symphony, turn the page and begin reading Chapter 1.

✔ To discover Lotus Documents, check out Chapter 4.

✔ To learn about Lotus Spreadsheets, skip over to Chapter 8.

✔ To discover Lotus Presentations, check out Chapter 14.

✔ To see what things you should consider before putting on a presentation, read Chapter 19.

Part I
Introducing IBM Lotus Symphony

The 5th Wave   By Rich Tennant

"We should cast a circle, invoke the elements, and direct the energy. If that doesn't work, we'll read the manual."

In this part . . .

You finally made it. You've now entered one of the most unique times of your life. When you make it through to the end of this part, your life will be changed. You'll look back and wonder how life was possible before you read this. Actually, you're just going to find out about IBM Lotus Symphony basics and how to use its help system. Consider yourself warned.

Chapter 1

Starting IBM Lotus Symphony

* *

In This Chapter

▶ Getting familiar with the Lotus Symphony user interface

▶ Exploring the Symphony toolbars

▶ Customizing programs

▶ Shutting down Lotus Symphony

* *

*I*BM Lotus Symphony is more than just a single program. It's a set of three distinct business-class applications that help you perform specific tasks. Each of the three applications is designed to create different types of documents and files, but they work closely with each other to allow you to share information between them. Lotus Symphony also is designed to work with other IBM and IBM Lotus applications, as well as IBM technologies such as their collaboration technologies.

With IBM Lotus Symphony, you get a word processing application, a spreadsheet program, and a presentations program. In addition to these programs, Lotus Symphony also includes a Web browser that enables you to navigate to Web sites and display Internet information.

In this chapter, I show how you can start using Lotus Symphony, including starting each application, using the Lotus Symphony interface, getting acquainted with the Symphony toolbars, customizing different parts of the Lotus Symphony program set, and shutting down Symphony properly.

Starting Lotus Symphony

Unlike other software suites, Lotus Symphony provides access to all of its separate applications from a single point. You start Lotus Symphony and then start the application you want to use. Figure 1-1 shows the initial window you see when you start Lotus Symphony.

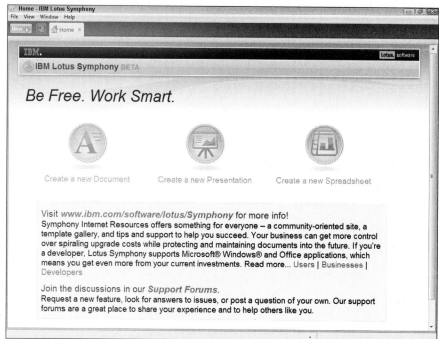

Figure 1-1:
The Lotus
Symphony
home page
window.

To start Lotus Symphony, you use the following steps:

1. **Click the Start button.**

2. **Navigate to the All Programs folder.**

3. **Click IBM Lotus Symphony.**

You can add a shortcut to Lotus Symphony to your desktop or Quick Launch toolbar. (It resides on your Windows task bar, if you have it turned on.) To do this, locate the IBM Lotus Symphony program icon in the All Programs folder, right-click it and drag it to the desktop or Quick Launch toolbar. Release the right mouse button and click Create Shortcuts Here from the pop-up menu that appears. Now you can quickly start Lotus Symphony by clicking the new shortcut.

When Lotus Symphony starts, the Lotus Symphony home page, shown in Figure 1-1, displays. The home page displays inside the Lotus Symphony main window. You may think it looks a lot like a regular Internet browser, such as Microsoft Internet Explorer or Mozilla Firefox. That's a good observation because the Lotus Symphony interface includes a Web browser that displays in the same environment as the Symphony application.

Each application and Web browser instance displays on a separate tab. At the top of the tabs, you can see the names of the tabs, such as Home, IBM Lotus Symphony - Support Forums, and New Document. Figure 1-2 shows an example of a Web page displaying in the Lotus Symphony window with each of the tabs named as just discussed.

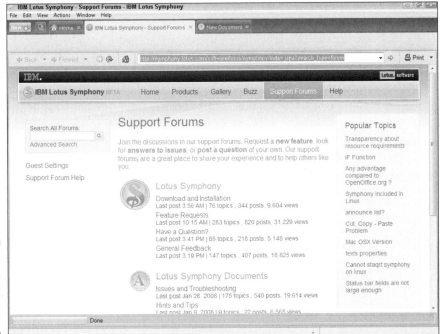

Figure 1-2:
The Lotus
Symphony
main
window.

Getting to Know the Lotus Symphony User Interface

After you have Lotus Symphony started, you need to decide what to do. For example, do you want to create a new word processing document? How about opening a spreadsheet file? Or simply navigating to a Web page on the Internet?

The main Lotus Symphony window includes four main areas. These areas help you navigate Symphony, start new documents, start a Web session, or simply get more information about contents that are displayed. The following list and Figure 1-3 explain each area:

A brief history of Lotus Symphony

Way back in the earlier days of computing — the 1980s — a company called Lotus released one of the earliest spreadsheet programs. It was called Lotus 1-2-3. A few years later, Lotus introduced Lotus Symphony, a program designed to run under an operating system called MS-DOS. That version of Lotus Symphony for DOS included five separate applications that resided in memory when you launched it. This was a revolutionary concept back then because it allowed users to work in these applications without closing one and then opening another one. These applications included the following:

✔ SHEET for spreadsheet work

✔ COMM for communications over a modem

✔ DOC for word processing work

✔ GRAPH for creating charts

✔ FORM for database work

Lotus Symphony for DOS distinguished itself from competitors at the time not by its individual programs (some of them weren't as robust as other offerings), but by its macro language. The macro language enabled users to create custom routines that automated repetitive and sometimes complex tasks, such as dialing up a stock market ticker service, downloading market information into SHEET, and creating custom reports from this data. Lotus discontinued Lotus Symphony for DOS when users migrated to a graphical user interface environment, such as Microsoft Windows 3.1.

A predecessor to the version of Lotus Symphony you're using today is the IBM Workplace application, which was introduced by IBM in 2002 and created on the Eclipse.org Rich Client Platform (RCP) application platform. Eclipse is built on top of Java.

✔ **Window** includes the main Lotus Symphony window that contains all of the individual Symphony applications: Web browser, Lotus Symphony Documents, Lotus Symphony Spreadsheets, and Lotus Symphony Presentations.

✔ **Menu bar** includes command menus that display commands relevant to the document you're creating or task you're working on. For example, when you choose to create a new Lotus Symphony Spreadsheets file, the set of menus that appear include File, Edit, View, Create, Tools, Manipulate, Layout, Window, and Help.

✔ **Tabs** are individual windows inside the main Lotus Symphony window. Each tab includes a Web browser window or Symphony document type, such as a Lotus Symphony presentation. You click each tab to switch between your open editing or browsing sessions.

✔ **Status bar** displays at the bottom of the main Lotus Symphony window to indicate different information about an open document or Web page.

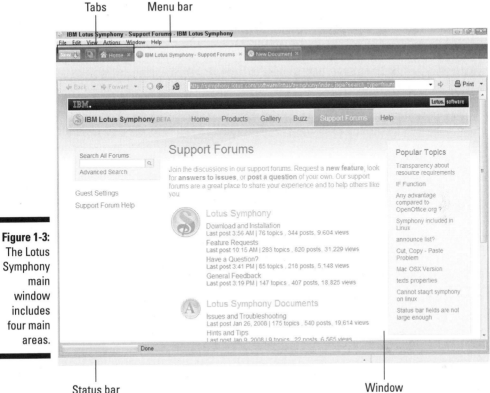

Figure 1-3:
The Lotus
Symphony
main
window
includes
four main
areas.

Tabs   Menu bar

Status bar   Window

Other features of the Lotus Symphony main window are common to most other windows you find in Microsoft Windows applications, such as the close button, scroll bars, restore button, and so on.

The main Lotus Symphony window includes the Home tab. This appears when you initially launch Lotus Symphony. On the Home tab are links to the following:

- ✔ **Lotus Symphony Documents:** A word processor application
- ✔ **Lotus Symphony Presentations:** A presentation (or slide show) application
- ✔ **Lotus Symphony Spreadsheets:** A spreadsheet application

The following sections describe the basic tasks you can perform after you start Lotus Symphony.

Discovering the Lotus Symphony Documents window

Lotus Symphony Documents is the word processor application included with IBM Lotus Symphony. A *word processor* is an application that enables users to create, edit, view, and print documents. Documents include memos, letters, reports, books, brochures, and similar items. With Lotus Symphony Documents, you can create documents from scratch, use prebuilt templates to help you design your documents, and modify existing documents.

Before you start using Lotus Symphony Documents, it's a good idea to get familiar with the Lotus Symphony Documents window and primary interface. Figure 1-4 shows the default Lotus Symphony Documents window.

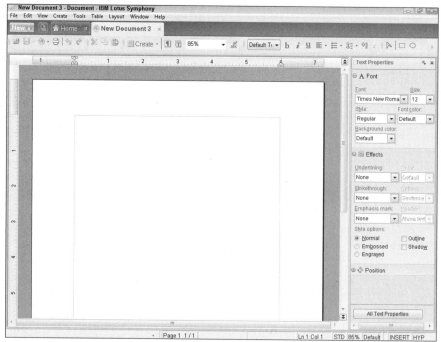

Figure 1-4: The Lotus Symphony Documents main window.

The Lotus Symphony Documents window displays the document, as well as features that help you work with your documents. The following list explains these features:

✔ **Title bar:** Displays the file path and name of the document. The default document name is New Document until you save the document with a different name. The title bar also displays the type of Lotus Symphony application in which you're working — in this case, Documents.

The *path* is simply the location of the saved file. For example, if your documents are stored in a subfolder named Documents, which resides in a folder named My Stuff stored on your C drive, the path is `C:\My Stuff\Documents`.

✔ **Menu bar:** Provides access to the Lotus Symphony Documents command menus. From these menus, you can select commands to help you perform tasks and actions to create, modify, display, and print your documents.

✔ **Lotus Symphony tabs:** These tabs display the open windows you're working on, such as documents, spreadsheets, or other items. Each document you open in Lotus Symphony appears on a separate tab.

✔ **Toolbars:** Display buttons you can click to quickly perform a word processing action. Toolbar buttons correlate to commands you can find in the Lotus Symphony Documents menus. For example, to open a document, you can click the Open toolbar button, or choose File➪Open➪File from the menu bar. As you learn in the Using the Symphony Toolbars section later in this chapter, toolbars can display on a single line or stacked in multiple lines in the window.

✔ **Document window:** Displays the open document, such as a blank document, template, or existing document on which you're working.

✔ **Sidebar:** Displays the Properties sidebar, which provides information and tools for modifying text attributes in your document. For example, you can change font size using the Size option under the Font category.

✔ **Status bar:** Displays information about the open document, including page numbers, line and column numbers, and other items.

You may also notice a few other items in the Lotus Symphony Documents window, such as scroll bars and rulers. The scroll bars are common Windows elements that appear any time you need to view information that displays outside the view of the current display. You simply slide vertical scroll bars up or down to move the current display up or down. Slide horizontal scroll bars right or left to view information that has moved off to the right or left of the screen.

Rulers are measurement tools that help you design and place text, graphics, and other objects on your document window. You'll see more about rulers in Chapter 4.

Discovering the Lotus Symphony Presentations window

Like the Lotus Symphony Documents window, the Lotus Symphony Presentations window includes a number of common features. In fact, some of the features are the same as the Lotus Symphony Documents window, except they adjust to show information about your presentations and slides.

You can see the Lotus Symphony Presentations window by clicking the Create a New Presentation button on the Lotus Symphony Home tab. The following list describes the features displayed in the Lotus Symphony Presentations window and shown in Figure 1-5.

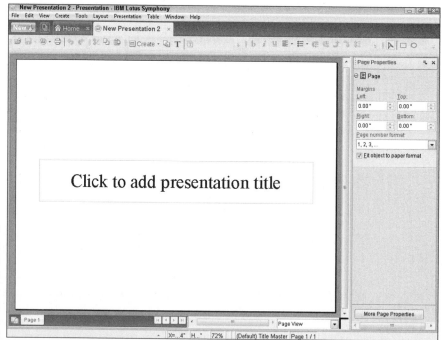

Figure 1-5:
The Lotus
Symphony
Presen-
tations main
window.

✔ **Title bar:** Displays the file path and name of the presentation. The default presentation name is New Presentation until you save the presentation with a different name. The title bar also displays the type of Lotus Symphony application in which you're working — in this case, Presentation.

✔ **Menu bar:** Provides access to the Lotus Symphony Presentation command menus. From these menus, you can select commands to help you perform tasks and actions to create, modify, display, and print your presentations.

✔ **Lotus Symphony tabs:** These tabs display the open windows you're working on, such as presentations, spreadsheets, or other items. Each presentation you open in Lotus Symphony appears on a separate tab.

✔ **Toolbars:** Display buttons you can click to quickly perform a presentation action. Toolbar buttons correlate to commands you can find on the Lotus Symphony Presentations menus. For example, to open a presentation, you can click the Open toolbar button, or choose File⇨Open⇨File from the menu bar. As you learn in the Using the Symphony Toolbars section later in this chapter, toolbars can display on a single line or stacked in multiple lines on the window.

✔ **Presentation window:** Displays the open presentation, such as a blank presentation, template, or existing presentation on which you're working.

✔ **Sidebar:** Displays the Page Properties sidebar, which provides information and tools for modifying page attributes in your presentation. For example, you can change how page numbering looks using the Page Number Format option under the Page category.

✔ **Page tabs:** Provides tabs to navigate between pages in your presentation. When you create a new presentation, only one page tab appears. This area also includes tools for switching to the Master view of a slide and changing to a different page view, such as Outline view.

✔ **Status bar:** Displays information about the open presentation, including slide page numbers, zoom size, and other items.

You'll find out more about the tools and how to navigate the Lotus Symphony Presentations window in Part IV of this book.

Discovering the Lotus Symphony Spreadsheets window

When you're ready to create a spreadsheet in Lotus Symphony Spreadsheets, you click the Create a New Spreadsheet button on the Home tab. Again, many of the same window features found on the previous two application windows appear on this window as well. See Figure 1-6 for a view of the default Lotus Symphony Spreadsheets window.

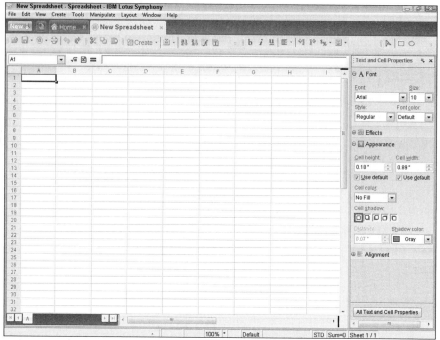

Figure 1-6:
The Lotus
Symphony
Spread-
sheets main
window.

✔ **Title bar:** Displays the file path and name of the spreadsheet. The default spreadsheet name is New Spreadsheet until you save the spreadsheet with a different name. The title bar also displays the type of Lotus Symphony application in which you're working — in this case, Spreadsheet.

✔ **Menu bar:** Provides access to the Lotus Symphony Spreadsheets command menus. From these menus, you can select commands to help you perform tasks and actions to create, modify, display, and print your spreadsheets.

✔ **Lotus Symphony tabs:** These tabs display the open windows you're working on, such as spreadsheets, documents, or other items. Each spreadsheet you open in Lotus Symphony appears on a separate tab.

✔ **Toolbars:** Display buttons you can click to quickly perform a spreadsheet action. Toolbar buttons correlate to commands you can find on the Lotus Symphony Spreadsheets menus. For example, to open a spreadsheet, you can click the Open toolbar button, or choose File➪Open➪File from the menu bar. As you learn in the Using the Symphony Toolbars section later in this chapter, toolbars can display on a single line or stacked in multiple lines on the window.

✔ **Spreadsheet window:** Displays the open spreadsheet, such as a blank spreadsheet, template, or existing spreadsheet on which you're working.

✔ **Sidebar:** Displays the Text and Cell Properties sidebar, which provides information and tools for modifying attributes in your spreadsheet. For example, you can change the height of a spreadsheet cell using the Cell Height option under the Appearance category.

✔ **Worksheet tabs:** Provides tabs to navigate between worksheets in your spreadsheet file. When you create a new spreadsheet, only one worksheet tab appears.

✔ **Status bar:** Displays information about the open spreadsheet, including insertion information, formula data, and more.

You find more about the spreadsheet window in Part III of this book.

Discovering the Lotus Web Browser window

The final window view you can use in Lotus Symphony is the Web Browser window. This window displays when you select the New drop-down button on the Home window and select Web Browser. Figure 1-7 shows the Web Browser window as it appears when you first open it.

Figure 1-7:
The Lotus Web Browser window.

Not much to see when you first open the browser. However, you can type a Web page address in the address box, press Enter, and click the Go button to link to and display a page in the browser window.

The common items found on the Web Browser window include:

- ✔ **Title bar:** Displays the title of the Web page displayed in the window. By default, the page is blank, so it shows about: blank as the name of the page.

- ✔ **Menu bar:** Provides access to the Web Browser command menus. From these menus, you can select commands to help you perform tasks and actions to navigate, open, and print Web pages.

- ✔ **Lotus Symphony tabs:** These tabs display the open windows you're working on, such as a Web page, spreadsheets, or other items. You can open multiple Web page tabs to display multiple Web pages, or use one tab to navigate to each page.

- ✔ **All Toolbars toolbar:** Displays buttons you can click to perform Web page actions. For example, to return to a Web page you have recently visited, click the Back button.

- ✔ **Document window:** Displays the open Web page.

- ✔ **Status bar:** Displays information about the open Web page, including the status of the Web page download.

Web page addresses are known as URLs, or Uniform Resource Locators. You may hear them pronounced as *earls,* but you can simply call them Web addresses if you like. Some common URLs include www.google.com, www.cnn.com, and www.IBM.com.

Using the Symphony Toolbars

Most Windows applications include toolbars to help you complete tasks, select items, and do other actions. Toolbars contain buttons that correspond to actions such as printing a document, opening a new spreadsheet, or saving a presentation. Generally, toolbars include the most frequently used commands in an application.

You can use toolbars in each of the applications in IBM Lotus Symphony. Although the toolbars don't take up much screen real estate, you do have the choice of turning off the toolbars, or moving them if you think they restrict some of the viewing area. The next two sections discuss how to turn on and off the toolbars, as well as move them.

Displaying toolbars

By default, the Lotus Symphony applications have some of their toolbars turned on. For example, in Lotus Symphony Documents, the following toolbars are activated by default:

✔ Context Sensitive

✔ Drawing

✔ Editing

✔ Main

✔ Universal

To turn on other toolbars — or the default ones, if they've been turned off — do the following:

1. **Start an application to display its window.**

   For example, click the Create a New Document button on the Home page to start Lotus Symphony Documents.

2. **Choose View⇨Toolbars and then the name of the toolbar.**

   The toolbar displays.

 Lotus Symphony is built on the IBM Lotus Expeditor and Eclipse.org developer platform. That means that many custom applications and add-ins are available for the Lotus Symphony environment. Some of these add-ins include new toolbars that users can activate using the information contained in this section. However, in some cases, you may need to activate the toolbars using different methods. In those cases, contact the developer of those toolbars to find out how to activate them.

To turn off a toolbar, repeat the preceding steps and choose a toolbar that has a check mark next to it. This deselects the toolbar and turns it off.

Moving toolbars

Lotus Symphony toolbars display on a single row below the menu bar. You can move the toolbars so they appear on multiple rows, stacked below the menu bar. This is handy if you can't see all the buttons on a toolbar when they appear on the same row. Sometimes when you have a smaller monitor, your Windows screen resolution is set so that your application windows display in a larger view, making them easier to see. The problem can be that you can't see some of the application items, most commonly, the toolbar buttons that are on the far right of a toolbar.

To move a toolbar, use the following steps:

1. **Start an application to display its window.**

   For example, click the Create a New Document button on the Home page to start Lotus Symphony Documents.

2. **Move the mouse pointer over the top of the left side of a toolbar until the pointer turns to a four-sided arrow.**

3. **Click and hold down the left mouse button.**

4. **Drag the toolbar down to the next row and release.**

   The toolbar appears on the second row.

When you move a toolbar, don't worry if you don't see a second row below the main toolbar. As you drag the toolbar down, a new row automatically appears, enabling you to insert that toolbar there.

Starting Lotus Symphony When Windows Starts

Because Lotus Symphony includes four of the most common business applications, you may find that you use it every day. In fact, except for e-mail, it may be the most common set of applications you use. For this reason, you may want to set up Lotus Symphony to start automatically in the background each time you start Windows.

This is helpful if you start Windows in the morning as you begin work, and then do a few administrative tasks before you actually begin work (such as get a cup of coffee, listen to voice mail, or chat with your cubicle neighbor). As Windows goes through its tedious, and sometimes lengthy startup process, Lotus Symphony will start up in the background so that when you launch Lotus Symphony from its desktop icon or Start menu area, the program starts faster for you.

To set up Lotus Symphony to start in the background when Windows starts, do the following:

1. **Make sure Lotus Symphony is started.**

2. **Choose File⇨Preferences.**

   The Preferences window appears.

3. **Select the Launch Lotus Symphony in the background when the operating system starts option.**

   Figure 1-8 shows the Preferences window with the background startup feature selected.

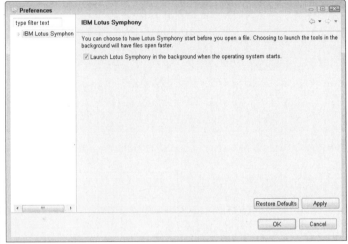

4. **Click Apply.**

5. **Click OK.**

Shutting Down Lotus Symphony

After you finish using Lotus Symphony, you can shut it down. When you do this, all four applications — Lotus Symphony Documents, Lotus Symphony Spreadsheets, Lotus Symphony Presentations, and the Web Browser — close.

To shut down Lotus Symphony, choose File⇨Exit. If you have any open documents, you're prompted to save them before Lotus Symphony closes down.

Another way to shut down Lotus Symphony is to use the Close button on the top-right corner of the main window. Again, you're prompted to save any unsaved documents.

Chapter 2

Switching to IBM Lotus Symphony

In This Chapter

▶ Choosing Lotus Symphony over other application suites

▶ Finding out what your new software can do

▶ Considering system requirements

▶ Getting your computer ready for the switch

▶ Moving encrypted and Open XML files to Lotus Symphony

▶ Finding familiar features

*A*s I discuss in Chapter 1, Lotus Symphony is more than just a single program. With a word processor, spreadsheet program, and presentation software, not to mention a Web browser, Lotus Symphony provides many of the everyday tools that professionals, students, and consumer users need. Aside from the powerful features that the suite provides, Symphony is based on a file format known as the Open Document Format (ODF). ODF uses non-proprietary formats for saving files. This means that you aren't locked in to one specific format, such as the document format in Microsoft Word (.doc), and you can share files with someone who doesn't have Lotus Symphony.

Another advantage of the ODF specification is related to software licenses and usage rights. Most commercial software requires you to purchase rights for using that software on your computer and for deploying it to other computers. Software that adheres to ODF specifications is free to all users to install on any computer.

This chapter discusses making the move to Lotus Symphony and some of the requirements for making this transition. As you decide to use Lotus Symphony — and perhaps present it as a choice for your company, educational institution, or organization — this chapter can help you make the switch.

Understanding Why You Want to Switch

Switching software programs can be a daunting and serious step. This is true for most any user, including:

- ✔ Business users, whether they work for small, medium, or large companies, domestic corporations, or global monoliths.

- ✔ Consumer users, such as home users and families.

- ✔ Students, such as elementary, secondary, and college-level students. Many consumer users also fall into this category as adult student populations grow.

- ✔ Organizations, whether they're not-for-profit organizations, churches, or youth groups.

To use IBM Lotus Symphony, you aren't required to give up your old suite. In fact, many users have multiple applications that perform the same tasks (such as multiple word processors) and multiple software suites installed on their systems. This allows them to pick the best solution for their needs. You may be in a similar situation, especially if you've invested in other applications (such as Microsoft Office) and don't want to lose that investment. Feel free to install Lotus Symphony to work alongside your other applications.

A brief history of ODF

The Open Document Format (ODF) specification got its start around the late 1990s when an XML (eXtensible Markup Language) format was developed by a company called Starfish Software. This company, and its StarOffice software, was subsequently purchased by Sun Microsystems. StarOffice was one of the first ODF applications available and found its way into several schools and businesses because of its cost — it was free to schools and was a low-cost alternative to Microsoft Office to businesses. Another benefit was its support of an open file format that other software manufacturers could support in their applications. This made it easier for users who had different applications and even different operating systems to share documents. For most people, StarOffice didn't become the de facto software suite (Microsoft Office, Lotus SmartSuite and Corel Office were the favorites), but it did become a favorite among many die-hard users. Sun Microsystems started the OpenOffice.org open source project by releasing most of the StarOffice source code. This led to many other companies and organizations getting involved to promote an open file format and produce software that met these specifications. In May 2005, the ODF specification was approved by the committee that drafted the standard, OASIS. Since that approval time, some applications that include ODF support have been released, including SoftMaker TextMaker 2006, IBM Workplace, KOffice 1.5, and, of course, IBM Lotus Symphony. To learn more about ODF, visit the OASIS Web page at www.oasis-open.org.

All of the preceding users may have different types of documents they produce using software. However, all users have the same general needs and goals when it comes to the software they adopt. For example, users usually expect *long-term data preservation* when they plan to adopt a new software program. This means that they want a program that creates documents, spreadsheets, and presentations in a file format that is usable now and in the future. The Open Document Format (ODF) specification addresses this expectation and promises to deliver on this.

The following sections provide some discussion on helping you understand some reasons for switching to Lotus Symphony.

Comparing Lotus Symphony to other suites

One way to compare Lotus Symphony to other software suites is by the number of software suite users. As you may be well aware of, Lotus Symphony is not the only software suite on the market. In fact, it isn't even the most popular one available.

Microsoft Office dominates the office suite market. A *Business Week* 2006 report listed Microsoft Office with a 95 percent market share. In addition, the W.P. Carey School of Business at Arizona State University listed an October 2007 analysis with the same market share. However, that number factors in only revenues for Office suites. Of course, free products, such as Lotus Symphony (which at that time was in a testing stage — called a *beta cycle),* aren't included in that analysis.

It's estimated that over 400 million users have Microsoft Office. An ODF product called OpenOffice has reached the 100 million download mark. Of course, the number of users who have downloaded multiple copies of OpenOffice can't be determined. But OpenOffice.org has estimated that their market share for *users* of office suites is about 20 percent. Remember, the 95 percent share that Microsoft Office claims is for *purchases* of office suites. Because Lotus Symphony is a new product, download numbers aren't available.

Another way to look at Lotus Symphony against other suites is by examining the applications other suites include as part of their packages. Table 2-1 lists some of the most popular office suites and their features.

As you can see, all suites include word processors, spreadsheet programs, and presentation tools. Some, like Microsoft Office and Corel WordPerfect Office, also include e-mail and database programs. If you need e-mail and database applications and you decide to adopt Lotus Symphony, you'll need to find other stand-alone products to fill those needs. For example, you may want to use Windows Vista's free e-mail program called Windows Mail (called

Table 2-1 **Office Suite Features**

Suite Name	Word Processor	Spread-sheet	Presen-tation	Web Browser	E-Mail	Data-base	Adobe PDF Support	Other	Cost
Lotus Symphony	*	*	*	*			*		Free
Microsoft Office	*	*	*		*	*	*	Multiple suites	$499
Microsoft Works	*	*						Sometimes included free with new PC purchases	$225
Corel Word-Perfect Office	*	*	*		*	*	*	Includes other tools	$149
Google Docs	*	*	*		*		*	Online only	Free
Zoho Office Suite	*	*	*		*	*	*	Online only	Free
ThinkFree Desktop	*	*	*				*		Free
OpenOffice.org	*	*	*		*	*	*		Free

Microsoft Outlook Express in Windows XP) for your e-mail application. For a database product, you can download a free version of OpenOffice.org's Base database (at www.openoffice.org), or you can purchase a database program such as Microsoft Access or Corel Paradox.

Project management is another unsupported feature in Lotus Symphony. With Microsoft Office Professional, Corel WordPerfect Office, and a few other Office suites, you can purchase a supporting project management application. These types of programs enable you to create files that help you manage, track, and analyze projects. A free alternative to these (somewhat) pricey commercial applications is OpenProj. OpenProj includes many project management features found in the for-cost programs. You can download a copy of it at http://openproj.org/openproj.

Understanding the benefits of Lotus Symphony

Lotus Symphony provides several benefits for the business, consumer, and student user. Some of the benefits you realize when switching to Lotus Symphony include:

- ✔ **Interoperability:** By supporting ODF (Open Document Format), Lotus Symphony provides users with applications that support many different formats for exchanging information. Businesses and organizations can share documents saved in ODF file formats with others who have programs that support ODF files. If a company or organization is not sure it has programs that support ODF formats, it should find out what file types its programs can open (using the File⇨Open command, for example) and which ones it can save to (using File⇨Save As).

- ✔ **PDF export capabilities:** With Lotus Symphony, you can easily, and without any additional cost or software, export a document to the Adobe Portable Document Format (PDF) file format. You can transfer PDF files to other users, who can read them on any computer running the Adobe Reader application (which is free).

- ✔ **Support:** Lotus Symphony supports online Web-based community groups and forums, like the one shown in Figure 2-1. These sites, which are listed in Chapter 20, are free and provide tips for using Lotus Symphony, answers to help solve system problems, places for you to post and download templates, and other helpful information.

- ✔ **Macros:** You can automate tasks by creating and running short little programs that you can create, called *macros*. Macros can be created in all three Symphony applications: Lotus Symphony Documents, Lotus Symphony Presentations, and Lotus Symphony Spreadsheets.

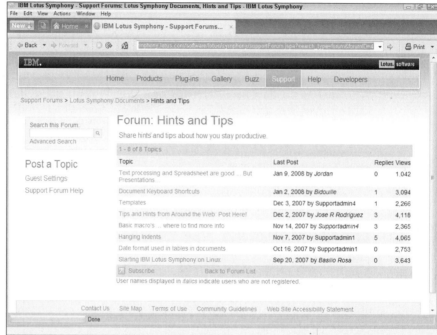

Figure 2-1:
Visit the
Symphony
Web sites
and forums
for additional
help and
information.

✔ **Support of Microsoft Office files:** Lotus Symphony provides support for Microsoft Office documents (Word), spreadsheets (Excel), and presentation files (PowerPoint).

Lotus Symphony doesn't currently support the Microsoft Office 2007 Open XML format (such as the .docx format that Microsoft Office Word 2007 uses), but support is pending. You can, however, save files within Microsoft Office applications to supporting formats (such as .doc in Microsoft Office Word 2007) and then import those files into Lotus Symphony. You can read more about preparing your documents for Lotus Symphony in the section, "Preparing your old documents for Lotus Symphony," later in this chapter.

✔ **Template organizer:** Lotus Symphony includes a template organizer to help you install, manage, and view file templates. You can use these templates in Lotus Symphony Documents, Lotus Symphony Spreadsheets, and Lotus Symphony Presentations.

✔ **Plug-ins:** You can add features and tools to your installation of Lotus Symphony via plug-ins. Programmers can create plug-ins using the Developer Toolkit and the Eclipse.org Integrated Development Environment (IDE), and you can integrate those plug-ins into your applications. An early example of a plug-in is the Lotus Quickr connector for Lotus Symphony, which provides support for working online or on a network with multiple users simultaneously (known in the computer world as *collaboration*) using features within Lotus Symphony.

Getting your hands on the toolkit

You can download the Lotus Symphony Developer Toolkit download from the IBM Lotus Symphony Developers Web site at `http://symphony.lotus.com/software/lotus/symphony/developers.jspa`. With the Toolkit, you can create links to other IBM software, such as IBM Lotus Notes, IBM WebSphere Translation Server, and other applications. While you're downloading the Toolkit, you also can download a tutorial to help you learn more about it. The tutorial is available at `http://symphony.lotus.com/software/lotus/symphony/developers.jspa`.

You can read more about plug-ins — and you can download shared plug-ins — at the Lotus Symphony Plug-Ins Web site at `http://symphony.lotus.com/software/lotus/symphony/plugins.jspa`.

The site also has a Post a Plug-In link for uploading plug-ins that you've created and want to share with other users.

✔ **Developer Toolkit:** Provides APIs (Application Programming Interfaces) for programmers to create plug-ins for the Lotus Symphony applications, as well as integration with other IBM applications.

✔ **Web browser:** Enables you to navigate to Web pages on the Internet, such as IBM Lotus Symphony support sites. To connect to a Web site, you can enter a Web address in the address toolbar or click a hyperlink ("link") in a Web page. At the time of this writing, you could not bookmark a page, such as you can save Favorites in Microsoft Internet Explorer.

Understanding Lotus Symphony requirements

As you decide to make Lotus Symphony a part of your application collection, you do need to take into consideration its system requirements. You don't want to get into the situation where you decide to use Symphony only to find out that it won't install or run properly on your computer.

The following list shows the system requirements for installing Lotus Symphony:

✔ **Operating system:** Microsoft Windows XP or Microsoft Windows Vista (a Linux version is available as well, but we do not cover that version in this book). Must have Administrator rights to install software.

✔ **Memory:** 512MB of random access memory (RAM) is the minimum, but 1GB is recommended.

🖊 **Free hard disk space:** 750MB.

🖊 **Internet Web browser:** Internet Explorer 5.5 or higher, Mozilla Firefox, or Opera. You need a Web browser to connect to and download the Lotus Symphony installer program.

🖊 **E-mail address:** Required for signing in to download the Lotus Symphony installer.

🖊 **Internet connection:** A high-speed Internet connection is recommended in order to download the IBM Lotus Symphony install program.

You can find additional information about installing and configuring Lotus Symphony in Appendix A.

Switching from Microsoft Office Applications

Many organizations, businesses, and consumers are looking for alternatives to the Microsoft Office suite of applications. One main reason for this evaluation focuses on costs associated with Microsoft Office. As updates are released, users incur additional costs (albeit lower than full version costs) that can have an impact on the decision to upgrade. When alternatives are available at a much lower cost (or free), businesses, organizations, and other users become interested. Lotus Symphony has sparked the interest in many of these areas because of its low cost, features set, and the backing of a giant corporation (IBM).

If you want to make the switch to Lotus Symphony and have documents in a Microsoft Office format, read the following sections to find out how to best transition to Lotus Symphony.

Preparing your computer for Lotus Symphony

The first step in preparing for Lotus Symphony — and this may sound counter-intuitive — is to keep all of your old applications installed. Do this because you may need to open those applications to convert files, view documents or files that you can't view in Lotus Symphony, or test different items that don't convert properly to Symphony.

Another step in preparing your computer for Lotus Symphony is to make backup copies of all of documents you plan to convert to Symphony files. Do this so that you can refer to the original files if something goes wrong during the conversion.

Finally, refer to Appendix A to install Lotus Symphony on your computer. You'll need to install it before continuing with the conversion process described in the following section.

Preparing your old documents for Lotus Symphony

When you're ready to use documents from a different application suite or application in Lotus Symphony, you may need to do some prep work in the original application before working on that file in Lotus Symphony.

Files saved in Microsoft Office using the Microsoft Office encryption feature are not supported by Lotus Symphony. You can't open or convert an encrypted Microsoft Office document. Before trying to open it in Lotus Symphony, open it in Microsoft Office (such as a document in Microsoft Word), and follow these steps:

1. **Choose File⇨Save As.**

   The Save As dialog box appears.

2. **Choose Tools⇨General Options in the bottom-right corner of the Save As dialog box.**

   (If you're using Word 2003 instead of Word 2007, you'll find the Tools drop-down list in the upper-right corner of the Save As dialog box.)

   The General Options dialog box appears.

3. **Highlight the passwords in the Password to Open and Password to Modify fields, delete them, and click OK.**

4. **Click the Save button to save your settings for this document.**

   It's now unencrypted, and you can convert it to a Lotus Symphony document.

Items and objects you create using advanced features in Microsoft Office don't convert to Lotus Symphony files. For example, Microsoft Excel spreadsheets with embedded macros don't convert to Lotus Symphony Spreadsheets files. You will need to re-create those macros in the Lotus Symphony Spreadsheets files to duplicate the feature found in the Excel spreadsheet. Also, graphics objects created using SmartArt, WordArt, and similar tools in Microsoft Word don't convert into editable objects in Lotus Symphony Documents. Again, re-create those objects in Documents, or leave them as embedded objects (that you can't edit) when you convert the files.

Table 2-2 shows the Microsoft Office file types supported by Lotus Symphony applications. Consult it when you encounter a file type you want to pull into Lotus Symphony. You can open these file types within Lotus Symphony without any additional steps. Simply use the File➪Open command in Lotus Symphony.

Table 2-2	Microsoft Office File Types Supported		
	Lotus Symphony Documents	*Lotus Symphony Presentations*	*Lotus Symphony Spreadsheets*
Microsoft Word	`.doc, .rtf, .txt`		
Microsoft PowerPoint		`.ppt`	
Microsoft Excel			`.xls, .csv`

The following steps show how to open a Microsoft Office PowerPoint `.ppt` file in Lotus Symphony Presentations:

1. **Start Lotus Symphony.**

2. **Choose File➪Open➪File.**

   The Open dialog box shown in Figure 2-2 appears.

   You don't have to be in the application in which you want to open a file. You can open any type from the Open dialog box.

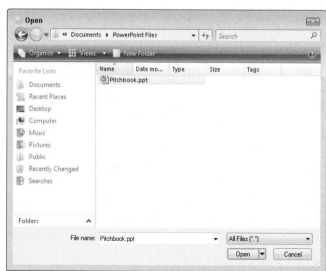

Figure 2-2: Use the Open dialog box to open a file supported by Lotus Symphony.

3. **Navigate to the drive, folder, and file you want to open.**

To narrow your search to just the file type you want to open, click the All Files button in the lower-right corner and select the file type you want to open. In the example shown here, I selected Microsoft Power-Point 97/2003/XP (*.ppt). Then the Open dialog box changes to show only files of that type.

4. **Click a file to open.**

5. **Click the Open button on the lower right.**

6. **If a message appears (see Figure 2-3) telling you that some features may not convert correctly when opening, click OK.**

Figure 2-3:
Some fea-
tures from
a Microsoft
Office file
won't open
correctly
in Lotus
Symphony.

The file, in this case a Microsoft Office PowerPoint 2003 file, opens in Lotus Symphony Presentations.

7. **Scroll through the presentation. Look for objects, text, or other items that are missing, displaying incorrectly, or unreadable. Correct any problems in the presentation.**

8. **Choose File➪Save As.**

The Save As command enables you specify a new file format for the presentation.

9. **From the Save As dialog box (see Figure 2-4), click the Save as Type drop-down list and select Open Document Presentation (*.odp).**

10. **Click Save.**

This saves the presentation in the OTP file format, which is the Lotus Symphony Presentations Open Document Presentation format.

For Microsoft Office 2007 files saved in the Open XML format, you need to resave those files in an earlier file format within the respective Microsoft Office application. For example, if you have a file with a .docx file extension, follow these steps:

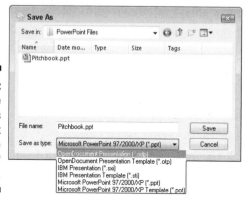

Figure 2-4:
Use the
Save As
dialog box
to save the
file in OTP
file format.

1. **Open the file in Microsoft Office Word 2007.**

2. **Choose File⇨Save As.**

   The Save As dialog box appears.

3. **From the Save as Type drop-down list, choose Word 97-2003 Document.**

4. **Click Save.**

5. **Open the file in Lotus Symphony Documents.**

Making the switch to Lotus Symphony

After you convert your old files into the Open Document Format (ODF), you can use Lotus Symphony applications to modify and read those files. Starting with Part II of this book, I show you how to use each of the individual Lotus Symphony applications to create, edit, view, and print files.

When you move to Lotus Symphony from Microsoft Office, you don't have to start at the lowest point on the learning curve. Many of the same skill sets you learned in Microsoft Office transfer to using the Lotus Symphony applications. For example, when formatting a document in Lotus Symphony Documents, you use the Bold, Italic, or Underline toolbar buttons, which are similar to the toolbar buttons found in Microsoft Word. In Lotus Symphony Presentations, when you want to insert a text box, simply click the Text Box toolbar button. This is the same action you do in Microsoft PowerPoint. And finally, when resizing a column in Lotus Spreadsheets, click and drag the borders of the column. Microsoft Excel uses the same action.

Lotus Symphony applications do have their own features and ways of doing things, however. For example, when inserting a graphic into your Lotus Symphony Documents document, you choose Create⇨Graphics. In Microsoft Word, however, you choose Insert⇨Picture⇨From File.

Chapter 3

Getting Help from Lotus Symphony

- -

In This Chapter

▶ Navigating the Help window

▶ Finding instructions with the search tool

▶ Going online for more information

▶ Telling IBM what you think

- -

*Y*ou may not know this, but most software companies invest a great deal of time, money, and resources putting together documentation to help users (like yourself) understand their products. With Lotus Symphony, for example, IBM has created a help system that installs on your local computer. When you encounter a task you aren't sure how to complete, simply access the help utility and look for the answer.

Likewise, online sources provide a great deal of information for helping you solve your Lotus Symphony application problems. A number of Web pages are available from the IBM Web site, as well as other sources. The Lotus Symphony help system includes a feature called the Workbench, which lets you get context-sensitive help called *Infopops*.

Finally, you can provide feedback to the IBM documentation and product staffs by using the Eclipse.org participation site on the IBM Web site. A link to this site is located in the Help system.

Browsing the Help Contents

Lotus Symphony includes a help system accessible from any part of the Symphony program. For example, if you're working in Lotus Symphony Presentations, you can access the help system. Likewise, if you've just started Lotus Symphony and are viewing the Home page, you can access the help system from there as well.

To open help, do the following:

1. Open Lotus Symphony.

2. Choose Help⇨Help Contents.

The Help – IBM Lotus Symphony window opens.

You can see in Figure 3-1 that the help system opens in a separate window from the main Lotus Symphony window. None of the normal tabs for the main Lotus Symphony window appear here. Instead, you see two panes, a search field, and some toolbar buttons.

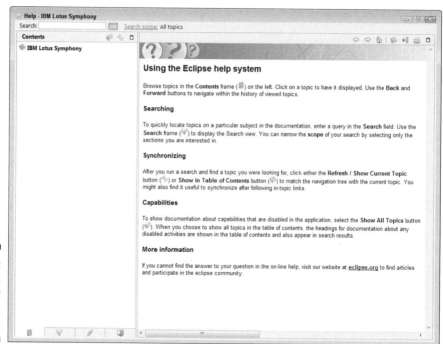

Figure 3-1:
The Lotus Symphony help window.

To switch between the Help window and main Lotus Symphony window, click the respective Windows taskbar button. Or you can press Alt+Tab on the keyboard until the task icon for the window you want to view is selected, and then release the keys.

As with any Microsoft Windows-compliant software, you can press the F1 key to open the help system while in the main Lotus Symphony window.

The left pane of the help window (Contents) contains a table of contents of the help topics available. The main topics in the help system appear with book icons next to them. In this case, the main help topic is called *IBM Lotus*

Symphony. The book icon next to it appears closed — or collapsed — with no subtopics below it showing.

Click the IBM Lotus Symphony item to expand the contents below it. The help item links appear with underlines when you hover your mouse over them.

If a topic is collapsed — that is, if you can't see any subtopics below it — click the plus sign (+) next to it to expand the topic. You then can see the subtopics below it. Sometimes a topic may have multiple subtopics, under which may appear other subtopics. You simply have to keep clicking the subtopic item until you come to a topic of interest.

If you click a subtopic heading, such as IBM Lotus Symphony Documents, you don't expand it to show subtopics and documents under it. Instead, you show the help information associated with that item. In this case, you can read information about Lotus Symphony Documents. You need to click the plus sign (+) next to the subtopic to expand it.

Help information is contained in *documents*. These appear next to icons that look like single sheets of paper. When you click a document name in the left pane, the information associated with that topic appears in the right pane.

Figure 3-2 shows the help system with subtopics showing in the left pane and a help document showing in the right pane. Read the help document for information about that topic.

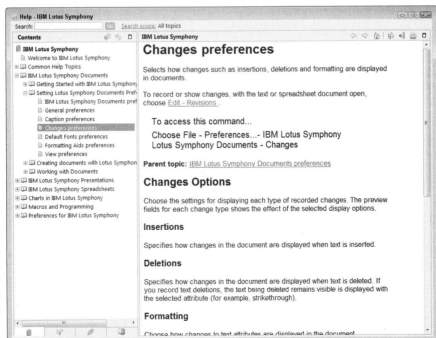

Figure 3-2:
The
Changes
Preferences
help
document.

Some help documents include links to other documents. These links appear like Web page links, as underlined blue text. (The blue text usually turns to purple after you click it once.) Click the links to take you to different help documents.

For example, in Figure 3-2, a link appears in the Changes Preferences document. The link is called Edit – Revisions. When you click it, you're taken to the Changes document, which discusses information relating to Lotus Symphony Documents revisions.

To navigate back to a previous help document, click the Go Back arrow on the toolbar on the right pane. Conversely, to move to a document you have jumped back from, click the Go Forward arrow.

Table 3-1 describes the help window's toolbar buttons.

Table 3-1		Toolbar Buttons Located in the Help Window
Icon	*Name*	*Description*
	Show All Topics	Displays all the topics and subtopics of the help system in the left pane, including topics about features you have disabled on your system. Click OK if you see the Confirmation dialog box.
	Refresh/ Show Current Topics	Displays topics for all the features currently configured on your system.
	Maximize	Maximizes the left pane. When you click this icon, the right pane is minimized so that only the left pane shows. Click the Restore button on the right side of the maximized pane to return the left pane to its normal size, and to reshow the right pane.
	Go Back	Returns you to the previously shown help document.
	Go Forward	Returns you to a page you have viewed already in this session. For example, if you clicked the Go Back button while viewing a document, you can then click the Go Forward button to re-view that page you just left.
	Home	Returns you to the help system home page, which is shown in Figure 3-1.

Icon	Name	Description
	Show in Table of Contents	Shows the currently selected help document in the table of contents. This is handy if you click a link while viewing a document and you want to know where in the help system this linked document appears. The left pane changes to show that location when you click the Show in Table of Contents button.
	Bookmark Document	Enables you to add this help document to a list of book-marked pages. You might do this if you want to quickly return to this document later and don't want to hunt it down. Just click the Bookmarks icon on the lower-left pane and see the topic listed in your bookmarks.
	Print Page	Prints the currently shown help document. The Print dialog box appears, from which you select a printer and then click Print to continue with the print job.
	Maximize	Maximizes the right pane. When you click this icon, the left pane is minimized so that only the right pane shows. Click the Restore button on the right side of the maximized pane to return the right pane to its normal size, and to reshow the left pane.
	Contents	Displays the help contents tab.
	Search Results	Displays the search results tab.
	Links	Shows links to a context-sensitive help item (called an *Infopop)* for a widget when you press the F1 key.
	Bookmarks	Shows bookmarks for help documents you have bookmarked.

Because IBM Lotus Symphony includes all three Symphony applications under one main window, you can access help for any application from this one help window. For example, to find help for Lotus Symphony Presentations, do the following:

1. **Open the help system window.**

2. **Expand the IBM Lotus Symphony help topic.**

3. **Expand the IBM Lotus Symphony Presentations help subtopic, as shown Figure 3-3.**

4. **Click a subtopic to view additional subtopics or documents for information about a Presentations feature.**

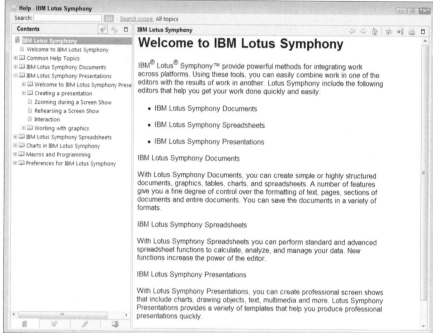

Figure 3-3:
Locating
help docu-
ments
for each
application.

Searching for Help Items

When you can't locate a help document using the table of contents, try searching for it. You can use the Search field on the Help – IBM Lotus Symphony window to do this. Searching returns a list of help topics that includes the word or phrase you enter as search criteria. The results are located in the Search Results pane of the help window. (See Figure 3-4.)

If no related topics are found, a Nothing Found label is returned.

If a keyword or phrase you're searching doesn't find any topics or if the located topics aren't exactly what you're searching for, try a different phrase or keyword. For example, if you search the phrase, *How do I create a formula*, you won't find anything. Instead, change the phrase to *Creating a formula*. That returns several documents in the help system. Also, be sure to check your spelling to ensure that you spell your search criteria words correctly.

To run a search for help documents, do the following:

1. **Open the help system window.**
2. **Click in the Search text box.**

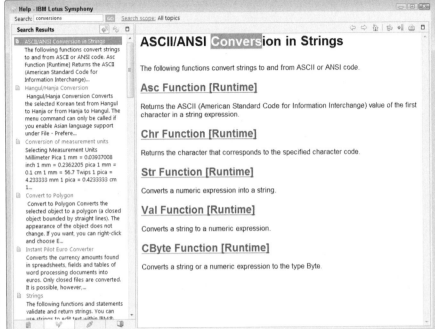

Figure 3-4:
The Search
Results
pane dis-
plays the
results of
your search.

3. Type a search keyword or phrase.

4. Click the Go button or press Enter.

The help system searches for matches to your keyword or phrase. Any documents matching your criteria return in the Search Results pane, as shown in Figure 3-4.

Matches to your search criteria display with the name of the help document followed by a short synopsis of the document. The document name is linked to the document, so you can click a document name to view its contents in the right pane. The Search Results pane remains active, and you can click another found item if the first one doesn't satisfy your needs.

When you display a document that you searched for, Lotus Symphony highlights the search keywords in the document that you view. For example, in Figure 3-5, the words *create* and *functions* are highlighted based on searching the phrase *creating functions*.

If you want to return to the table of contents without losing your search documents, click the Contents icon on bottom of the left pane. This displays the Contents pane, but your search documents are still available in the Search Results pane. Click the Search Results icon on the bottom of the left pane to see it.

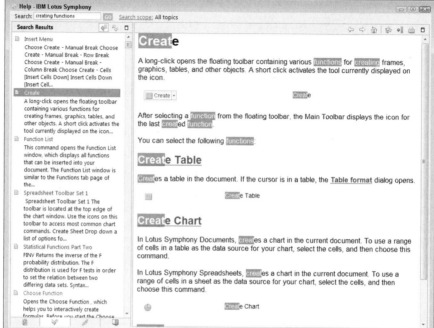

Figure 3-5:
Keywords
are high-
lighted in
the docu-
ments you
search for.

You can also search for help documents when you don't have the help window open. To illustrate, first close the help window (if you have it open) by clicking the close button on the right side of the window.

Next, do the following:

1. **Open Lotus Symphony.**

   You can open an application, such as Lotus Symphony Spreadsheets, or keep the Home page active.

2. **Choose Help⇨Search.**

   The Search pane appears on the right side of the Lotus Symphony window, such as the one shown in Figure 3-6.

3. **Type a keyword or phrase in the Search expression field.**

4. **Click Go or press Enter.**

   The Search pane shows documents containing your keyword or phrase.

5. **Click a document to view its contents. The keyword or phrase you searched appears highlighted in the document.**

6. **Click the Back button to return to your search results.**

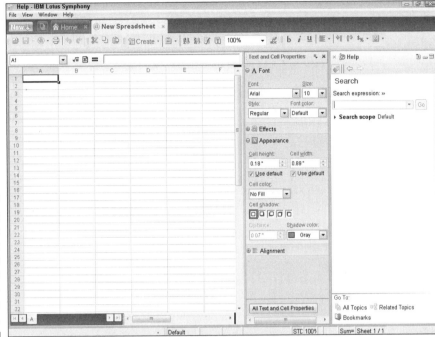

Figure 3-6:
The Search
pane shown
in the Lotus
Symphony
Spread-
sheets
window.

The Search pane menu

When you have the Search pane open on the right side of the main document window, and are viewing a document, spreadsheet, or presentation, you have access to the Search pane menu. This menu appears when you click the Menu icon at the top-right part of the pane. The commands are also available at the bottom of the Search pane when you're viewing a document. Menu choices include:

✔ **Related Topics:** Displays items from your search list that are related to the help document you're viewing.

✔ **All Topics:** Shows the IBM Lotus Symphony help system topics. These are the same topics that appear in the help system table of contents.

✔ **Search:** Displays your current search list.

✔ **Bookmarks:** Shows your saved bookmarks.

To close the Search pane, click the close button on the left side of the pane. Any searches you've made are deleted. However, you can click the down arrow on the Search expression field and see any previous search criteria you've entered. Select that criteria and click Go to rerun that search.

Using Online Resources for Help

A number of online resources are available to help you figure out how to use Lotus Symphony and its applications. The Lotus Symphony Home tab is the first place to look for help. (See Figure 3-7.) It includes links to IBM Lotus Symphony support forums and information pages.

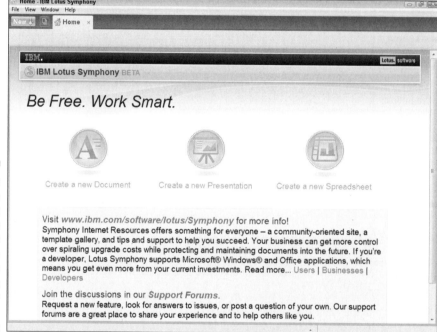

Figure 3-7: Find more information about Lotus Symphony by starting with the Lotus Symphony Home tab.

Another way to access Lotus Symphony online resources is via the Symphony Help menu. Here's how to access it:

1. **Open Lotus Symphony.**

2. **Choose Help➪Lotus Symphony Internet Resources.**

   The Lotus Symphony Web site (see Figure 3-8) appears. By default, the Web pages appear in a separate browser window, such as in Internet Explorer.

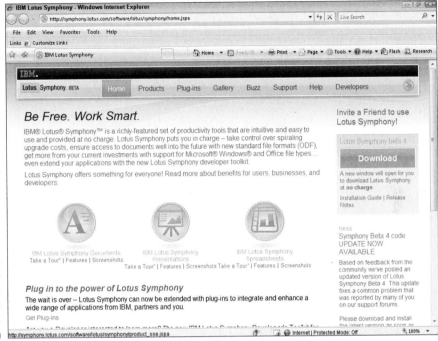

Figure 3-8:
This Web
site appears
when you
select
the Lotus
Symphony
Internet
Resources
menu item.

You can navigate the Web pages as you do any Web site. Some of the key places you may want to hit include these pages:

✔ **Products:** Click the Products tab at the top of the page. The Products page provides helpful links for each of the three Lotus Symphony applications.

✔ **Support:** Click the Support tab at the top of the page. The Support page links you to product support pages for each of the applications. For example, click the Issues and Troubleshooting link under the Lotus Symphony Documents section to see posted topics relating to problems and issues other users have had with Lotus Symphony Documents.

✔ **Gallery:** Click the Gallery tab at the top of the page. You can find uploaded templates, sample documents, and other files that you can download to use on your computer.

For more information about different Web sites relating to Lotus Symphony, see Chapter 20.

Submitting Feedback to IBM

IBM provides a way for you to submit feedback to help Lotus Symphony become a better product, and it enables you to submit problems or errors you've found in the Symphony help system. There are links called Help Feedback and Product Feedback for submitting your findings to IBM.

To access the feedback tool, do the following:

1. **Open Lotus Symphony.**

2. **Choose Help⇨Help Contents. The Help – IBM Lotus Symphony window appears.**

3. **Click any help topic, such as Common Help Topics.**

4. **Scroll to the bottom of the document in the right pane.**

5. **Click the Help Feedback or Product Feedback link, shown in Figure 3-9.**

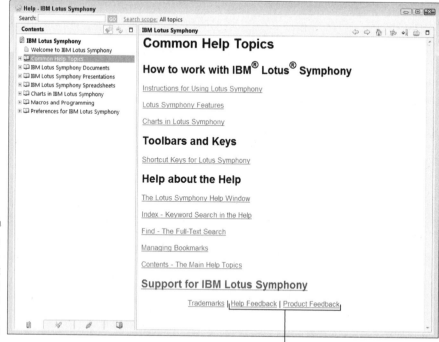

Figure 3-9:
The feedback links at the bottom of any help page.

Feedback links

The page associated with the link you click, such as Help Feedback, appears. Figure 3-10 shows the Help Feedback page.

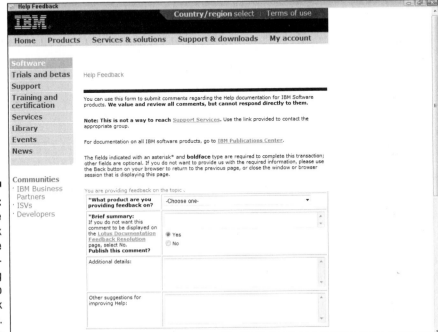

Figure 3-10: Provide feedback about the Help feature using the Help Feedback Web page.

6. **Fill out the feedback form by doing the following:**

   • Select the product you want to discuss (Lotus Symphony in this case, of course).

   • Enter a summary of the feedback you want to provide.

   • Include additional details about the product or help item that you want to discuss.

   • Enter other suggestions for improving the help system.

   • Fill out the survey at the bottom of the form.

7. **Click the Submit button at the bottom of the page.**

   Your feedback is sent to the IBM Feedback staff for review.

When you open the Help Feedback or Product Feedback pages, they're usually shown in a small window. You can resize the window by dragging its sides or corners to make it a different size. Or simply click the Maximize button in the top-right corner of the window to enlarge the window to fit your screen size. That's the size you see in Figure 3-10.

Part II

Using IBM Lotus Symphony Documents — the Word Processor Application

The 5th Wave — By Rich Tennant

"They won't let me through security until I remove the bullets from my Documents."

In this part . . .

You might think you don't need to read this part, and maybe you don't. But I will tell you one thing: Where else will you read about my fantastic trip to planet Lotus Symphony Documents? I was nervous at first, but I've gotten over it. And you might, too. Be sure to read about how to create documents, set up complex documents, and use the Template Organizer.

Chapter 4

Creating a Document

. . . .

In This Chapter

▶ Opening Lotus Symphony Documents and creating a file

▶ Saving in the Documents, PDF, and DOC formats

▶ Entering and editing content

▶ Finding your way around

▶ Previewing and printing your documents

. . . .

*O*ne of the first applications most users become familiar with is a word processor. Word processors enable you to create and edit letters, memos, flyers, brochures, resumes, and other types of documents. You also can view documents created by other users or saved on your computer or other devices (such as network drives or flash drives). For the most part, word processors are easy to use — you simply type in your information, format it (if you like), and save it. If you want a hard copy of the document, you send it to a printer.

Lotus Symphony includes Lotus Symphony Documents, a word processor application, which provides features found on the top-selling word processors on the market. With it, you can create documents from blank documents, templates, or from other documents. With its built-in conversion tools, you can open documents saved in the Microsoft Word format (.doc), Lotus Word Pro format (.lwp), and many more.

In this chapter, I show you how to start using Lotus Symphony Documents to create, view, navigate, edit, and save documents, as well as set up tables and print your documents.

Starting Lotus Symphony Documents

Before you can start working on a Lotus Symphony Documents file, you must start Lotus Symphony Documents. Before you can do that, however, you must start Lotus Symphony. (See Chapter 1 for more on how to do this.)

The most common way to start Lotus Symphony Documents after Symphony is started is to click the Create a New Document link on the Lotus Symphony Home tab. This launches a new document window on the New Document tab, as shown in Figure 4-1.

By default, the first blank document you open in the current Lotus Symphony *session* (that is, since you started Lotus Symphony) appears as New Document. Subsequent documents you start appear as New Document 2, New Document 3, and so on. These are just temporary names until you save the document with a new filename. Learn more about saving documents later in this chapter in the section called "Saving Your Documents."

Another way to start a new document is by using the Windows context menu you can see from the Windows Desktop and other areas. To use this method, right-click the Windows Desktop and choose New⇨OpenDocument Text. Lotus Symphony appears with the New Document tab showing. This command is also located from a Windows Explorer or My Documents File menu.

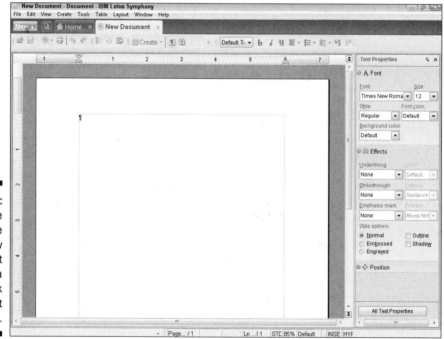

Figure 4-1:
Click the
Create
a New
Document
link and a
new blank
document
appears.

You can start a new blank document from the Home tab, as discussed in the previous section, but you also can start a blank document from the Lotus Symphony menus. In fact, you can use either of two different menus to do this, as follows:

1. **Start Lotus Symphony.**

2. **Choose File⇨New⇨Document.**

   Or click the New button to the left of the Home tab and click Lotus Symphony Documents.

   Either way, a new document opens on a new tab.

If you have a Lotus Symphony Documents file saved to your system, such as to your Windows Desktop or a different folder, you can double-click the file (or a shortcut to it) to launch Lotus Symphony, and then a Lotus Symphony Documents tab appears automatically with the selected file open.

Windows enables you to set file types that automatically launch the correct application when you double-click a file. When you install IBM Lotus Symphony on your computer, the Setup program automatically sets files with the filename extension of .odt to launch Lotus Symphony and to display in a Lotus Symphony Documents tab. As I discuss later in this chapter, the .odt extension stands for Open Document Text.

Creating a Lotus Symphony Documents Document

Before you begin typing text into a document, you need to first decide which type of document you would like to use. Lotus Symphony Documents supports the following general types:

- ✔ **Blank document,** which displays a new, unformatted, blank screen for you to work on.

- ✔ **Document from a template,** which provides boilerplate formatting, text, graphics, and other basic items for a document type.

- ✔ **Document from another document,** which enables you to save an existing document to a new name (thereby creating a copy of it) and then modify the new document.

Each of these methods is shown in the following sections.

Creating a blank document

When you need to start a document from scratch — that is, one without a specific format or one that isn't based on another document — use the blank document method. A blank document is just that; it contains no text, formatting, or other objects. This way is handy if you aren't sure what the final document should look like but you want to get down your information and build the document as you go.

Not every document needs to have some kind of formatting or other fancy stuff added to it. Sometimes you need to create a quick document just to save some text. In these cases, a blank document works great. For example, you may want to save the text from an e-mail message you've received, but you want it in a Lotus Symphony Documents file. In these cases, open a blank Lotus Symphony Documents file, copy and paste the information into the document, and save the file.

To find out how to save files in Lotus Symphony Documents, read "Saving Your Documents" later in this chapter.

Essentially, when you start the Lotus Symphony Documents application from the main Lotus Symphony window, as described in the previous section, you create a blank document. (Refer to Figure 4-1.)

When your blank document is created, you can begin filling it with content — text, graphics, tables, bulleted lists, and more.

Creating a document using a template

A template provides you a head start in getting a portion of your document completed. Sometimes a template simply provides common formatting, such as margin settings, heading styles, or logos. Other times, you can use a template that has everything you need entered except for variable text, such as a person's name, address, and phone number. An example of the latter is a form letter.

Examples of templates can include:

- Memos containing boilerplate text, business or departmental logos, signature lines, and date areas.
- Form letters that include standard text, formatting, signature lines, and fields that automatically fill in with variable data.

Downloading templates

Templates aren't just files you create. You can download them from Web sites, share them with colleagues, and have them sent to you via e-mail. In fact, some users on the Lotus Symphony support Web sites (see Chapter 20) have uploaded templates that work with Lotus Symphony Documents. As Lotus Symphony becomes more popular, look for additional templates that you can use.

✔ Calendars for monthly, quarterly, or annual events. For example, you can create a template for a company calendar that includes holidays, company events, and employee information.

✔ Resumes that you update with your work history, education, and other information that changes over time. Standard information, such as name, address, contact info, and past work history can remain in your resume template, and you can update it only when necessary.

✔ Newsletters containing masthead, column placements, standard graphics, address information, and graphic boxes.

When you want to use a template to create a new document, access the Template Organizer. From there, pick a template file (with a .ott file extension), open it in Lotus Symphony Documents, make your changes, and then save the document. When you save the document, Lotus Symphony Documents automatically knows you want the file to be a document, not a template. A document file is stored on your system. The original template file doesn't change; you can then re-use it the next time you want a document in this format.

To start a document that uses a template, follow these steps:

1. **Start Lotus Symphony.**

2. **Choose File⇨New⇨From Template⇨Document.**

   The New from Template window appears. The first time you use the Template Organizer, a message appears informing you that the Organizer doesn't include any templates at this time. The next few steps show how to populate the Template Organizer for the first time.

3. **Click OK.**

   The New from Template window appears. (See Figure 4-2.)

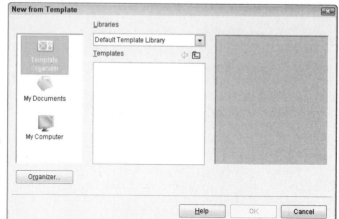

4. **Click the Organizer button.**

   The Template Organizer window appears.

5. **Click Actions⇨Import Template.**

   The Insert dialog box appears.

6. **Navigate to a folder that includes a Lotus Symphony Documents template file and select it.**

   If you don't have a template file on your system, you can download one from the IBM Lotus Symphony Gallery Web page at `http://symphony.lotus.com/software/lotus/symphony/gallery.jspa`.

7. **Click Insert.**

   The Template Organizer window appears, with the template added to the list of available templates. Continue adding templates as needed. (See Figure 4-3.)

8. **Click OK.**

   The New from Template window appears again, as shown in Figure 4-4, this time with document templates you can select.

9. **Select a template.**

10. **Click OK.**

    A new document appears with the formatting, boilerplate text, and other objects stored in the template you choose to start with. In the template we show in Figure 4-5, for example, you can start writing a business plan using the objects and text included in the template file.

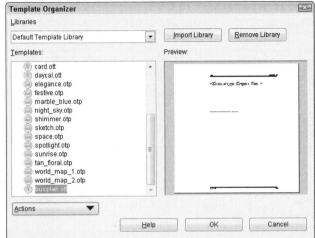

Figure 4-3:
The
Template
Organizer.

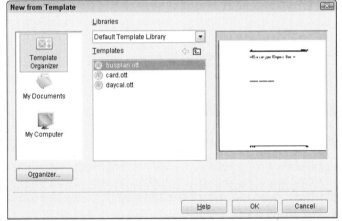

Figure 4-4:
Only Lotus
Symphony
Documents
templates
appear
in the
New from
Template
window.

After you have templates in the Template Organizer, you don't have to go through all the steps you just went through. You can go from Step 2 to Step 9. Of course, any time you want to import new templates into the Template Organizer, follow Steps 3–8.

For information on creating templates and working with the Template Organizer, see Chapter 5.

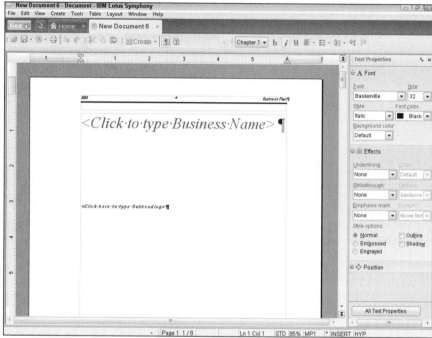

Figure 4-5:
Some templates even include helpful hints to guide you through creating the document.

Creating a document from another document

Finally, another way to create your own document is to use another Lotus Symphony Documents document. You can overwrite the information in the document, save the document with a different name (or leave it the same as the original if you like), and by golly, you got your document.

To do this, get another document, such as a document you created from a template file, and follow these steps:

1. **Start Lotus Symphony Documents.**

2. **Choose File⇨Open⇨File.**

   The Open dialog box appears.

3. **Select the document.**

4. **Click Open.**

   The document opens in the Lotus Symphony Documents tab.

How often should I save?

"How often should I save?" is a common question I'm asked. My typical reply is "As often as you can." When I'm working on a document, I save about every minute or two. You never know when the power may go out or an electrical event may occur. When this happens, your computer will shut down (unless you have a battery backup such as while using a laptop), and all of your unsaved modifications will be lost. A good recommendation is to save every time you make extensive changes to a document and don't want to redo those changes later in the event of an electrical outage.

---

5. **Choose File⇨Save As.**

   The Save As dialog box appears.

6. **Enter a new filename in the File Name field.**

7. **Click Save.**

   A new document is created.

Saving Your Documents

As you create new documents and modify existing ones, you need to make sure that you save any changes. This means that you take the information that appears on the monitor and make a permanent copy of it on your hard disk or other drive (such as a network drive or flash media device). You can continue to work on the document, but you should periodically take the time to save your changes.

When you use Lotus Symphony Documents to create or work on files, you have a few options for saving the file. You can save files in these formats:

- ✔ Open Document Format (`.odt`)
- ✔ Microsoft Word format (`.doc`)
- ✔ Adobe Portable Document Format (`.pdf`)
- ✔ IBM Word Processing Document (`.sxw`)
- ✔ Rich Text Format (`.rtf`)

 When saving documents, you also can save them as template files. For Lotus Symphony Documents templates, you save them as Open Document Text Templates with an `.ott` file extension. You also can save files in the IBM Word Processing Document Template format (which uses the `.stw` extension). For more about templates, see Chapter 5.

Saving in Open Document format

The primary format for saving Lotus Symphony Documents files, Open Document Format, provides a way for other Open Document-compliant applications to read Lotus Symphony Documents files. For example, the OpenOffice product, available from OpenOffice.org, supports Open Document files. Likewise, Sun Microsystems provides Open Document support in its StarOffice product.

You may wonder why you should care if a document is supported by other programs. One primary reason is document sharing. When you create a document in a proprietary format (such as Microsoft Word's .doc format), anyone who wants to read or edit that document must have a product that's compliant with that proprietary format. Sometimes this requires obtaining add-ons, or even paying for a license for the program (such as Microsoft Word). With the Open Document format, many of the products that can read and edit those documents are free, letting you share documents with others and not worry that the other person will have to invest in a new application (or suite of applications).

By default, when you save a new document in Lotus Symphony Documents, the Open Document format is automatically selected. To save in Open Document format, follow these steps:

1. **Open a new Lotus Symphony Documents document.**

2. **Enter some text in the window.**

   The section called "Entering Content" discusses this in more detail, but for now, you can type any characters you want. If you don't add new text, the Save command on the File menu (see Step 3) doesn't display.

3. **Choose File⇨Save.**

   The Save As dialog box appears. (See Figure 4-6.)

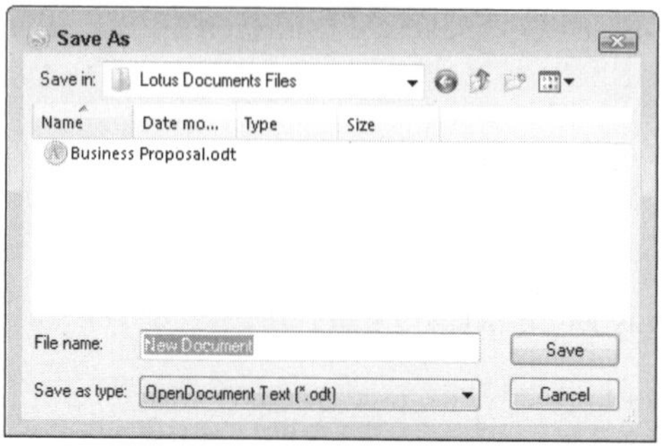

Figure 4-6:
By default,
Documents
files are
saved
in Open
Document
Text format.

4. **Type a name for the file in the File Name field.**

5. **Click Save.**

   The document is saved in the .odt file format.

 If the Open Document Text (*.odt) format doesn't show up as the default file format, you can click the down arrow and select the Open Document file format.

Saving in PDF format

As mentioned before, many users need a way to share documents with other users. One way to share documents requires all users to have common applications, such as Lotus Symphony, Microsoft Word, or Corel WordPerfect. But what if you just need to share information and don't need others to modify the document's content? That's when you may want to consider saving your documents as Adobe PDF, or Portable Document Format files.

Users who receive PDF files simply need the Adobe Reader (which is available for free on Adobe.com) to read the contents of the file. Granted, they can't make edits to the document, but that's okay in many cases. For example, you may have a press release put out by your marketing department. The content includes information about a new product that you want to announce to the world; you don't want anyone editing the document, just reading it. Saving the document from Lotus Symphony Documents into the PDF format makes a lot of sense.

PDF files are created using a built-in tool provided for free with Lotus Symphony Documents. Create your document in Lotus Symphony Documents, save it as a Lotus Symphony Documents file so you can edit it later if you want, and then convert it to PDF format when it's finalized.

 To read documents saved in PDF format (which is .pdf, by the way), you need a free program called Adobe Reader. You can download it from Adobe. com. Many companies and organizations install it as a one of the primary applications on their users' machines. Even if you don't receive PDF files from someone using Lotus Symphony Documents, you'll undoubtedly run into them from other users, Web sites, and software or hardware vendors. For example, many software companies include their documentation on CD-ROMs or Web sites in PDF format.

To save a Lotus Symphony Documents file in PDF format, use these steps:

1. **Open a document in Lotus Symphony Documents.**

2. **Choose File⇨Save to save the document in Lotus Symphony Documents format.**

3. **Choose File⇨Export.**

   The Export dialog box appears, with the Portable Document Format (.pdf) format selected.

4. **Type a name for the document in the File Name field.**

   The name can be the same as you used for the original Lotus Symphony Documents file.

5. **Click Save.**

   The PDF Options dialog box appears. (See Figure 4-7.)

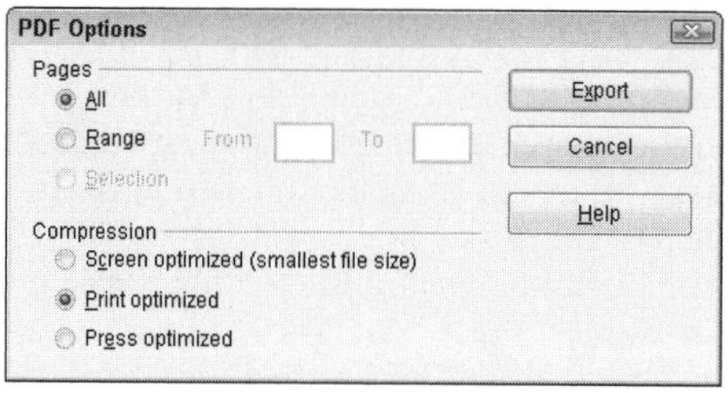

Figure 4-7:
You can set some PDF file options in this dialog box.

PDF Options

Pages
- ◉ All
- ○ Range   From [ ] To [ ]
- ○ Selection

Compression
- ○ Screen optimized (smallest file size)
- ◉ Print optimized
- ○ Press optimized

[Export]
[Cancel]
[Help]

6. **Keep the default options, as they export the entire document and optimize the document for viewing onscreen and printing.**

7. **Click Export.**

   Lotus Symphony Documents converts the document into PDF format and saves the file to your system. You can open the document by locating it on your hard drive (or whichever location it was saved to) and double-clicking it. The file appears in the Adobe Reader window. (See the previous tip for information on acquiring the free Adobe Reader program).

Saving in Word DOC or other formats

Microsoft Word remains the most popular word processor in the market, even with a long list of free or nearly free alternatives. Because of this, other word processors remain competitive by providing support for the .doc format (Word's native file format). Lotus Symphony Documents includes support for saving in .doc format.

Currently, Lotus Symphony Documents supports only the Word 97/2000/XP .doc file format. The latest Word format, called .docx for Open XML, isn't supported. If you need to get a document into .docx format and you have access to Microsoft Word, save the Lotus Symphony Documents file to `.doc`, open the file in Word, and do a File➪Save As command to save in Word Document format (or `.docx`).

You can also save your documents in other file formats, including IBM Word Processing Document (`.sxw`), Microsoft Rich Text Formatting (`.rtf`), or Text (`.txt`). The first two formats aren't used as much as the Microsoft Word (`.doc`) or Open Document format. However, the Microsoft Rich Text Formatting format is used a lot for sharing documents that have some formatting inside them (such as bulleted lists), but some higher-end formatting may be lost.

A Text file (`.txt`), however, probably is the most used document in the computing world. They have been used since the first micro-computers (which is what a desktop or laptop PC is) and even used during the larger mainframe and mini-computer days. Text files contain just text — no graphics, pretty bullets, tables, or other extended characters.

To save in one of these formats, use the following steps:

1. **Open a document in Lotus Symphony Documents and enter some text.**

2. **Choose File➪Save As.**

   The Save As dialog box appears.

3. **Click the down arrow on the Save as Type field to see a list of file types.**

4. **Choose a file type, such as Microsoft Word 97/2000/XP (*.doc) or Microsoft Rich Text Format (*.rtf), as shown in Figure 4-8.**

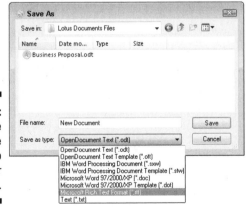

Figure 4-8:
Select the file type you want to convert your file to.

5. Click Save.

Lotus Symphony Documents converts the file to the file you choose.

 If you save the file in Microsoft RTF format, you'll see a message informing you that some of the content and formatting may be lost during the conversion. Click OK to continue the conversion process. In the document shown in Figure 4-8, for example, when I converted this document, the content, graphic, and paragraph formatting stayed the same. However, the background (which is blue) disappeared when I opened the converted Microsoft Rich Text Formatting file in Microsoft Word.

Entering Content

By now (if you read the first part of this chapter), you know how to start Lotus Symphony, launch Lotus Symphony Documents, and display a blank new document. In the next section of this chapter, you learn how to input content and manipulate it once it's in there.

Typing new text

When working in a Lotus Symphony Documents file, you can add text. To add text, you simply click inside the document window to set your insertion point (cursor) and begin typing. The insertion point appears as a flashing vertical bar. As you type text into the document, the insertion point moves to indicate where the next character is to appear. The insertion point automatically flows to the next line when you reach the right margin.

Margins dictate the parameters of the document area in which you can insert text or other document items. A document has four margins. The top margin sets the amount of space from the top edge of the paper to the first line of text. The bottom margin sets how far up on the page from the bottom edge of the paper text stops. The left and right margins set how close to the left and right edges of the paper the text can get. You can set the margins to different measurements depending on the look of the finished document you want. The default margin settings are $1^1/_2$ inches for the left and right margins, and 1 inch for the top and bottom margins.

To add a new paragraph to the document, press the Enter key. A gap appears between the first paragraph and the insertion point.

That gap between paragraphs is called *paragraph spacing,* or *spacing,* as in single-spacing, double-spacing, and so on. Also, some people refer to it as "adding paragraph returns" to the document, similar to hitting the return key on the old-fashioned typewriters. You may want to add a few more paragraph returns in some parts of your documents to add more space between paragraphs, depending on your design needs. Chapter 5 discusses more about how to set up paragraph spacing and other style issues.

Embedding graphics and clip art

Not only can you insert text into your documents, but you also can add pictures to them. Pictures, also called "graphics," include:

- ✔ Photographs
- ✔ Drawings
- ✔ Technical drawings
- ✔ Borders
- ✔ Charts
- ✔ Animations
- ✔ Line art
- ✔ Clip art

Graphics that are included in a document are said to be *embedded,* meaning they are part of the document. Because Lotus Symphony Documents is a word processor and not a graphics editor, you cannot make changes to a graphic inside Lotus Symphony Documents. Instead you can double-click an embedded graphic and edit it in an outside graphics program, such as Adobe Photoshop (if that program is installed on your computer).

Lotus Symphony Documents comes bundled with a number of free-to-use images. When you work through the following steps, you are shown how to use one of these images to embed into a document. If you have your own images saved to your system, feel free to use one of those images as well.

To embed a graphic in a document:

1. **Open a document in Lotus Symphony Documents.**
2. **Choose Create⇨Create Graphics.**

   The Create Graphics dialog box appears.

3. Locate the graphic you want to embed into your document.

In our example, we looked in the Architecture folder for the Lighthouse. wmf file.

4. Click Open.

The selected graphic embeds into your document.

Chapter 5 discusses how you can resize, position, and remove graphics from your documents.

Editing Text

Unless you are a brilliant writer or just do not care what you write, at some point you will need to correct something in your document. Part of the process of creating documents includes editing text. Lotus Symphony Documents provides several ways to edit text, including manually modifying text, using the built-in automatic correction tool Instant Corrections, and a spell-checker.

Modifying text manually

When you make or find an error in your documents, you can modify your text as follows:

- Select a character (such as a letter or number), word, or multiple words or paragraphs, and press Delete. This erases your selection.

- Press the Delete key. This deletes the character to the right of the insertion point.

- Press the Backspace key to delete the character to the left of the insertion point.

- Select a character, word, multiple words, or paragraph, and enter new text. The new text appears in place of your selection.

- Copy some information to the clipboard using the Edit⇨Copy command. Select the text you want to remove and choose Edit⇨Paste. The pasted information appears where your selected text was.

You will want to be careful when you insert new text into a document to ensure you have the Insert key enabled on your keyboard. It appears above the Delete key on a normal size keyboard. What this does is allow new text to be inserted, while existing text remains untouched. If the Insert key is turned off, the Overwrite feature is enabled, meaning new text overwrites existing text. You can tell the Insert key remains enabled by looking on the Lotus Symphony Documents Status bar (at the bottom of the Lotus Symphony Documents window). The word STATUS appears when enabled. If it says OVER, the Overwrite feature needs turned off by pressing the Insert key on the keyboard.

Another way to change text in documents uses the Instant Corrections feature. This feature automatically changes text as you enter it, such as changing commonly misspelled words or phrases to their correct spellings. Lotus Symphony Documents provides dozens of replacement words for misspellings, and you can add your own.

Checking your documents for spelling errors

One of the most useful tools for word processors has to be the spell checking tool. This tool goes through your document — and even runs as you type your text looking for Instant Correction replacements — and checks the spelling for accuracy. When it finds a word that it does not recognize, it displays the Spellcheck dialog box.

To run the Spell Check tool, perform the following steps:

1. **Make sure you have a document in Lotus Symphony Documents created. Also, make sure some text appears in the document.**

2. **Choose Tools⇨Spell Check.**

3. **Click Yes if you are prompted to start checking from the beginning of the document.**

    If the Spell Check discovers a misspelled word, the Spellcheck dialog box appears.

The red squigglies

After you run Spell Check on a document, you may see red squiggly lines appear under some words. These words are coming up as misspelled ones, and the red squiggly lines help you identify them quickly. Right-click the word, select a suggested new spelling from the context menu that appears, or click Ignore to ignore the word. You also can add words to your dictionary here, by clicking the Add button.

4. Look at the word in the Word field. Do one of the following:

- Is the word misspelled? If yes, click a suitable replacement in the Suggestions area and click Replace. If no, click Ignore.

- Is the word misspelled but no suggestion matches the correct spelling (or what you think it might be)? Type a new spelling into the Word field. Click Replace.

- Is the spelling correct for the word? Click Close to retain the word's spelling. Why do this? Some words, such as product names, do not appear in the Spell Check dictionary. For these cases, you can close the Spellcheck dialog box without making any changes. Or click the Add button to add that word to the dictionary so that Lotus Symphony Documents will know that you do not want to be prompted on that spelling again.

 You can run Spell Check at any time; you don't have to wait until you finish writing your document. In fact, you may find it convenient to run Spell Check on a word or two if, as you're writing or performing other daily tasks (such as adding text to a graphic in Adobe Photoshop) where an electronic dictionary comes in handy. Simply type the word or phrase you want to check and then run Spell Check to verify if your spelling is correct.

Navigating a Document

As documents grow in size, you'll need a way to move around the document. You can

- ✔ Move within a page.

- ✔ Go from page to page.

- ✔ Jump from any place in the document to the end of the document.

- ✔ Return to the beginning while positioned any place in the document.

 This chapter focuses on using basic commands to navigate through a document. To learn about a more powerful navigation tool — the Lotus Symphony Navigator — see Chapter 6, "Designing Complex Documents."

Using the mouse to move through a document

To get around any document in Lotus Symphony, the mouse probably provides the most convenience and flexibility. Here are some of the things it can do:

✔ Click the left mouse button on the scroll bars on the side of the document to move up and down a document that stretches beyond a single Lotus Symphony Documents window. A scroll bar can also appear on the bottom of the document's window if the document spans wider than the window. Use that scroll bar to move left or right in a document.

✔ With the scrolling wheel found on many new mouse designs, use the wheel to quickly scroll through a document line by line, multiple lines at a time, or page by page.

✔ Use the mouse to set the insertion point (the cursor) anyplace inside your documents.

Using the keyboard to move through a document

Some users prefer to keep their hands on the keyboard as they work, minimizing the repetitive action of moving one hand to the mouse and back to the keyboard. Although this appeals to the more efficiency-minded users, it can pose a few hurdles for navigating through a document.

Some of the commands for keyboard navigation are as follows:

✔ **Enter:** Press this to move the insertion point down and to create a new paragraph.

✔ **Home key:** Press this key to move the insertion point to the beginning of the current line.

✔ **End key:** Press this key to move the insertion point to the end of the current line.

✔ **Ctrl+Home:** Press this keyboard combination to move the insertion point to the top of the first page.

✔ **Ctrl+End:** Press this keyboard combination to move the insertion point to the bottom of the last page.

✔ **Shift+Home:** Press this keyboard combination to highlight all text from the insertion point to the beginning of the current line.

✔ **Shift+End:** Press this keyboard combination to highlight all text from the insertion point to the beginning of the current line.

✔ **Page Up key:** Press this key to display the previous page.

✔ **Page Down key:** Press this key to display the next page.

✔ **Arrow keys:** Use these keys to move the insertion point one position up, down, right, or left.

Viewing Text

Lotus Symphony Documents displays documents at a percentage of their normal size. Sometimes the percentage is 100 percent, while other times it's set to a higher or lower value. These settings are established in the Zoom drop-down toolbar feature or the Zoom dialog box.

Besides changing zoom settings in your documents, you also can view rulers that help you place text and other items in specific locations on your document. Keep reading for more details.

Using zoom settings

You can see the current zoom setting by looking in two places. First, you can look on the document window status bar, located at the bottom of the window. You'll see a number followed by a percentage, such as 125%, telling you the zoom factor. Double-click that number to display the Zoom dialog box. (See Figure 4-9.) Select a predefined zoom setting and click OK, or select Variable to type in a zoom value and then click OK.

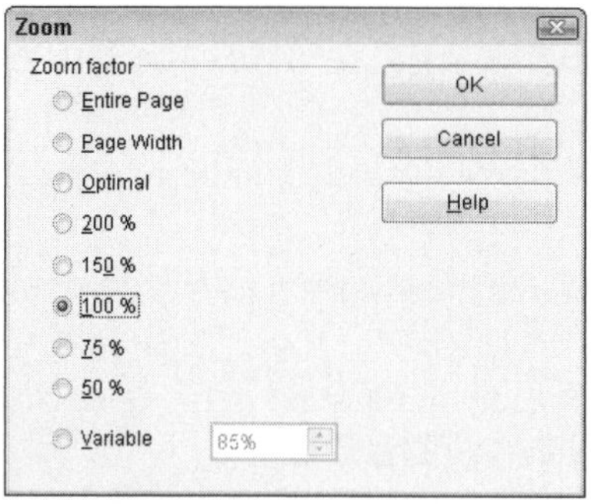

Figure 4-9:
Use the
Zoom dialog
box to set a
zoom factor.

You also can see it in the Zoom toolbar drop-down tool on the Main toolbar. This provides a handful of predefined settings, but you also can type in a value and press Enter for that setting to be applied to your document.

Turning on/off rulers

Lotus Symphony Documents includes two rulers that enable you to place precisely text and other objects you insert into your documents. The vertical ruler appears on the left side of the document window. It provides measurement values for vertical placement of objects in your documents. For example, use this ruler if you want to place an object 1.5 inches from the top of the page.

The horizontal ruler appears at the top of the document window. You use it to position objects relative to the left or right side of your documents. For example, if you want a text box to appear 3.25 inches from the left side of the page, use the horizontal ruler to help you line up that text box on the page.

If the rulers aren't turned on — which they should be by default — you can turn them on manually. To do this, choose View➪Ruler➪Horizontal Ruler for the horizontal ruler. Or choose View➪Ruler➪Vertical Ruler for the vertical ruler. A check mark appears next to the rulers that you've turned on. Repeat the process to turn off the rulers you want to remove from the document window.

Outputting Your Documents

You can output Lotus Symphony Documents documents a few different ways, including

✔ Preview mode

✔ To a printer

✔ Reused in other documents

I discuss each of these in the upcoming sections.

Previewing your documents

As you create documents, you can preview how they'll look if you print them. With the Print Preview, Lotus Symphony Documents shows 100 percent of your document, and it can even show multiple pages at 100 percent. Of course, as the zoom percentage increases, the size of each document decreases, so reading documents in Print Preview mode may be difficult at times.

Print Preview provides a big-picture view of what your final, printed document will look like.

Just because something doesn't show up in Print Preview mode, it doesn't mean that it isn't in your document. Sometimes your video hardware can display only so much information from a document. In those cases, some items may not appear in the Print Preview mode. Or they may appear difficult to see or grayed out. The only way to really see how a document looks printed out is to print it out. You learn about printing documents in the next section.

To use Print Preview to take a look at how your document will print, do the following:

1. **Open a document in Lotus Symphony Documents.**

2. **Choose File⇨Print Preview.**

   The Print Preview window appears, like the one shown in Figure 4-10.

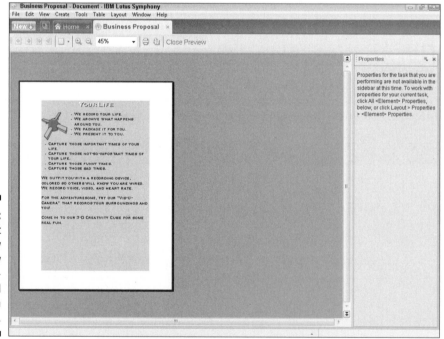

Figure 4-10:
Print Preview shows how your document will look when printed.

3. **Click the Next Page button to navigate from page to page. Or click the Last Page button to jump to the end of the document.**

4. **Click the Close Preview button to close the Print Preview window and to return to the normal document editing window.**

Printing documents

In many cases, you'll want to make a hard copy of your final document, or print a version of the document in progress. To do this, you use a printer connected to your computer and send the document to it from Lotus Symphony Documents.

To print a document:

1. **Open a document in Lotus Symphony Documents.**

2. **Choose File⇨Print. The Print dialog box appears. (See Figure 4-11.)**

3. **Set these print options:**
   - The Name drop-down list provides a list of printers connected to your computer.
   - Print range options let you select the entire document (All) to print, or you can specify a range of pages to print (using the Pages field).
   - The Number of Copies field enables you to set a value for the number of copies you want to make.

4. **Click OK. Your document is sent to the selected printer.**

Saving documents for reuse in other documents

As you find in the "Saving in PDF format" section earlier in this chapter, you can output your Lotus Symphony Documents files into a format that is suited for online dissemination. For example, you can create a document in Lotus Symphony Documents and save the file to a PDF format. You can then upload the PDF file to a network location, such as on an internal LAN (local area network) or WAN (wide area network). Web pages can include hyperlinks to that PDF file so that other users can access it.

Chapter 5

Formatting for Style

In This Chapter

▶ Formatting your text

▶ Creating and modifying lists

▶ Understanding your templates and styles

▶ Working with the Template Organizer

▶ Formatting your graphics

▶ Making subscripts and superscripts

*I*f you've followed along to this point, you probably have a document or a set of documents with content in them, such as text and graphics. You may also have done a little formatting to help make the document more presentable. This chapter shows you how to apply formatting elements, such as templates, font characteristics, lists, and more, to make your documents have more pizzazz.

With a little work, anyone can create easy-to-read documents that have some aesthetic appeal to them. Not only does formatting provide stylistic detail to a document, but it also can make information easier to locate and understand. Whether you're a professional at your job or even a volunteer worker at your local church, Lotus Symphony Documents allows you to spend just a few moments — or hours, if you like — making your documents look more appealing.

Along with just looking pretty, stylized documents can help make getting your point across a whole lot easier. Imagine the book you're holding in your hands without any stylistic elements: no graphics added and resized, no headlines to break up the different sections, and no bulleted points to help break up a large amount of text. Also consider reading through a set of steps without numbers to guide you from one action to the next. You may get through the material eventually, but doing so probably would require lots of concentration and may get frustrating at some point. With a clean design, consistent elements, and overall appealing layout, readers can concentrate on the content of the pages, not work at deciphering if a heading is an instructional step or a section break.

Formatting Text

How you present information means a great deal to your audience. As an example, read the following passage:

```
Self Evaluation Take a few minutes to assess
yourself. 1 is the low score and 5 is the
high score. After you finish, total the values
and insert the amount at the bottom. Personal
Life Attitude 1 2 3 4 5 Life Skills (Self
discipline, self confidence, self image) 1 2 3
4 5 Habit 1 2 3 4 5 Desire 1 2 3 4 5 Enthusiasm
1 2 3 4 5 Focus 1 2 3 4 5 Professional Life
Come to work mentally prepared. 1 2 3 4 5
Have a written plan and follow it daily. 1
2 3 4 5 Fill my day with sales producing
activities. 1 2 3 4 5 Database Management 1 2
3 4 5 Marketing 1 2 3 4 5 Job vs. Career 1 2 3
4 5 Outlook 1st impression & Greeting 1 2 3 4
5 Building Rapport & Investigating 1 2 3 4 5
Presenting & Demonstrating 1 2 3 4 5 Closing 1
2 3 4 5 Bypassing & Handling Objections 1 2 3
4 5 Service Walk / Evidence Manual 1 2 3 4 5
Follow-Up 1 2 3 4 5 Prospecting 1 2 3 4 5
```

Now look at the following same content as earlier but with a little formatting added:

Take a few minutes to assess yourself — 1 is the low score, and 5 is the high score. After you finish, total the values and insert the amount at the bottom.

Self Evaluation

Area To Evaluate	Item To Evaluate	Scoring
Personal Life		
	Attitude	1 2 3 4 5
	Life skills (Self-discipline, self-confidence, self-image)	1 2 3 4 5
	Habit	1 2 3 4 5
	Desire	1 2 3 4 5
	Enthusiasm	1 2 3 4 5
	Focus	1 2 3 4 5

Area To Evaluate	Item To Evaluate	Scoring
Professional Life		
	Come to work mentally prepared	1 2 3 4 5
	Have a written plan and follow it daily	1 2 3 4 5
	Fill my day with sales-producing activities	1 2 3 4 5
	Database management	1 2 3 4 5
	Marketing	1 2 3 4 5
	Job versus career	1 2 3 4 5
Selling Outlook		
	First impression and greeting	1 2 3 4 5
	Building rapport and investigating	1 2 3 4 5
	Presenting and demonstrating	1 2 3 4 5
	Closing	1 2 3 4 5
	Bypassing and handling objections	1 2 3 4 5
	Service walk/evidence manual	1 2 3 4 5
	Follow-up	1 2 3 4 5
	Prospecting	1 2 3 4 5
	Total	

Which assessment would you rather read? Of course, most of us would rather work through the latter assessment. That's a simple example of what can be done with formatting, which is easy to apply to the documents you create in Lotus Symphony Documents.

The following few sections show how to use fonts and styles to modify document layout.

Changing the font

When you look at a document, whether it's on-screen or printed as hard copy, each character of text has a typeface. *Typefaces* are shapes (actually, they're called *glyphs*) given to specific characters. *Fonts* are a family of typefaces that make characters (such as letters, numbers, and symbols) appear in a certain way. You can select different fonts, font sizes, and font enhancements to format text in your documents. Figure 5-1 shows several different fonts used to format the same sentence.

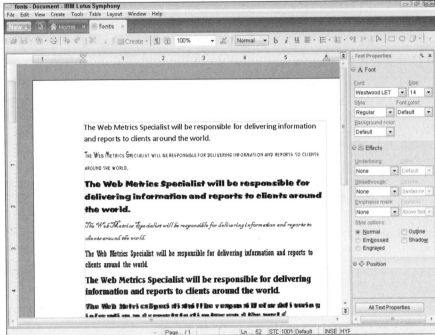

Figure 5-1:
Here are some different fonts and how they make the same text look different

Lotus Symphony Documents enables you to change the font for any character in your document by using the fonts installed on your computer. Fonts are stored in the operating system (Microsoft Windows) with different names to help distinguish them from other fonts, but fonts can be accessed from the Text Properties Sidebar in Lotus Symphony Documents. Some common fonts include

- ✔ Arial
- ✔ Times New Roman
- ✔ Courier
- ✔ Bookman
- ✔ Calibri
- ✔ Futura
- ✔ Wingdings

You can find all the fonts stored on your computer by accessing the Fonts folder. Choose Start➪Control Panel➪Fonts to see this folder. From the File menu, the Install New Font command enables you to manually install new fonts (such as those you download from the Internet). However, most new fonts users receive are included as part of other applications. During the initial installation of those applications, any new fonts are installed automatically for you.

Fonts: size and kerning

Besides the different look of each font in Figure 5-1, you may also have noticed that some lines appear longer (or *bigger*) than others and that some lines have more space between characters and words than other lines. For the figure, I used the same font size (14 point) for all characters, regardless of font. The differences among the ways each line looks in regard to spacing relates to kerning. *Kerning* is how much space a single character (including a space) consumes on the line in relation to a character next to it.

You can adjust kerning of characters in Lotus Symphony Documents by expanding or condensing the kerning of characters. Unless you plan to create high-end graphics, designed documents, or layout, the normal kerning values are usually adequate even for serious business documents and memos. You can, however, experiment with the kerning settings (discover how to adjust font settings in the following section) for those situations in which you must pay attention to character spacing and alignment.

Although aesthetically-speaking you should limit the number of different fonts you use in a document (some designers suggest using no more than three to five different fonts in a document), you can use as many as you want. Each word in your document could have a different font — that would make your document look like one of those motion-picture ransom letters, but Lotus Symphony Documents would let you do it.

To change the font, do the following:

1. **Start Lotus Symphony Documents.**

2. **Open a document that has some text, or create a new document and enter a few lines of text.**

3. **Select some text.**

   The current font for your selected text appears in the Font drop-down list.

4 **From the Text Properties sidebar, choose the Font drop-down list (see Figure 5-2).**

5. **Select a different font.**

   The font changes for the selected text and displays your text with that font.

When you change fonts for selected text, the next characters you type after the selected text use that new font. If you want to start a new document and change the font for all the text you plan to enter, select the font from the Fonts drop-down list before you enter any new text. Then as you enter text, the text uses the new font.

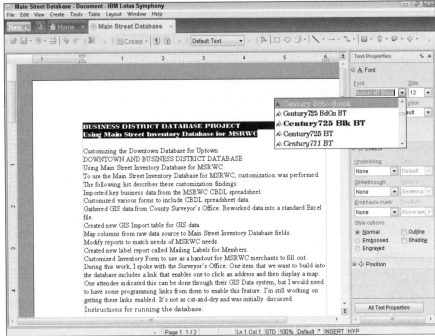

Figure 5-2:
Use the
Font drop-
down list
on the Text
Properties
sidebar to
choose a
font.

All new Lotus Symphony Documents use the Times New Roman font as their default fonts. You can change this by changing the new blank document template that displays every time you start a new document. However, you may want to consider creating your own template (with different default fonts) and using it for your new documents. This way you don't run the risk of corrupting the master template. Read how to save your own templates in the "Saving your own templates" section later in this chapter.

Changing the font size

Lotus Symphony Documents enables you to change font size for any font used in your document. Popular font sizes for standard documents, such as memos, business reports, and similar documents, include 10 point and 12 point. Headings and special text items (such as callouts) tend to be larger font sizes, such as 16 point for the Heading 1 style used by the default template in Lotus Symphony Documents. You can actually set up font sizes to just about any size (I entered a point size of 2000, but the text flowed over to numerous pages!) in Lotus Symphony Documents. Figure 5-3 shows some examples of different font sizes applied to text.

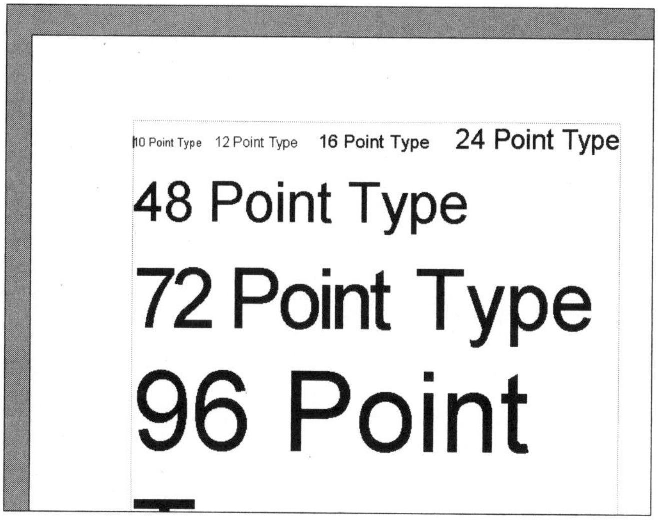

10 Point Type   12 Point Type   16 Point Type   24 Point Type

48 Point Type

72 Point Type

96 Point

Figure 5-3:
You can
vary the
sizes of
fonts in your
documents.

Points are a measurement of the size of typeface displayed on a screen or printed material. One point equals $1/72$ of an inch.

To change the font size of text, use the following steps:

1. **Start Lotus Symphony Documents.**

2. **Open a document that has some text, or create a new document and enter a few lines of text.**

3. **Select some text.**

   The current font size for your selected text appears in the Size drop-down list.

4. **From the Text Properties sidebar, choose the Size drop-down list.**

5. **Select a different size.**

   The font size changes for the selected text and displays your text with that setting.

When you design documents, use different font sizes to differentiate between body text and other text, such as titles, headings, sub-headings, and similar text. Usually titles, such as chapter titles, have larger font sizes than headings, which have larger font sizes than sub-headings. In turn, sub-headings generally have slightly larger font sizes than body text.

Changing other text properties

Along with font and font size, you can change other text properties. Table 5-1 describes text properties accessible from the Text Properties sidebar and the Text Properties dialog box. To access the Text Properties dialog box, click the All Text Properties button on the Text Properties sidebar.

A number of formatting options are available by selecting text or paragraphs and right-clicking. You can, for example, use the Align Text options to align text on the page (left align, right align, center, or justify). The Line Spacing command (with single, 1.5, and double spacing options) can be found on the contextual menu as well.

To get familiar with Lotus Symphony Documents text properties, you may want to spend some time working with them. Apply some of these effects to sample text to see how the effect looks in your documents. The shadow and engraved style options, for example, can be used for different words or phrases placed on your documents, but you probably shouldn't use them for a ten-page report. Also, the strikethrough effect performs the function of allowing you to keep text on a page so that it's readable, but still shows that you plan to remove it for a final draft. Strikethrough is handy when you're routing a document for review to several people or departments.

Table 5-1	Lotus Symphony Documents Text Properties
Property	*Description*
Style	Includes settings for emphasizing a character with **bold**, *italic*, ***bold italic***, or regular (sometimes called Roman) typeface.
Font color	Enables you to set different colors for your text, such as red, blue, white (you better have a dark background to see this), and so on.
Background color	Lets you set the background color of your text. This option just sets the color behind the text you specify, not for the entire page.
Underlining	Enables you to underline selected text.
Color	Sets the color for the underlined text.
Strikethrough	Enables you to use the strikethrough mark for selected text. Lotus Symphony Documents includes single, double, bold, / and X strikethrough marks.
Options	Sets options for the strikethrough setting, such as sentence or word only.

Property	Description
Style options	Includes options for adding effects to your text, such as normal, embossed, engraved, outline, and shadow.
Font position	Enables you to set text as normal, superscript, or subscript. You can read more about this setting in the section "Using Subscript and Superscript" later in this chapter.
(Font position) Change by	Sets subscript and superscript percentage values. You can read more about this setting in the section "Using Subscript and Superscript" later in this chapter.
Font spacing	Provides settings for expanding or condensing the space between characters.
(Font spacing) Change by	Enables you to set the font spacing values for expanding or condensing the space between characters.
Rotate text	Enables you to rotate selected text clockwise by 90 or 270 degrees.
Scale width	Enables you to stretch or compress selected characters.
Language	Sets the language for the selected text, such as English (USA), Latin, Armenian, and so on. Use this option when you want a word or group of words to be in a language different than the rest of the document. Language doesn't translate your text but does apply proper language syntax for the language you select. Found only on the Font tab of the Text Properties dialog box.
Emphasis mark	Enables you to display dots, circles, discs, or accents above or below a selection. Use the Position drop-down list along with the Emphasis mark option. These settings are found only on the Effects tab of the Text Properties dialog box.
Effects	Provides options to set the font to different capital letter effects. For example, you can use the Small capitals option to display a selection of lowercase letters as all capital letters, but sized as if they were lowercase letters. You may hear this referred to as *small caps*. This setting is found only on the Effects tab of the Text Properties dialog box.

To set different options for text properties, do the following:

1. **Start Lotus Symphony Documents.**

2. **Open a document that has some text, or create a new document and enter a few lines of text.**

3. **Select some text.**

4. **Select options on the Text Properties sidebar.**

   For example, Figure 5-4 displays a document with several options from the sidebar. The following lists each of the properties used in Figure 5-4:

   A. Arial font, font size 26, black background with white font

   B. Arial font, font size 16, double-underlined, condensed font by 1.7 points

   C. Arial font, font size 14, small capitals

   D. Arial font, font size 12, double strikethrough word only

   E. Arial font, font size 12, circle emphasis mark above text

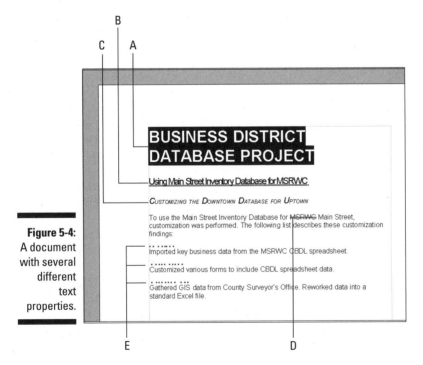

Figure 5-4:
A document
with several
different
text
properties.

Lotus Symphony Documents Formatting with Lists

Bulleted and numbered lists help you display content in an easy-to-read and follow format. A group of steps, such as those found in the tutorial sections of this book, lets readers quickly recognize step-by-step procedures and provides them a way to see each specific step needed to perform a specific task. Without steps, readers could be left wondering which part of a procedure to perform next.

Similarly, bulleted lists provide you with a way to pull out a group of related items and format them outside the normal paragraph format. By doing this, readers can easily grasp that the items are part of a list and have some relationship to each other. List items buried within a paragraph can be lost as pertinent information the author is attempting to convey to the readers.

Lotus Symphony Documents makes it easy to add the bulleted and numbered list formats to your documents. The next sections show how to create and modify these types of lists.

Creating a bulleted list

Bulleted lists make reading a set of related items easier. Figure 5-5 shows the same text in two formats. The top area shows text in paragraph format. The bottom shows the same text as a bulleted list. As you can see, the bulleted list makes the text easier to read, thereby your reader has to work less to get the same information. Hopefully this results in better grasp of the information as well as longer retention of it.

To create your own bulleted list, do the following:

1. **Open Lotus Symphony Documents.**
2. **Create a new document or open an existing one.**
3. **Input a few items you want to create as a bulleted list.**
4. **Select those items.**
5. **Click the Bullets toolbar button on the Context Sensitive toolbar.**

   You may need to move the Context Sensitive toolbar down to its own toolbar layer in order to see the Bullets toolbar button. To do this, select the toolbar and drag it down.

   Your text changes to show round bullets to the left of the selection.

These are tasks I performed. Imported key business data from the MSRWC CBDL spreadsheet. Customized various forms to include CBDL spreadsheet data. Gathered GIS data from County Surveyor's Office. Reworked data into a standard Excel file. Created new GIS Import table for GIS data. Map columns from raw data source to Main Street Inventory Database fields. Modify reports to match needs of MSRWC needs. Created new label report called Mailing Labels for Members. Customized Inventory Form to use as a handout for MSRWC merchants to fill out.

These are the tasks I performed:

- Imported key business data from the MSRWC CBDL spreadsheet.
- Customized various forms to include CBDL spreadsheet data.
- Gathered GIS data from County Surveyor's Office. Reworked data into a standard Excel file.
- Created new GIS Import table for GIS data.
- Map columns from raw data source to Main Street Inventory Database fields.
- Modify reports to match needs of MSRWC needs.
- Created new label report called Mailing Labels for Members.
- Customized Inventory Form to use as a handout for MSRWC merchants to fill out.

Figure 5-5:
A document with unbulleted and bulleted text.

Modifying a bulleted list

Bulleted lists come standard with a 10-point dot as the bullet. You can modify this feature by changing the Numbering and Bullets dialog box options. You can use another symbol for the bullet style, such as a circle, arrow, or check mark. Or you can use graphics as the bulleted style, which gives several more options and also allows the bulleted items to have color.

Bullets that use color don't show up on printouts unless you print to a color printer. Also, light-colored bullets, such as those that are yellow, may be difficult to see on black-on-white printouts. However, color bullets are a nice touch for documents viewed on-screen or for those you plan to convert to Web pages. See Chapter 17 for information on creating Web pages.

To modify a bulleted list, do the following:

1. **Open a document with a bulleted list.**

2. **Select the bulleted list you want to modify.**

3. **Click the Numbering and Bullets toolbar button. The Numbering and Bullets dialog box appears (see Figure 5-6).**

   This button displays at the far right of the Context Sensitive toolbar.

4. **On the Bullets and Numbering tab, click a bullet symbol. Alternatively, click the Graphics tab to see the types of graphics you can use as bullets and then click a graphic that you like.**

5. **Click OK.**

   The bulleted list changes to reflect the new bullet you selected.

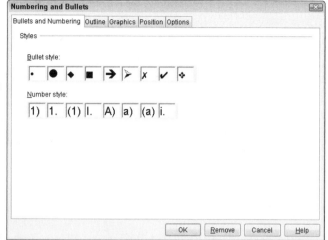

Figure 5-6:
The
Numbering
and Bullets
dialog box
provides
options for
modifying
bullets.

Your lists can use different bullets for each item. Simply select one list item, modify its bullet to use a different bulleted symbol or graphic, and then repeat the process for each list item choosing different bullet symbols or graphics for each one.

Creating a numbered list

Numbered lists are similar to bulleted lists in that they separate a specific type of text from a normal paragraph. For numbered lists, you usually have items that have a sequential relationship to each other. A procedure for baking a cake, for instance, makes a wonderful numbered list. The ingredients you need, on the other hand, could fit into a bulleted list.

You create a numbered list similar to a bulleted list, as follows:

1. **Open a document that includes a list of items you want to include as a numbered list.**

2. **Select the list.**

3. **Click the drop-down arrow on the right side of the Bullets toolbar button.**

   A drop-down list appears.

4. **Click Numbers.**

   The selected list changes to a numbered list.

You can place numbered lists inside bulleted lists or vice versa. Simply create a list, such as a numbered list. For those items you want as bulleted lists, select them and then click Bullets from the drop-down list of the Bullets and Numbering toolbar button. You may want to indent the toolbar button to tab in those bulleted list items to indent them from the numbered list items. The numbered items that are below the bulleted list renumber to fall in sequence with the rest of the numbers.

Modifying a numbered list

By default, numbered lists use the *1.* format (a number followed by a period). You can modify this style with the Numbering and Bullets dialog box, which you can see in Figure 5-6 earlier in this chapter. The styles you can choose from include numbers, Roman numbers, and letters (such as *A., B.,* and so on).

To modify a numbered list, do the following:

1. **Open a document with a numbered list.**

2. **Select the numbered list you want to modify.**

3. **Click the Numbering and Bullets toolbar button.**

4. **The Numbering and Bullets dialog box appears.**

5. **Select a Numbering style.**

6. **Click OK.**

   The numbered list changes to reflect your choice.

Understanding Templates and Styles

Many of the formatting options you apply to documents are done manually, such as when you want to format a specific word or sentence. However, you can automate some of your formatting work by creating and using styles. *Styles* are collections of formatting settings in a template that apply to entire documents, headings, specific text, and other objects. For example, the default Lotus Symphony Documents template that displays a new blank document includes the following styles:

✔ 1. Heading 1

✔ 1. Heading 2

✔ Bullet 1

- Bullet 2
- Default Text
- First Line Indent
- Heading 1
- Heading 2
- Number List 1
- Text Body Indent
- Text Body Single
- Title

These styles apply specific formatting to selected text or to the paragraph to which you apply them. For example, when you use the Heading 2 style, Lotus Symphony Documents automatically changes the selection to have the following characteristics:

- Arial font
- 14 point
- Italic
- Bold

Other styles apply different formatting options.

It's a good idea to use styles for all your standard documents (such as all your business correspondence or professional writings) rather than modify individual words or paragraphs with ad hoc formatting. This way if your document is long and you need to change the formatting of a specific type of object, such as a first-level heading (that is, Heading 1), simply modify the style that applies to that type of object and instruct Lotus Symphony Documents to apply the formatting changes to the entire document. All the objects formatted with that style are quickly updated to match your new style settings.

Using styles to format documents

Styles provide a way for you to apply consistent formatting for documents. Your documents should also have a consistent use of formatting throughout them. All your main headings should use one type of formatting, your body should use a single font family, and the like. Documents that don't adhere to consistent usage of formatting can become difficult to follow, and at the very least look unprofessional.

The advantage of styles

Styles not only allow you to apply multiple formatting settings with a single click, but they also eliminate the need to remember formatting you applied to similar text. For example, as you work at creating a document, you may get six pages-deep in the document and want to format a new heading. Unless you remember exactly that you used Arial 16 point, bold, italic, underline formatting for your previous headings, you may need to flip back to an earlier heading and examine it for formatting details. Instead, create a style for this heading and apply it each time you need a heading formatted.

To apply styles to a document, do the following:

1. **Open a document in Lotus Symphony Documents.**

2. **Select a paragraph of text.**

3. **Choose the Apply Style drop-down list.**

   A list of styles appears, as shown in Figure 5-7.

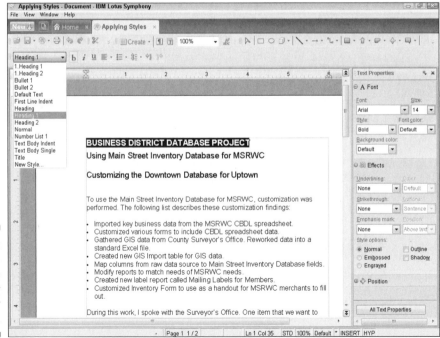

Figure 5-7: You can use styles to quickly format your documents.

4. **Choose a style, such as Heading 1.**

The selected text's formatting changes to match the style's formatting settings.

Creating new styles

Not only can you use built-in styles, but you also can create your own styles or modify existing ones. If you want to modify the Heading 2 style to use the Calibri font instead of Arial, change that in the style definition (the place in which styles store their formatting instructions) and Lotus Symphony Documents uses that new setting for that style. In fact, Lotus Symphony Documents matches existing content in the current document to the changes you just performed on the style.

Styles are part of the template file. When you create a style, it belongs to the template in which you're currently working. I show you how to save your own template later in the "Saving your own templates" section.

To create a new style, use the following steps:

1. **Open a document in Lotus Symphony Documents.**

2. **Choose Layout⇨Style List.**

The Style List appears (see Figure 5-8), which shows styles in the current document template as well as buttons for modifying and creating styles.

Figure 5-8:
The Style List.

3. **Click the New button.**

   The Style dialog box appears. (See Figure 5-9.)

4. **Type a name for your style, such as Headline, Body Text Modified, or similar.**

5. **Choose a style from Following style drop-down list.**

   This style automatically applies to the next new paragraph or object after you apply the new style.

6. **Choose a style from the Derived From drop-down list on which to base your new style.**

   You don't necessarily have to choose a style from the Derived From drop-down list; however, if a style exists that includes many of the same formatting options, you should choose it.

7. **Click the Indents & Spacing tab.**

8. **Choose options for specifying the amount of indenting and paragraph spacing for your new style.**

9. **Choose the Fonts tab.**

10. **Choose the font and other font properties for your new style.**

11. **Click OK to save your style.**

    The Styles dialog box appears.

12. **Choose All Styles from the View by list to see all styles in the Style List, including your new style.**

Your new style can now be used to format your document. From the Style List, double-click your new style, or click it and then click Apply.

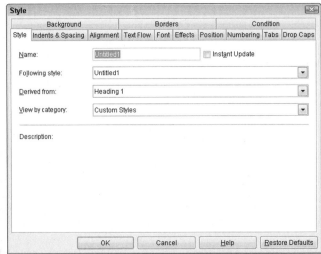

Figure 5-9:
The Style dialog box lets you set up options and proper-ties for your new style.

You can work inside your document with the Style List open. This is a handy way to create content and apply styles without the hassle of opening the Style List each time you need to apply a new style. Just keep the Style List sitting on the side of the document window.

In the Style dialog box, you can use any of the tabs to set properties for your new style. Before creating a style, you may want to work inside a document to design your style. After you get the look you want, select the word or paragraph. Right-click and choose Create Style from Selection. The Create Style dialog box appears. Type a name for the style and click OK. Your new style appears in the Style List.

Modifying existing styles

Sometimes you want to change something in a style definition. For example, you may grow tired of a font or need to indent a heading level another quarter-inch. You can modify styles easily with the Style List.

Lotus Symphony Documents lets you modify the styles in the default blank document. For example, you can modify the Heading 1 style to fit your needs. However, instead of modifying one of them, consider creating your own new styles that are similar to the default ones.

To modify a style, perform the following:

1. **Open a document in Lotus Symphony Documents.**
2. **Choose Layout⇨Style List.**

   The Style List appears (refer to Figure 5-8).
3. **Select a style you want to modify, such as the one you created earlier.**
4. **Click Modify.**

   The Style dialog box appears.
5. **Choose the new style properties using the tabs and their options on the Style dialog box.**
6. **Choose OK to save the settings for the style.**

Saving your own templates

Templates provide pre-built document settings for new documents. Some templates include placeholders for text, styles, boilerplate text, header and footer information, standard graphics, and more. Use templates to help you speed up the process of creating documents that you have to create multiple times. Templates also allow you to standardize a document format that you can then share with other users, such as a project team or sales force.

Downloading templates

You can download templates from the Lotus Symphony Galley Web site. See Chapter 20 for information on how to access the Lotus Symphony Web sites. Some of the templates you can download include

✔ Calendars

✔ Memos

✔ Invoices

✔ Budgets

✔ Resumes

✔ Resignation letters

✔ Business correspondence

You can create your own templates and save them (and perhaps submit them to the Lotus Symphony Gallery Web site to share with others) using the OpenDocument Text Template (.ott) format. The biggest difference between saving a template file and saving a regular document relates to what you put in the template file. For templates, you put all the information, design elements, graphics, and other objects that you want repeated in all documents based on this template. Everything else — the actual content of the document — remains out. When users open the template file, the content can be added and saved as an OpenDocument Text .odt file.

To save a document as a template file, use the following steps:

1. **Open a document in Lotus Symphony Documents.**

2. **Add some design elements, custom styles, and boilerplate text that you want as your template content.**

   Figure 5-10 shows an example of a document I'll turn into a template.

3. **Chose File➪Save As.**

   The Save As dialog box appears.

4. **Choose OpenDocument Text Template (.ott) from the Save As drop-down list.**

5. **Use the Save In drop-down list to navigate to a location on your system where you want to save your template.**

   Be sure you know where you save the template file.

6. **Type a name in the File Name box.**

7. **Click Save.**

   Lotus Symphony Documents saves the file as an OpenDocument Text Template.

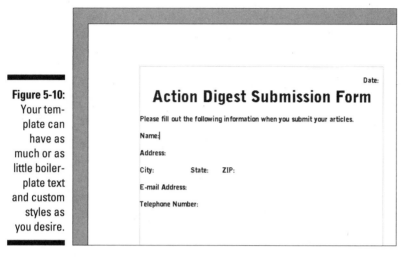

The following section describes how to use the Template Organizer to store, access, and organize your templates.

You can open a template file without using the Template Organizer. To do this, open Lotus Symphony Documents and choose File⇨Open⇨File. From the All Files drop-down list, choose OpenDocument Text Template (.ott) to show only files with the .ott extension. Choose your template file and click Open. Modify the document and choose File⇨Save As. Give your document a name. Your document automatically saves to the OpenDocument Text (.odt) file format. Notice that the Save feature doesn't display when you go to save a template file. This is because template files are *read-only,* meaning you must save any changes to a different file. Your original template file remains unchanged.

Using the Template Organizer

The Template Organizer stores Lotus Symphony templates saved to your system and lets you quickly find templates for Lotus Symphony Documents, Lotus Spreadsheets, and Lotus Presentations.

Chapter 4 includes a section on creating a document based on a template. That section also includes details on setting up Template Organizer for the first time. If you haven't set up Template Organizer to use a template, see that chapter's discussion.

Accessing the Template Organizer

When you want to use a template saved in the Template Organizer, choose File⇨Template Organizer⇨Launch. The Template Organizer appears, as shown in Figure 5-11.

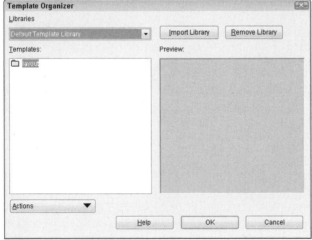

Figure 5-11:
The
Template
Organizer
organizes
your
templates.

Choosing a template

When you're in the Template Organizer, you can access the templates stored there. Templates are stored in folders, such as the Layout folder shown in Figure 5-11. Double-click the folder (or folders if you have multiple folders set up) to display your templates. Figure 5-12 shows a list of templates stored on my system. I selected one to show a sample view of it in the Preview window.

Click a template and then click OK to open that template in Lotus Symphony Documents.

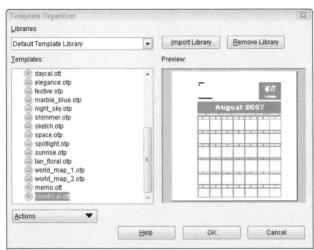

Figure 5-12:
The
Template
Organizer,
displaying
a list of
templates
on my
system.

Saving a new template to the Template Organizer

You can create a new template (like I discuss in the "Saving your own templates" section earlier) and then save it directly to the Template Organizer. This way you don't have to import it later while in the Template Organizer.

To save a new template to the Template Organizer, do the following:

1. **Open Lotus Symphony Documents.**

2. **Create or open a document template.**

3. **Choose File⇨Template Organizer⇨Save File To.**

   The Save File to dialog box appears.

4. **Type a name in the Template Name field. Make sure you retain the** **.ott file extension for document templates.**

5. **Click Save.**

Formatting Graphics

In Chapter 4, I show you how to embed graphics (pictures, clip art, photographs, and similar objects) into your Lotus Symphony Documents files. After those images are in your documents, you may want to perform some simple formatting. You can perform color correction, resize graphics, position them around your documents, and delete them. The following sections show how to perform these tasks.

Lotus Symphony doesn't provide too many tools for editing graphics, such as editing layers of an image or eliminating red-eye. For those duties, you need a graphics- or picture-editing application, such as Corel PaintShop Pro, Windows Paint, or Adobe Photoshop. If you need some basic editing done and you have Windows Vista, look at the Windows Photo Gallery application. It allows you to *fix* photographs, such as adjusting exposure and color settings, cropping a picture, and fixing red-eye.

Additional graphics information can be found in Chapter 7. In Chapter 7, for example, you discover how to prepare graphics that are in your Web pages for publishing to the Web.

Resizing graphics

To resize graphics in your documents, perform the following steps:

1. **Open a document with an embedded graphic.**

2. Click the graphic.

Lotus Symphony Documents displays sizing handles around the graphic, as shown in Figure 5-13.

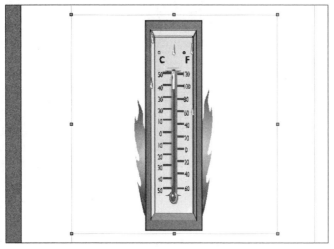

Figure 5-13:
Use the resizing handles to enlarge or shrink embedded graphics.

3. With the mouse, drag the lower-right corner of the graphic up and to the left of the graphic. Stop when the graphic is about half its normal size and then release the mouse.

Positioning graphics

Lotus Symphony Documents enables you to position graphics so text flows around, beside, on top of, or below them. For example, you may want to include a graphic that sits next to a paragraph of text. You can fit the graphic so that the paragraph flows around the outside of the graphic or you can sit the graphic so it sits at the top of a paragraph. Lotus Symphony Documents provides the Wrap options for controlling these settings.

To configure positioning options for embedded graphics, do the following:

1. Open Lotus Symphony Documents with an embedded graphic.

2. Resize the graphic so you can insert text to the left of the graphic.

3. Type a paragraph of text next to the graphic, as shown in Figure 5-14.

You may need to experiment with the size of the image to get enough space to add some text next to it.

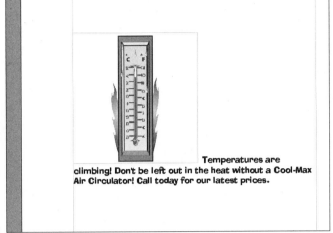

Figure 5-14:
You can
add text and
graphics to
your docu-
ments.

4. **Click the graphic.**

5. **Choose Layout⇨Anchor⇨To Paragraph.**

   The graphic anchors to the paragraph you just entered. The text moves
   below the graphic at this point.

6. **Click the graphic again.**

7. **Choose Layout⇨Wrap⇨Optimal Page Wrap.**

   Lotus Symphony Documents arranges the text to the left or right of the
   graphic in the most optimal placement, such as shown in Figure 5-15.
   That is, if the graphic displays closer to the right edge of the page, the
   text moves to the left side of the graphic, and vice versa as well.

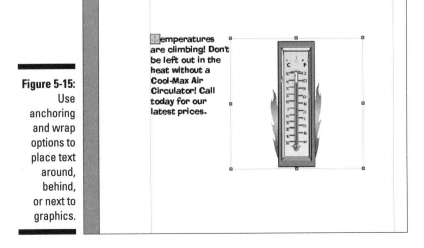

Figure 5-15:
Use
anchoring
and wrap
options to
place text
around,
behind,
or next to
graphics.

You may have noticed a small anchor icon next to the graphic after you select the Anchoring option. This icon shows you that the selected graphic is anchored to the text. When you click off the graphic, the anchor icon disappears until the next time you select the graphic. By the way, when you print your document, the anchor icon doesn't print.

Deleting graphics

Lotus Symphony Documents makes it easy to remove graphics from your documents. When you no longer need or want a graphic in your document, click the graphic and press the Delete key, or right-click the graphic and choose Cut.

Using Subscript and Superscript

Sometimes you need to add accompanying information with your main text in the form of subscripts and superscripts. These items can be in the form of

- Reference information
- Web site addresses for additional information
- Scientific annotations
- Chemical compounds
- Mathematical formulas

Lotus Symphony Documents makes it easy to format text in subscript or superscript properties.

Anchoring

The ability to position graphics, paragraphs, or other text is *anchoring*. For many documents, you use graphics that are somehow connected or related to the text around them. So if the text flows to a different page (such as from page 2 to 3), you want the graphic to flow with the text as well. You can anchor the graphic to the paragraph. With the Graphics Properties dialog box, you have the options of anchoring graphics in these ways:

- To page
- To paragraph
- To character
- As character

Making text subscript

Subscript appears as text smaller than the text around it and in a position lower than other text. The text appears below the baseline of the normal text. For example, chemical formulas appear with subscripts, such as the chemical makeup of water, as shown in Figure 5-16.

To apply subscript to a character, word, or group of words, do the following:

1. **Select what you want to subscript.**
2. **Right-click the selection.**
3. **Choose Style⇨Subscript from the contextual menu.**

   Lotus Symphony Documents applies the subscript formatting to the selection.

Figure 5-16:
Subscripts usually appear in chemical formulas and math equations.

H_2O

Making text superscript

Superscript appears as text smaller than the text around it, and in a position slightly above other text. For example, when you add annotation for a footnote, the annotation appears as a superscript number or character next to the word it annotates. Figure 5-17 shows an example of a superscript character.

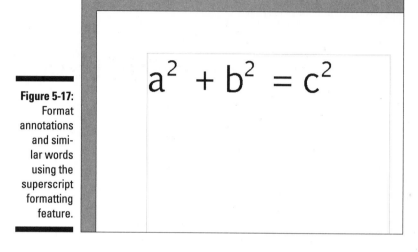

Figure 5-17:
Format annotations and similar words using the superscript formatting feature.

To apply superscript to a character, word, or group of words, do the following:

1. **Select what you want to superscript.**

2. **Right-click the selection.**

3. **Choose Style⇨Superscript from the contextual menu.**

   Lotus Symphony Documents applies the superscript formatting to the selection.

Chapter 6

Designing Complex Documents

· ·

In This Chapter

▶ Identifying complex documents

▶ Setting up and modifying tables

▶ Using captions for your graphics or tables

▶ Creating, updating, and removing cross-references

▶ Inserting fields, footnotes, and endnotes

▶ Creating a table of contents and an index

· ·

*A*s you put together a number of documents and grow more familiar with Lotus Symphony Documents, you may want to venture into some more complex document features. With these features, you can create tables, indexes, cross-references, and bookmarks, as well as insert fields. Fields provide pre-built codes that are placeholders for text and data that changes from document to document (such as the current date).

This chapter helps you understand some of the basics of these features and assists you in starting to build your own complex documents. I cover creating tables, adding captions to tables, inserting graphics, indexes, footnotes, cross-references, and more.

Recognizing Complex Documents

Complex documents include more than just plain text and simple graphics. When you employ Lotus Symphony Documents's intermediate and advanced features while creating your documents, you can safely assume you've started creating complex documents.

The following are some examples of complex documents you can create in Lotus Symphony Documents:

✔ Documents with tables of information

✔ Documents that use captions to describe graphics and tables

✔ Documents that include a table of contents (TOC) and index sections

✔ Documents with fields and macros

✔ Documents with footnotes and endnotes that add supporting and reference information

Figure 6-1, for instance, shows a document with a table of contents created at the beginning of the document.

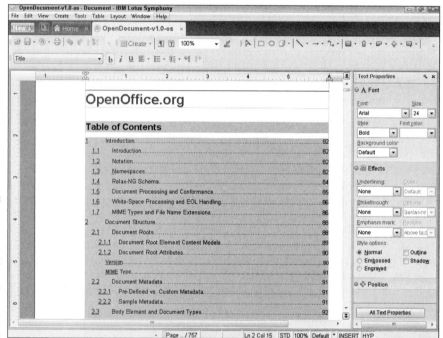

Figure 6-1: Creating a complex document with the table of contents feature.

Creating Tables

You can probably classify tables as an intermediate feature. However, their impact on a document (if used sparingly and with some consideration for design) can greatly impact any document. Tables can help you design and present information in a more professional and expert way. With Lotus Symphony Documents, you can quickly set up, modify, and add content to tables.

Tables enable you to organize content in a series of rows and columns. Columns display vertically, and rows display horizontally. Where rows and columns intersect, they create cells. You enter text, graphics, and other objects into these cells.

The following sections describe how to set up a table, enter data into that table, and modify a table.

Setting up a table

Before setting up a table, consider the following questions:

- ✔ How many rows do you need?
- ✔ How many columns do you need?
- ✔ How large does each cell need to be?
- ✔ What types of text or objects will be entered in the table?

These questions can help you design your table even if it's a design you keep in your head until you see it on the Lotus Symphony Documents screen. You might, however, sketch out the table freehand on a sheet of paper to get an idea of the shape and size of the table. You can then translate those sketch details to the electronic table within Lotus Symphony Documents.

 As I discuss in the "Modifying a table" section, later in this chapter, even if you think out every possibility before setting up your tables, you can still go back and change them later. For example, Lotus Symphony Documents makes it easy to add rows and columns to your tables, remove items you no longer want, and resize columns in your tables.

To set up a table in Lotus Symphony Documents, do the following:

1. **Open a new document in Lotus Symphony Documents.**

2. **Choose Table⇨Create Table.**

   The Create Table dialog box appears (see Figure 6-2).

3. **Enter a name for the table, such as New_Services.**

4. **Specify the number of columns in the Columns box.**

   This example uses three columns.

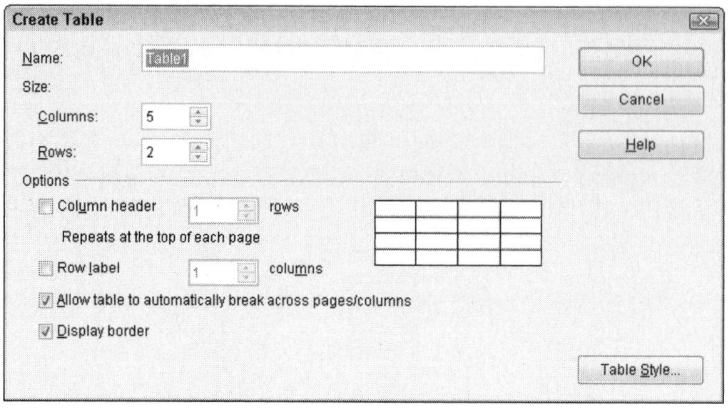

Create Table

Name: `Table1`

Size:

Columns: 5

Rows: 2

Options

☐ Column header   1   rows

Repeats at the top of each page

☐ Row label   1   columns

☑ Allow table to automatically break across pages/columns

☑ Display border

OK

Cancel

Help

Table Style...

Figure 6-2:
The Create
Table dialog
box.

5. **Specify the number of rows in the Rows box.**

   This example uses six rows.

6. **Choose the Column Header option to add a header row above the top.**

7. **Click the Table Style button.**

   The Instant Format dialog box appears.

8. **Select a table style from the Format list and click OK.**

   The Create Table dialog box appears again.

9. **Click OK.**

   Lotus Symphony Documents creates the new table and applies any formatting to it according to the Instant Format options you chose.

Tables in Lotus Symphony Documents contain a name property. You can use the default name, such as `Table1`, but you may want to get in the habit of naming the table something more descriptive. The name property can be used to reference that table someplace else in the document. For example, the table itself can be referenced by an index or a table of contents, not just the table's content.

After you create a table, you can enter text in the cells by doing the following actions:

- ✔ Click inside a cell and type.
- ✔ Press the Tab key to move to the next cell in the table.
- ✔ Press Shift+Tab to move back to the previous cell in the table.
- ✔ Double-click inside a cell to select all its content.

Figure 6-3, for example, shows my new table filled out with new information.

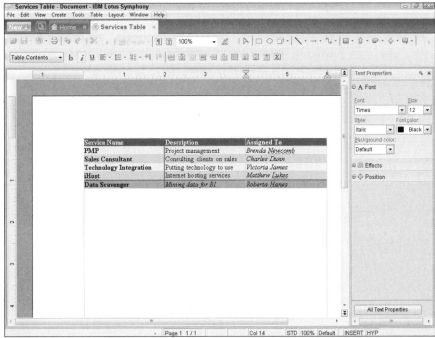

Figure 6-3:
My new
table with
information
added to it.

Modifying a table

Lotus Symphony Documents provides several tools to let you modify tables and their content. In the example shown in Figure 6-3, some features of the Instant Format option I chose don't fit well with my content. The bottom row, for instance, includes a heavy bold border between it and the row above it. In addition, the middle cell in that row has italics added to its text. These items are there because the Instant Format design assumes the table information contains numeric values, with the bottom row used for summing the values in the columns.

Because I'm using the table to list and describe services and assignments, I want to modify the design to my liking. Use the following steps to see how these changes can be made:

1. **Select the entire bottom row of the table.**

   To do this, put the insertion point to the left of the first word, hold down the left mouse button, and drag to the end of the row.

2. **Right-click and choose Table Properties from the menu that appears.**

   The Table Properties dialog box appears.

3. **Click the Borders tab in the Table Properties dialog box.**

4. **Select the None option in the Style box.**

   This turns off the border between the bottom row and the row above it.

5. **Click OK to save your changes.**

6. **Select the second cell on the bottom row and then right-click and choose Table Properties.**

7. **Click the Border tab, and in the User-Defined area, click the left side of the graphic to add a new border there.**

8. **Click the Color drop-down button, select the Yellow 7 option, and click OK.**

   Lotus Symphony Documents adds a new border to the left side of the second cell. This new border should match the border that appears in the cells directly above it.

9. **Select the content in the second cell again.**

10. **Choose Regular from the Style drop-down list on the Text Properties sidebar.**

    The regular style replaces the italics style on the phrase "Mining data for BI."

Lotus Symphony Documents enables you to format cells with different shades, fills, and colors. You can, for instance, use a background color in specific cells to emphasize those cells or use colors to design your tables for more visual impact. To modify cell properties, right-click a cell, choose Table Properties, and click the Cell tab.

Using Captions for Graphics or Tables

Lotus Symphony Documents enables you to add captions to graphics you embed in your documents and to tables you create. Captions allow you to add a description or other text that accompanies the graphic or table. Captions also provide sequential numbering for the item, such as sequential numbers for graphics in a document.

Captions provide a few benefits over using normal text entries for your captions. For one, when you enter captions, caption numbering updates automatically to keep the numbers in proper order. This may not sound like a big deal until you've entered a dozen or so graphics and decide to add or remove a graphic from the middle of the document. If you manually added captions and numbers, you'd need to go through and manually change the numbers to be sequential again. With the Lotus Symphony Documents Caption feature, the renumbering happens automatically.

Creating captions

To enter a caption, you must have a table or graphic in your document. I use the previous document that has a table entered, but you can use one that has a graphic in it. Simply select that graphic to activate the caption command.

Use the following steps to create a caption for a table:

1. **Open Lotus Symphony Documents with a document that includes a table.**

2. **Click inside the table.**

3. **Right-click and choose Add Caption.**

   The Create Caption dialog box appears, as shown in Figure 6-4.

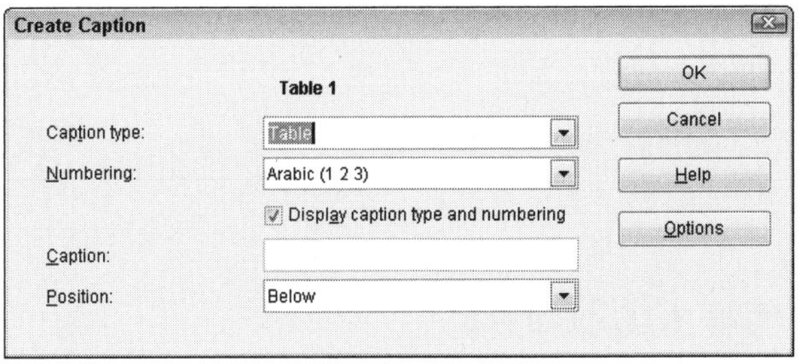

Figure 6-4:
Use the
Create
Caption
dialog box
to insert a
new caption
with your
table.

Create Caption		
	Table 1	OK
Caption type:	Table	Cancel
Numbering:	Arabic (1 2 3)	Help
	☑ Display caption type and numbering	Options
Caption:		
Position:	Below	

4. **Select Table from the Caption Type list (it's selected automatically to this type, but double-check to ensure it's selected).**

5. **Type a caption in the Caption box.**

   The caption should be short but descriptive. For example, my table includes a caption that reads *New services for Fiscal 2010.*

6. **Select the placement for the caption from the Position drop-down list.**

   Below is the default, but you can also choose to place the caption above the table.

7. **Click OK.**

   Lotus Symphony Documents adds the caption to the table, as shown in Figure 6-5.

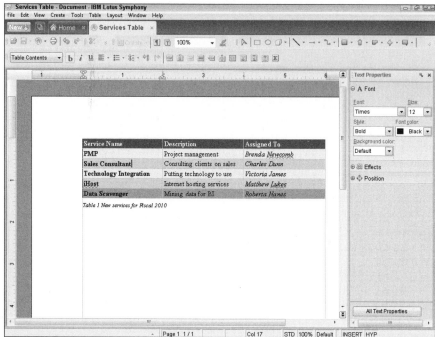

Figure 6-5:
The new
caption
added to the
table object.

Modifying captions

To modify a caption, such as change its text or text properties, select the caption and type in new text or select different text properties. In Figure 6-6, for example, I selected the caption that I added in the preceding section and performed the following edits to it:

✔ Changed the font to Accent SF

✔ Increased the font size to 12

✔ Aligned the caption in the center of the page

To remove a caption, use one of the following procedures depending on the object that the caption is added to:

✔ **For tables,** select the entire caption text and press Delete.

✔ **For graphics, text boxes, and shapes,** select the frame in which the caption is inserted, right-click, and choose Cut.

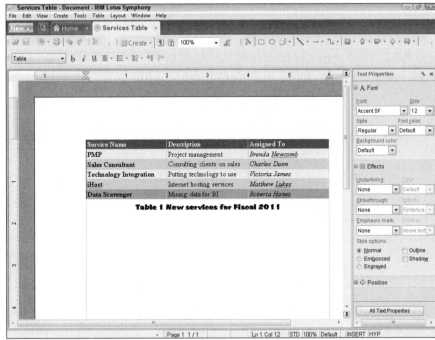

Figure 6-6:
Notice
the edits I
performed
on the table
caption.

Setting Up Cross-References

Lotus Symphony Documents enables you to create cross-references in your documents. *Cross-references* include hyperlinks that enable you to "jump" to that other cross-reference within the document. If you've ever used the Internet to navigate between Web pages by clicking links on the pages, you know how to navigate cross-references in Lotus Symphony Documents.

What you may not know yet is how to actually set up these cross-references. You discover how to do that in the following sections, as well as how to update a cross-reference and how to remove one.

Objects you insert in your documents can be cross-referenced, as well as text of course. To set up cross-references for objects, such as tables and graphics, make sure you include a caption with them. Otherwise, Lotus Symphony Documents doesn't allow you to cross-reference those objects.

Creating cross-references

When you create cross-references, you insert the following two items:

- ✔ **Target** specifies the text, table, graphic, or other object you want to link to. Lotus Symphony Documents refers to this as the *selection*.

- ✔ **Cross-reference** specifies where you place the link to the target.

Lotus Symphony Documents must be set to Hyperlink mode to allow you to click the cross-reference link item. To enable Hyperlink mode, make sure the status bar has the HYP signifier showing. If the SEL signifier shows instead, click it once to toggle it to HYP. The SEL mode enables you to edit hyperlinks.

To create a cross-reference, do the following:

1. **Open a document that has several pages in it.**

   By using a long document, one that has at least three or four pages, you can realize how powerful the cross-reference feature works to allow you to jump from one place in your document to another.

2. **Select a target, which is the text or object to which you want to link, and then choose Create⇨Cross-Reference.**

   The Create Cross-Reference dialog box appears (see Figure 6-7).

3. **Type a name for the target in the Name box and click Insert.**

   Lotus Symphony Documents adds the new target to the Selection list.

4. **Click Close.**

5. **Find the location in the document where you want to create the cross-reference and then choose Create⇨Cross-Reference.**

6. **From the Type list, select Insert Reference.**

7. **From the Selection list, select the target.**

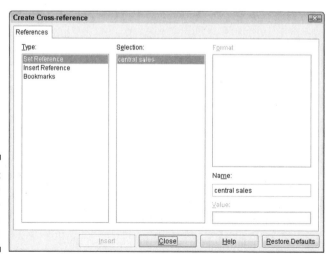

Figure 6-7:
The Create
Cross-
Reference
dialog box.

8. **From the Format list, choose the format type for the cross-reference and then click Insert.**

   The cross-reference appears in your document at the insertion point.

9. **Click Close.**

Lotus Symphony Documents inserts a cross-reference based on the format you selected in Step 8. You can then click that cross-referenced item to jump to the target.

The types of cross-reference formats you can choose are described in the following list:

- **Page:** Displays the page number of the target
- **Chapter:** Displays the chapter number of the target
- **Above/Below:** Displays whether the target appears before (above) or after (below) where you insert the reference
- **As Page Style:** Displays the page number of the target using the style set for that page

Updating cross-references

When you move around any of the text or objects that contain targets or references to those targets, your cross-references must be updated. Suppose, for example, that you set up a target that appears on page 4 of your document. After some editing and moving around, that same text appears on page 12 of the document. Any references to that target now must be updated to know that the target appears on page 12, not page 4.

With Lotus Symphony Documents, cross-references using fields can be updated easily. To update cross-references, press F9 or choose Tools⇨Update⇨Fields.

Removing cross-references

To remove cross-references, you need to remove the field from your document. The easiest way to do this is to turn on the fields in your document and to turn on field shadings. The Field Shadings function applies a gray shade to all the fields in your document. Use the following instructions to do both of these actions:

- **To turn on fields, choose View⇨Fields.**
- **To turn on shading, choose View⇨Field Shadings.**

After you turn on these options, your cross-reference fields are easier to see and select. Select one of them and press the Delete key to remove it from your document.

Inserting Fields

Lotus Symphony Documents enables you to use fields in your documents to help streamline your work. You read a little about fields in the preceding section on cross-references. But what are fields?

Fields are placeholders in your documents for information that normally changes routinely. Many documents include the Date field as a common field. The Date field updates automatically with the correct date when a document opens and closes (when saved). Many users prefer the field because it doesn't require them to change the date when a new printout of the document occurs. They just let Lotus Symphony Documents handle that part of the work.

Some common fields include

- ✔ Date
- ✔ Time
- ✔ Page numbers

To insert a field in your document, perform the following steps:

1. **Open a document in Lotus Symphony Documents.**

2. **Place your cursor where you want the field inserted.**

3. **Choose Create⇨Fields and then choose the name of the field.**

    In this example, I chose the Date field to insert into my document. The date appears in the document.

You can manually update fields — that is, update a field result before Lotus Symphony Documents automatically updates the field. For example, say you inserted a Time field that shows seconds and minutes. If you want to update that field to show the most current time, choose Tools⇨Update⇨Fields or press Ctrl+F9 to update just the inserted fields in your documents.

You can press F9 to update all the fields in your document, including cross-references, links, indexes, and other items. You can read more about indexes later in this chapter in the "Creating Indexes" section.

Inserting Footnotes

Some documents include information that needs to be cited for bibliographic or reference reasons. Lotus Symphony Documents enables you to set up footnotes for this type of information. When a topic on a page requires a footnote, you can set up a footnote that appears at the bottom of that page, allowing the readers to quickly and easily access that information.

When you create footnotes, Lotus Symphony Documents automatically generates the numbers for you to make keeping track of your footnotes and related text easy. A superscript number appears next to the text in the body of the document — this is the *anchor* of the note — with that same number appearing as a superscript next to the footnote.

Lotus Symphony Documents automatically renumbers footnotes when you create new ones. For example, you might have a footnote numbered as 3 but then decide to add a new footnote to a passage that falls between the second and third footnotes. No problem. Insert the new footnote, and Lotus Symphony Documents numbers that new footnote 3 and bumps up the old number from 3 to 4.

Creating footnotes

To create a footnote, you need to know where you want to place the footnote citation (such as after a passage you quote from another source) and what the footnote text should be. Then use the following steps to create the footnote:

1. **Open a document that includes a passage of text you want to footnote.**

2. **Click where you want the anchor of the footnote to appear.**

3. **Choose Create⇨Footnote.**

   The Create Footnote dialog box appears (see Figure 6-8).

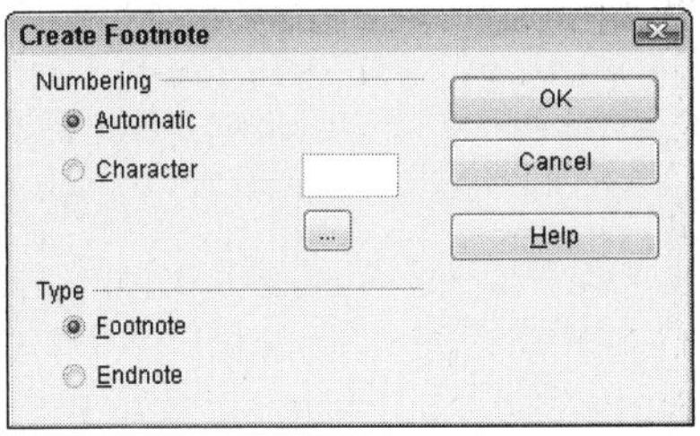

Figure 6-8:
The Create
Footnote
dialog box.

Create Footnote

Numbering

- Automatic
- Character

OK

Cancel

Help

Type

- Footnote
- Endnote

Using symbols or other number formats in footnotes

To use different number formats or symbols for your footnotes, open the Create Footnote dialog box. Click Character and then click the button with the ellipsis (. . .) on it. This opens the Special Characters dialog box. Select the character you want to use and click OK. You then click OK on the Create Footnote dialog box to apply that character to your footnote and anchor.

4. **Select Automatic in the Numbering area to instruct Lotus Symphony Documents to use normal numbering for your footnotes.**

5. **Select Footnote in the Type area and then click OK.**

   Lotus Symphony Documents adds the footnote number to the anchor and to the footnote area at the bottom of the page.

6. **Type the footnote text next to the footnote number you just created.**

   Figure 6-9 shows an example of a finished footnote.

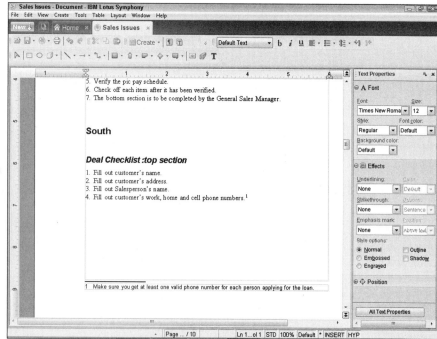

Figure 6-9: Footnotes are handy for adding citations and additional information to your documents.

Modifying footnotes

To modify a footnote, click in the footnote area and make changes to the footnote information as you do regular body text. You might, for instance, need to insert additional text about a reference or delete outdated information from a footnote.

If you have several footnotes on a page, you can click the anchor (the number 1, in this case) in the body text and Lotus Symphony Documents automatically puts the insertion point down at the beginning of the related footnote.

You also can click the footnote number to move the insertion point up to the anchor within the body of the document.

When you move the mouse pointer over top of an anchor or footnote number, the pointer changes to a hand.

Formatting footnotes

Lotus Symphony Documents enables you to format footnotes using styles set up for footnotes. You use the Style List to apply the styles for the footnotes. To format your footnotes, do the following:

1. **Click inside the footnote at the bottom of the page and select a word or two from the footnote text.**

2. **Choose Layout⇨Style List, or press F11.**

   The Style List appears.

3. **Choose Text Styles from the Style Type drop-down list.**

4. **Choose Hierarchical Styles from the View By drop-down list.**

5. **Right-click Footnote Characters from the list of styles and choose Modify.**

   The Style dialog box appears (see Figure 6-10).

6. **Choose a tab (such as the Font tab) and make changes to the style.**

   In this example, I'm changing the font to Arial and the size to 10.

7. **Click OK and then click Apply.**

   The selected text in the footnote changes to reflect the updated style modifications.

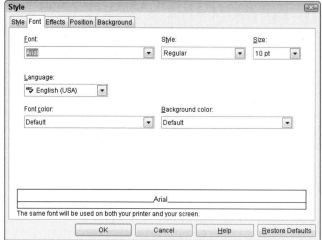

Figure 6-10:
You can
modify
footnotes
by changing
the Footnote
Character
style.

You can change the paragraph style for your footnotes as well. From the Style List, choose Paragraph Styles from the Style drop-down list. Right-click the Footnote style and choose Modify. Use the tabs and options to make changes to the Footnote style. Click OK and then Apply to make your changes take effect on your footnotes.

You can modify the text area of the footnotes by using the Page Properties dialog box. To open this box, choose Layout⇨Properties⇨Page Properties. Click the Footnote tab, and the Page Properties dialog box appears, as shown in Figure 6-11. You can make changes to the area of the footnote text (such as make it have a maximum height, as well as change the properties of the separator line).

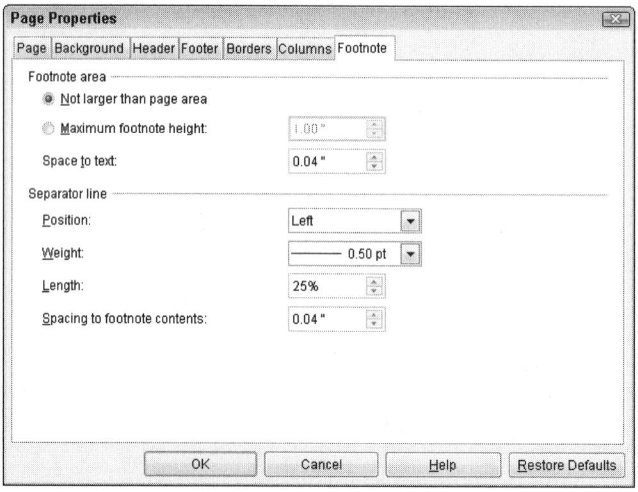

Figure 6-11:
The Page
Properties
dialog box.

Inserting Endnotes

Endnotes are similar to footnotes except they appear at the end of the entire document, not at the bottom (or foot) of a page. Some of the same concepts you may have read about in the preceding section on footnotes can be applied here as well.

Creating endnotes

To create endnotes in your documents, use the following steps:

1. **In a document, click where you want the anchor of the endnote to appear.**

2. **Choose Create⇨Footnote.**

   The Create Footnote dialog box appears.

3. **Select Endnote from the Type area and then click OK.**

   Lotus Symphony Documents creates a new endnote on a new page at the end of the document.

You can add text to the endnote as you did the footnotes earlier.

Modifying endnotes

To modify endnotes, use the same principles you use for editing standard body text and for footnotes. For example, to delete a word or phrase in an endnote, select what you want to delete and press Delete. Conversely, to add new information to the endnote, you can click inside the endnote you want to expand and enter the new text.

Formatting endnotes

As you read in the "Modifying footnotes" section earlier in this chapter, you can modify the styles that define formatting for footnotes. Those same principles apply to modifying endnote styles as well.

Follow the same steps in the "Modifying footnotes" section, but instead of choosing Footnote Anchor or Footnote Character from the Text Style options or the Footnote style from the Paragraph Style options, choose Endnote Anchor, Endnote Character, and Endnote.

Creating a Table of Contents

With Lotus Symphony Documents, you can create tables of contents that automatically generate and update while you work on your document. Tables of contents are used at the beginning of documents to list the major sections of the document and to display the page numbers where these sections begin.

When you want a table of contents as part of your document, you do need to do a little extra work besides just creating the content. You need to apply style headings to each section you want to appear in the table of contents. The best way to do this until you get more experienced with tables of contents is to use the built-in styles that Lotus Symphony Documents provides — headings, such as Heading 2, 1. Heading 3, and so on.

Setting up tables of contents

To set up your document for a table of contents, go through the entire document and apply heading levels to your major sections. For example, the following provides a simple example of the types of headings and sections you may have in your document:

- Heading 1: Chapter title
- Heading 2: Main section title
- Heading 3: Subsection title

After your document has the section headings applied, use the following steps to create your table of contents (TOC):

1. **Place the insertion point where you want the table of contents to appear.**

   Usually you want it at the top of the document after the title of the document and any front matter information you may have.

2. **Choose Create⇨Index and Table⇨Indexes and Tables.**

   The Insert Index/Table dialog box appears, as shown in Figure 6-12.

3. **Click the Index/Table tab.**

4. **Type (if it's not already there) Table of Contents in the Title box.**

5. **Select Table of Contents from the Type drop-down list.**

6. **Select Outline from the Create From area.**

   You can click the ellipsis (. . .) button to choose additional outlining styles you want to appear on the table of contents. Click OK to return to the Insert Index/Table dialog box.

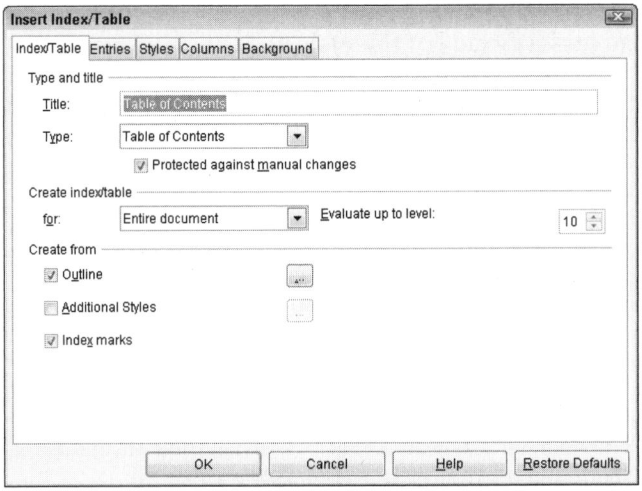

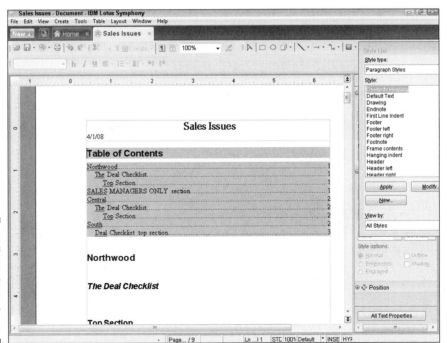

Figure 6-12:
The Insert
Index/Table
dialog box.

7. Click OK.

Lotus Symphony Documents creates your table of contents and places it
at the insertion point, such as the one shown in Figure 6-13.

Figure 6-13:
Table of
contents
make any
long docu-
ment easier
to navigate.

If the styles you use for the table of contents don't show up when you create it, return to the Insert Index/Table dialog box. Click the Index/Table tab and then select the Additional Styles option. Click the ellipsis (. . .) button to open the Assign Styles dialog box. Select those styles you want to include in your table of contents and click the >> button to arrange each style as you want it to appear in the table of contents. Click OK twice to create your table of contents.

Updating tables of contents

As you add to, move, delete, and revise your document, make sure the page numbers and table of contents information remain updated. You can manually update the table of contents by choosing Tools⇨Update⇨All Indexes and Tables. (You also can press F9.) This refreshes the content as well as any page number changes that need to be made.

As you may have found out already, you can't make changes directly to the table of contents area. Instead, if you need to change the name of a section item listed in the table of contents, click the blue link in that listing in the table of contents to jump to that item in the document. Make your changes in the section name and save your document. Check the table of contents — if it hasn't updated automatically with your new information, press F9 or choose the Update⇨All Indexes and Tables to manually update the table of contents.

Using tables of contents

The easiest way to use a table of contents while reading the document on your computer takes advantage of the hyperlinking capabilities of Lotus Symphony Documents. Each item listed in the table of contents includes a hyperlink to the section to which it refers. Click that hyperlink to jump to that section of your document.

Creating Indexes

Indexes provide a way for readers of your documents to find the page numbers of topics discussed in your document. Indexes are usually helpful for documents that end up being long, such as over ten pages. Any shorter than this and users may not take the time to refer to the index, essentially rendering your work worthless in the long run.

Creating useful indexes

Creating useful and complete indexes can be frustrating at times. You don't want to repeat everything from the document in the index. However, you want to make sure key words, terms, and phrases are indexed. Professional indexers have both a technical grasp of the content and an artful skill in the way they code indexes. If your indexes aren't the greatest things you've seen or used, don't beat yourself up too much — it takes time to figure out how to create dynamic indexes.

When you set up an index in Lotus Symphony Documents, you set up index entries in the document on the word or term you want to index. When you create the index part of the document, you specify that Lotus Symphony Documents uses those index entries to create the index. Lotus Symphony Documents automatically figures out the page number.

Setting up index entries

To set up index entries in your document, follow these steps:

1. **Open the document you want to index.**

2. **Select a word or phrase to index.**

3. **Choose Create⇨Index and Table⇨Entry.**

   The Insert Index Entry dialog box appears (see Figure 6-14).

4. **Type a new entry word or phrase if the selected one doesn't match what you want to appear in the index.**

   For example, instead of sales manager, you may want to put manager, sales.

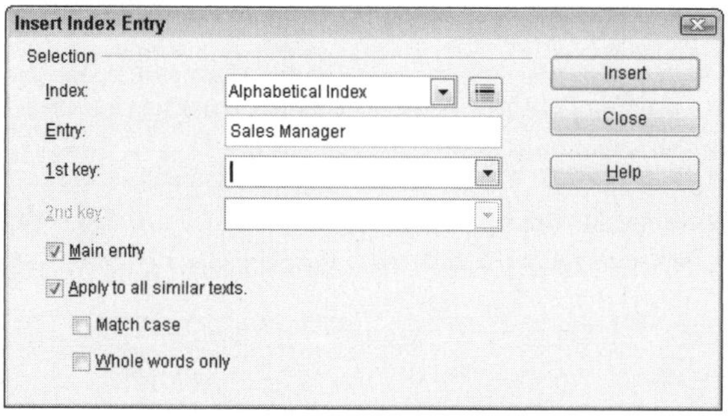

Figure 6-14: The Index Entry dialog box.

5. **Select Main entry to set this entry as the main entry for other entries to fall under.**

6. **Select Apply to all similar texts to make sure words and phrases that match this entry are indexed as well.**

   If you don't use the Apply to all similar texts option, you need to manually create entries for similar words and phrases throughout your document. Lotus Symphony Documents can't do it for you automatically.

7. **Click Insert and then click Close.**

8. **Repeat the process after you select another word or phrase for which to create an entry.**

Continue creating entries for the entire document. When you finish, read the "Creating Indexes" section earlier in this chapter to find out how to generate your new index.

A great way to discover how to index your own documents is to find out from others. For example, turn to the index in this book. Notice how keys are used to create entries, subentries, and sub-subentries. Also look at how some entries use different, but related, words to index items in the book. When you create index entries, try to guess what readers will want to look up and how those words or phrases match the information in your document.

Creating indexes

After you create index entries for your document, you're ready to create your index. To create an index, do the following:

1. **Place the insertion point at the end of the document.**

2. **Choose Create⇨Index and Table⇨Indexes and Tables.**

   The Insert Index/Table dialog box appears (refer to Figure 6-12).

3. **Type Index in the Name field.**

4. **Choose Alphabetical Index from the Type drop-down list and click OK.**

   Lotus Symphony Documents builds your index and places it at the end of the document (see Figure 6-15).

To update the index, make the changes to the body of the document and add any new entries you need to. You can then update the index by pressing F9.

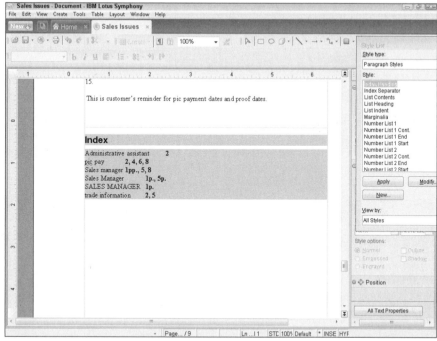

Figure 6-15:
An example
of some
index
entries
created
in my
document.

Automating Repetitive Tasks with Macros

You can use macros in your Lotus Symphony Documents to allow you to automate repetitive or complex tasks. Macros are routines, like mini-programs, you create that perform tasks automatically in your documents.

To create a macro, use the following steps:

1. **Open the document in which you want to create a macro. Make sure the document has been saved to a file name you can remember.**

2. **Choose Tools⇨Macros⇨Record Macro.**

   The Record Macro window appears.

3. **Perform a task you want to record as a macro.**

   As an example, enter a paragraph of text that can be boilerplate text, then format it with a crazy looking font, such as Comic Sans.

4. **Click Stop Recording.**

   The Macro dialog box appears (see Figure 6-16).

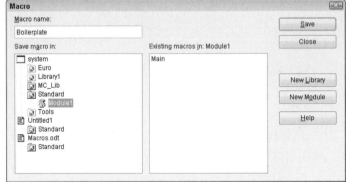

Figure 6-16:
Use the
Macro
dialog box
to name and
store your
new macro.

5. Type a name for the macro in the Macro name box.

We use the name `Boilerplate`.

Macro names cannot include spaces.

6. Select the folder that is named after the document, such as Macros.ods in our case.

7. Click Save.

8. Click Yes if prompted to overwrite the Main macro.

9. Choose File⇨Save to save your document with the new macro.

After you create a macro, you can run it.

When we saved the new macro, it was in the `Macros.ods` file. We need to re-open that document and then we can run the macro from that document.

To run a macro, do the following:

1. Open the document in which you stored the macro.

2. Choose Tools⇨Macros⇨Macros.

The Macro dialog box appears.

3. Select the macro from the Macro from list.

4. Choose Run.

The macro executes, performing the procedure you recorded earlier.

Chapter 7

Working with Other Document Types

In This Chapter

▶ Dealing with files from other word processing programs

▶ Opening Word, IBM, and Lotus document types

▶ Transferring spreadsheet data to Documents files

*N*ot all the documents you encounter in your work or personal life are going to be Lotus Symphony Documents ones. In fact, by popularity, the most numerous documents are probably Microsoft Word documents. You need a way to convert these documents into a format that Lotus Symphony Documents handles so you can view and edit them. Fortunately, Lotus Symphony Documents has a built-in converter for most Microsoft Word documents.

In addition to working with Microsoft Word, Lotus Symphony Documents supports converting other types of document files, such as rich text formatted documents. You can import, read, and modify those documents, and then you can save the finished document in Lotus Documents's Open Document Text format — or even to an Adobe Portable Document Format (PDF) file.

In this chapter, you find out which file formats Lotus Symphony Documents supports, as well as how to import documents and use spreadsheet information in your Lotus Symphony Documents files.

Understanding the Types of Documents Lotus Symphony Documents Handles

At one time or another, you probably will come across a file type that isn't native to Lotus Symphony Documents. That is, the file has been saved in a format other than the Open Document Text format, which uses the .odt file extension. ODT files follow a file format specification written by the OASIS (Organization for the Advancement of Structured Information Standards) Open Document specification committee.

Not all `.odt` files are created using Lotus Symphony Documents. Other Open Document-compliant programs write to that file format as well. Some of these other programs include OpenOffice.org, KOffice, Google Docs, and Zoho. Using the specifications published in the OASIS Open Document Format for Office Applications, the `.odt` format provides support of a number features and benefits, including:

- eXtensible Markup Language (XML)
- Text and graphics
- Font characteristics
- Database content access
- Table building and editing
- List creation and editing

You can download the specification from the OASIS Open Org Web site at `www.oasis-open.org/committees/tc_home.php?wg_abbrev=office`.

Document files

Some of the file types that Lotus Symphony Documents converts that you're likely to encounter include:

- Microsoft Word format (`.doc`)
- IBM Word Processing Document (`.sxw`)
- Lotus WordPro (`.lwp`)
- Text (`.txt`)
- Microsoft Rich Text Format (`.rtf`)

When you convert documents in Lotus Symphony Documents, you may experience some changes from the original document to the converted one. For example, some features found in one document format may not be directly supported by Lotus Symphony Documents.

For example, a Word 2003 formatted document that I have on my system includes a few lines of text and a macro that automatically embeds a table into the document. When I run the macro in Lotus Symphony Documents, the new document changes a little. The table embeds almost exactly as in the original Word file, only one of the fonts changes from bold to Roman in the converted one. That's a pretty good conversion.

If you save the file in Microsoft RTF format, you see a message informing you that some of the content and formatting may be lost during the conversion. Click OK to continue the conversion process. Usually, the text and layout remain the same in Lotus Symphony Documents as they appear in the original RTF file; however, some features, such as the background color, may be lost or somewhat changed.

In cases in which some items don't convert, you can open the document in its original application, such as Microsoft Word. If you don't have access to the original application, you'll have to obtain a copy of the original application or simply leave out the feature or object in the converted Lotus Symphony Documents file. In many cases, you can re-create the same feature (for example, an index that doesn't convert properly) in Lotus Symphony Documents.

Importing Specific Document Types

The following sections describe how to import specific document types into Lotus Symphony Documents. By *import,* I simply mean opening a document in Lotus Symphony Documents and letting Lotus Symphony work in the background a little to attempt to bring in as much text, formatting, graphics, and other elements from the original document as possible. Sometimes the entire document displays just fine, while other times you may just get the text and some freaky looking formatting.

Working with Microsoft Word files

As mentioned earlier in this chapter, Microsoft Word remains the most popular word processor in the world. Because of this, you probably encounter several Word documents that you need to import into Lotus Symphony Documents.

In some cases, however, Microsoft Word features don't convert as nicely as this one. The following describes some of the items that may not convert:

- ✔ Tables, frames, and multi-column formatting
- ✔ Microsoft Office form fields
- ✔ Hyperlinks and bookmarks
- ✔ Revision marks you add using the Track Changes features in Word
- ✔ Objects you embed in the document

- ✔ Symbol fonts
- ✔ Some macro features
- ✔ Indexes you create
- ✔ Animated text and characters
- ✔ Microsoft graphics, such as WordArt graphics and AutoShapes

Lotus Symphony Documents supports importing Microsoft Word 97/2000/XP files only. It doesn't currently support importing the latest version of Word, Microsoft Office Word 2007. That version of Word uses a proprietary format called the Office Open XML format. The file for that type of document uses a file extension of `.docx`. When you see these types of documents, you must convert them to `.doc` file formats before importing them into Lotus Symphony Documents.

To import a Microsoft Word document, use the following steps:

1. **Open Lotus Symphony.**

2. **Choose File⇨Open⇨File.**

   The Open dialog box appears. (See Figure 7-1.)

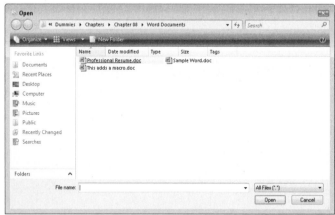

Figure 7-1:
The Open
dialog box.

3. **Click the drop-down arrow on the All Files button.**

4. **Choose the Microsoft Word 97/2000/XP (*.doc) option.**

   The Open dialog box limits the list of document types visible to just those with `.doc` file extensions.

5. **Select a Microsoft Word document.**

6. **Click Open.**

   The Lotus Symphony warning box message appears.

7. **Click OK.**

   The warning box disappears and Lotus Symphony Documents imports the Microsoft Word document.

If you have access to Microsoft Office Word 2007, you can save Word files to either .doc or .docx format. Be sure to save them to .doc format (rather than the .docx format) if you plan to convert them to the Lotus Symphony Documents format or send them to someone who uses Lotus Symphony instead of Office. To do this in Word 2007, choose File⇨Save As and choose the Save to Word 2003 and Earlier format. Some Word 2007 features aren't supported by Word 2003 (or Lotus Symphony Documents).

With the Word document in the Lotus Symphony Documents window, you can modify the document as needed. You may need to replace any missing elements that didn't convert, or clean up any problems that are introduced into the document during conversion. One such problem you may experience relates imported text or other elements appearing in incorrect positions on the page. Also, paragraph spacing and line indents may not convert 100 percent accurately.

After you make your changes, you can save the file to Lotus Symphony Documents format using the following steps:

1. **Choose File⇨Save As.**

   The Save As dialog box appears. (See Figure 7-2.)

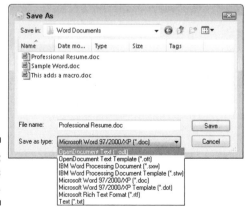

Figure 7-2:
The Save As
dialog box.

2. **Click the Save as Type drop-down list.**

3. **Choose OpenDocument Text (*.odt).**

4. **Click Save.**

   Lotus Symphony Documents saves the file to the Open Document Text format.

Working with Lotus and IBM word processing files

Lotus Symphony Documents supports importing other Lotus and IBM word processing files. These include:

✔ IBM Word Processing document (`.sxw`)

✔ Lotus Word Pro (`.lwp`)

Lotus Word Pro originally was named Ami Pro. If you use an older version of Ami Pro, convert those files to Lotus Word Pro or Microsoft Word `.doc` format before importing into Lotus Symphony Documents. Then import them into Lotus Symphony Documents.

You use the same method for importing Lotus Word Pro and IBM Word Processing documents as you do with Microsoft Word files. The following steps show how:

1. **Open Lotus Symphony.**

2. **Choose File⇨Open⇨File.**

   The Open dialog box appears. (Refer to Figure 7-2.)

3. **Choose the drop-down arrow on the All Files button.**

4. **Select IBM Word Processing Document (*.sxw) or Lotus Word Pro (*.lwp) from the menu.**

5. **Click Open.**

   Lotus Symphony Documents opens the IBM Word Processing document.

Working with spreadsheet files in Lotus Symphony Documents

For the most part, when you open a spreadsheet file in Lotus Symphony, you do so in the Lotus Symphony Spreadsheets application. However, you can use spreadsheet information inside of your Lotus Symphony Documents files.

You might, for instance, want to display a list of products in your document. The list of products might be stored in a spreadsheet file that updates automatically each time a new product arrives in the company database. You can embed that list into your document and it will update as the data in the original spreadsheet file updates.

When you first start using data from a spreadsheet in a document, start out small. That is, experiment with a small chunk of data and work your way up to long lists and other features, such as data pilot information. By starting small, you can easily see how the data works inside your document. With large collections of data, you become overwhelmed by the multiple document pages that can result when you have hundreds of rows and columns of data.

To use spreadsheet information in your documents, do the following:

1. **Start a blank Lotus Symphony Documents document or open a document in which to embed the spreadsheet data.**

2. **Open the spreadsheet file you want to use as the data source.**

3. **Select the data you want to copy.**

   In Figure 7-3, for example, I selected the data in the Quarters table.

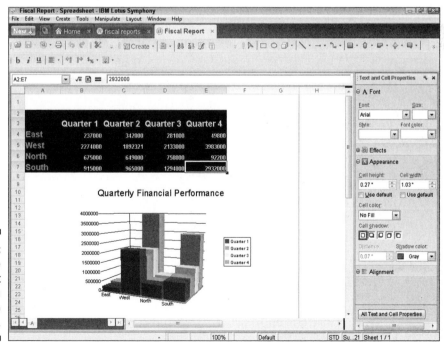

Figure 7-3:
Select the spreadsheet data you want to copy.

4. Choose Edit➪Copy or press Ctrl+C on the keyboard.

The selected information copies to the Windows Clipboard.

5. Switch to the document window.

6. Click inside the document at the point you want the spreadsheet data to reside.

7. Choose Edit➪Paste Special.

The Paste Special dialog box appears. (See Figure 7-4.)

If you simply want to paste the data to the Lotus Symphony Documents file and not have it update when the source information updates, choose Edit➪Paste. The data pastes into the document and no links are retained back to the Lotus Symphony Spreadsheets file.

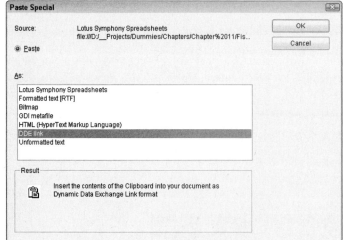

Figure 7-4:
The Paste
Special
dialog box.

8. Select DDE Link.

9. Click OK.

The data pastes into the document, as shown in Figure 7-5. When the data in the original spreadsheet changes, the changes reflect in the document as well.

When you use the Paste Special command, be aware that the source file needs to remain on your system for this "linking" to work. If the source file would happen to be deleted or moved, the link is broken and the document cannot be updated automatically anymore.

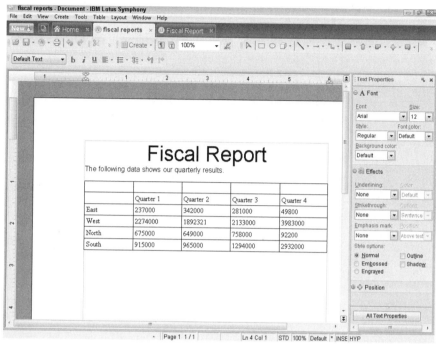

Figure 7-5:
Embedding spread-sheet data in a Lotus Symphony Documents file.

Part III

Using IBM Lotus Symphony Spreadsheets — the Spreadsheet Application

The 5th Wave   By Rich Tennant

"I started running 'what if' scenarios on my spreadsheet, like, 'What if I were sick of this dirtwad job and funneled some of the company's money into an off-shore account?'"

In this part . . .

Sometimes life throws you a curveball when you're expecting a high fastball. But it doesn't really matter if you strike out a lot. You wouldn't have hit that curveball anyway. So roll up your sleeves and get ready to find out about spreadsheets — stuff like ranges, absolute references, and DataPilots. After the chapters in this part, you might just be good enough to hit that curveball after all. So just turn the page and read.

Chapter 8

Creating a Spreadsheet

· ·

In This Chapter

▶ Opening the program

▶ Creating a spreadsheet from a blank document or template

▶ Looking at the basic structure of a spreadsheet

▶ Entering data manually and automatically

▶ Finding your way around

▶ Selecting data

▶ Working with third-party spreadsheet files

▶ Working with word processor files

· ·

*O*ne of the most popular types of business software on the market is a class of products called spreadsheets. Spreadsheets are the electronic versions of the old ledger sheets — but with much more power and versatility. With electronic spreadsheets, you can maintain lists of data on which you can perform calculations both simple (such as summing a list of values) and complex (such as running what-if analyses on dozens of rows of values and variables).

Lotus Symphony includes Lotus Symphony Spreadsheets as a spreadsheet application. It includes many of the same powerful features that other more costly programs include. Throughout this chapter and the following four chapters, you're introduced to Lotus Symphony Spreadsheets and shown how to use many of its features.

In this chapter, I show you how to start using Lotus Symphony Spreadsheets to create, view, navigate, and edit spreadsheets. I also show you how to select data, embed data into your spreadsheet, and save your spreadsheets.

Starting Lotus Symphony Spreadsheets

Before you can start working on a Lotus Symphony spreadsheet file, you must start Lotus Symphony Spreadsheets. Before you can do that, however, you must start Lotus Symphony.

Unlike some other Office suites, Lotus Symphony has one primary application window. From this window, you launch each application by clicking the appropriate link, such as Create a New Spreadsheet for Lotus Symphony Spreadsheets. Program icons for each of these applications don't reside in a Lotus Symphony program folder accessible from the Windows Start menu. Instead an icon called IBM Lotus Symphony found on the Start⇨All Programs menu lets you start Lotus Symphony.

The most common way to start Lotus Symphony Spreadsheets after Symphony is started is to click the Create a New Spreadsheet link on the Lotus Symphony Home tab. This launches a new spreadsheet window on the New Spreadsheet tab, as shown in Figure 8-1.

By default, the first blank spreadsheet you open in the current Lotus Symphony session (that is, since you started the current session of Lotus Symphony) appears as New Spreadsheet. Subsequent spreadsheets you open appear as New Spreadsheet 2, New Spreadsheet 3, and so on. These are just temporary names until you save the spreadsheets with new filenames. Find out more about saving documents later in this chapter in the section "Saving Your Spreadsheets."

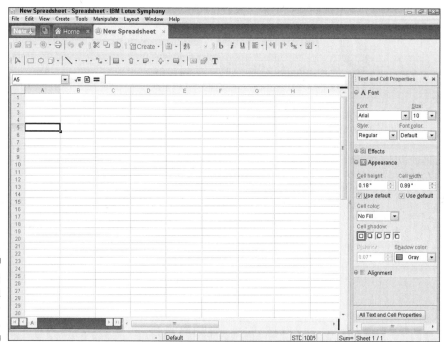

Figure 8-1:
A new blank spread-
sheet.

You can also start a new spreadsheet by using the Windows context menu you can see from the Windows Desktop and other areas. To use this method, right-click the Windows Desktop and choose New➪OpenDocument Spreadsheet. Lotus Symphony appears with the New Spreadsheet tab showing. This command is also located from Windows Explorer or the My Documents File menu.

Starting Lotus Symphony Spreadsheets from a menu

You just read how to start a new Lotus Symphony Spreadsheets blank document from the Home tab. You also can use Lotus Symphony menus to start a new document. In fact, you can use two different menus to do this:

1. **Start Lotus Symphony.**

2. **Choose File➪New➪Document.**

   Or click the New button to the left of the Home tab and click Lotus Symphony Spreadsheets.

   Either way, a new spreadsheet opens on a new tab.

Starting Lotus Symphony Spreadsheets from a spreadsheet file

Another way to start Lotus Symphony Spreadsheets requires that you already have a Lotus Symphony Spreadsheets file saved to your system, such as to your Windows Desktop or a different folder. You can double-click the file (or a shortcut to it) to launch Lotus Symphony, and then a Lotus Symphony Spreadsheets tab appears automatically with the selected file open.

Windows enables you to set file types that automatically launch the correct application when you double-click a file. When you install IBM Lotus Symphony on your computer, the Setup program automatically sets files with the filename extension of .ods to launch Lotus Symphony and display in a Lotus Symphony Spreadsheets tab. (The .ods extension stands for Open Document Spreadsheets.)

Starting Lotus Symphony Spreadsheets from a document attached to an e-mail message

An e-mail message you receive may include an attached Lotus Symphony Spreadsheets file that you need to review, edit, or print. To read it in Lotus Symphony, you can open the file from the e-mail application, or save the file to your system and then launch the file as explained in the preceding section.

To start from the e-mail application:

1. **Open the e-mail message that contains the attached Lotus Symphony Spreadsheets file.**

2. **Double-click the attached filename.**

   The spreadsheet opens on a Lotus Symphony Spreadsheets tab.

The preceding steps show an example of how to launch a Lotus Symphony Spreadsheets file as an attached e-mail file. This example uses Microsoft Office Outlook 2007 as the e-mail application. Your e-mail program may or may not use the same steps for completing this kind of task. Consult the documentation or help system for your e-mail program to understand the proper steps for your situation.

Creating a Lotus Symphony Spreadsheets Spreadsheet

Before you begin typing data into a spreadsheet, you need to first decide which type of spreadsheet you'd like to use. Lotus Symphony Spreadsheets supports the following general types:

- ✔ **Blank spreadsheet,** which displays a new, unformatted, blank screen for you to work on.

- ✔ **Spreadsheet from a template,** which provides boilerplate formatting, text, graphics, and other basic items for a document type.

- ✔ **Spreadsheet from another spreadsheet,** which enables you to save an existing spreadsheet to a new name (thereby creating a copy of it) and then modify the new spreadsheet.

I show each of these methods in the following sections.

Creating a blank spreadsheet

When you need to start a spreadsheet from scratch — that is, one without a specific format or one that is not based on another spreadsheet — use the blank spreadsheet method. A blank spreadsheet is just that; it contains no data, text, formatting, formulas, or other objects. This is handy if you aren't sure what the final spreadsheet should look like, but you want to get your information down and build the spreadsheet as you go.

Not every spreadsheet needs to have some kind of formatting or other fancy stuff added to it. Sometimes, you need to create a quick spreadsheet just to save some data or a list of items. In these cases, a blank spreadsheet works great. For example, you may want to save a list of data you downloaded from an online database, but you want it in a Lotus Symphony Spreadsheets file. In these cases, open a blank Lotus Symphony Spreadsheets file, copy and paste the information into the document, and save the file.

To see how to save files in Lotus Symphony Spreadsheets, read "Saving Your Spreadsheets," later in this chapter.

Essentially, when you start the Lotus Symphony Spreadsheets application from the main Lotus Symphony window, you create a blank spreadsheet. Here's how:

1. **Open Lotus Symphony.**
2. **Click Create a New Spreadsheet.**

    A new blank document opens in the New Spreadsheet tab.

As you find out in the "Entering Content" section of this chapter, you can begin filling your blank spreadsheet with data — values, text, calculations, graphics, objects, and more.

Creating a spreadsheet using a template

A template provides a head start in completing some of your spreadsheet. Sometimes, a template simply provides common formatting, such as cell formatting, column and row headings, and standard graphics (such as a company logo). Other times, you can use a template that has everything you need (including standard formulas) entered, except for variable data, such as interest rates, starting balances, and the like.

Examples of templates can include:

- ✔ Invoices
- ✔ Interest rate calculators

- ✔ Mortgage calculators
- ✔ School grade books
- ✔ Purchase orders

Templates are not just files you create. You can download them from Web sites, share them with colleagues, and have them sent to you via e-mail. In fact, some users on the Lotus Symphony support Web sites (see Chapter 20) have uploaded templates that work with Lotus Symphony Spreadsheets. As Lotus Symphony becomes more popular, look for additional templates that you can use.

When you want to use a template to create a new document, you access the Template Organizer. From there, you pick a template file, open it in Lotus Symphony Spreadsheets, make your changes, and then save the spreadsheet. When you save the spreadsheet, Lotus Symphony Spreadsheets automatically knows that you want the file to be a spreadsheet, not a template, and a spreadsheet file is stored on your system. The original template file doesn't change; you can then reuse it the next time you want a spreadsheet in this format.

To start a spreadsheet that uses a template, first set up your Template Organizer with template (after you set them up once, you don't have to do this again) using the following steps:

1. **Start Lotus Symphony.**

2. **Choose File⇨New⇨From Template⇨Spreadsheet.**

   The New From Template window appears. The first time you use the Template Organizer, a message appears informing you that the Organizer doesn't include any templates at this time. The next few steps show how to populate the Template Organizer for the first time.

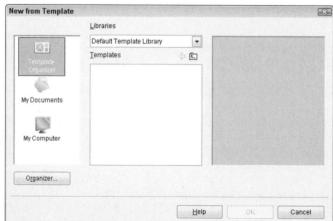

Figure 8-2: An empty Template Organizer.

3. **Click OK.**

   The New From Template window appears (See Figure 8-2.)

4. **Click Organizer.**

   The Template Organizer window appears. (See Figure 8-3.)

5. **Click the Actions drop-down list shown in Figure 8-3 and select Import Template.**

   The Insert dialog box appears. (See Figure 8-4.)

Figure 8-3:
You can import templates using the Template Organizer window.

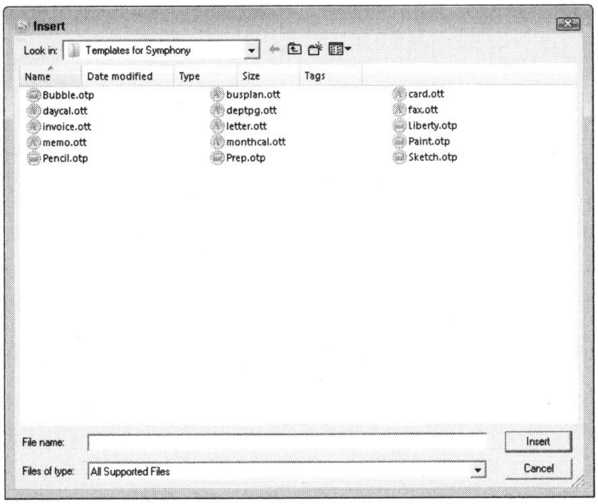

Figure 8-4:
You use the Insert dialog box to specify the templates to import into the Template Organizer.

6. **Navigate to a folder, using the Look In drop-down list, that includes a template file and select it. (Template files have .ots file extensions.)**

   If you don't have a template file on your system, you can download one from the IBM Lotus Symphony Gallery Web page at `http://symphony.lotus.com/software/lotus/symphony/gallery.jspa`.

7. **Click Insert.**

   The Template Organizer window appears, with the template added to the list of available templates. Continue adding templates as needed.

8. **Click OK.**

   The New From Template window appears again, this time with document templates you can select.

After you set up your Template Organizer with templates, you can select a template to use for a new document. Here are the steps for that process:

1. **Start Lotus Symphony.**

2. **Choose File⇨New⇨From Template⇨Spreadsheet.**

   The Template Organizer displays.

3. **Select a template.**

4. **Click OK.**

   A new spreadsheet appears with the formatting, boilerplate text, and other objects stored in the template you choose to start with. In the template shown in Figure 8-5, for example, you can create an invoice using the objects and data included in the template file.

 When you have templates in the Template Organizer, you don't have to go through all the steps you just went through. You can go from Step 2 to Step 9. Of course, any time you want to import new templates into the Template Organizer, follow Steps 3–8.

Creating a spreadsheet from another spreadsheet

Finally, another way to create your own spreadsheet is using another spreadsheet. You can overwrite the information in the spreadsheet, save the spreadsheet with a different name (or leave it the same as the original spreadsheet, if you like), and by golly, you got your spreadsheet.

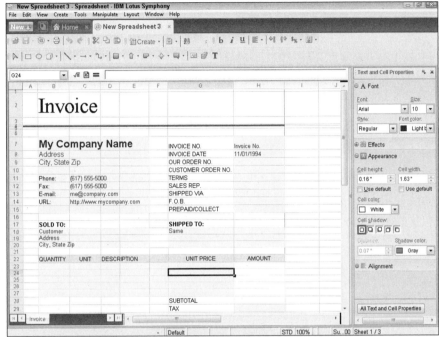

Figure 8-5:
Some templates include boilerplate text that you don't change each time you open the file.

To do this, get another spreadsheet file, such as a spreadsheet file you created from a template file, and follow these steps:

1. **Start Lotus Symphony or have Lotus Symphony Spreadsheets open.**

2. **Choose File⇨Open⇨File.**

   The Open dialog box appears.

3. **Select the spreadsheet.**

4. **Click Open.**

   The spreadsheet opens in the Lotus Symphony Spreadsheets tab.

5. **Choose File⇨Save As.**

   The Save As dialog box appears.

6. **Enter a new filename in the File Name field.**

7. **Click Save.**

   A new spreadsheet is saved.

Entering Content

If you've read the first part of this chapter, by now you know how to start Lotus Symphony, launch Lotus Symphony Spreadsheets, and display a blank new spreadsheet. In the next section of this chapter, you learn how to input content and manipulate it once it's there.

Cells, rows, and columns

Before I get too far into the discussion of entering data, I need to pause and introduce three of the most important concepts in spreadsheets. When you look at a spreadsheet, you see a bunch of vertical and horizontal lines and some empty boxes on-screen. Figure 8-6 shows them.

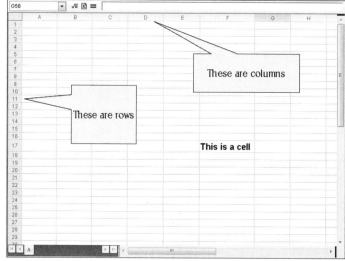

Figure 8-6:
The primary look of a spreadsheet shows rows, columns, and cells.

Cells are the rectangles where vertical rows and horizontal columns in the spreadsheet meet. *Columns* are denoted by letters, such as A, B, C, and so on. *Rows* are denoted by numbers, such as 1, 2, 3, and so on.

Another important feature of spreadsheets includes how each cell is named. All cells have a unique address on the spreadsheet. The naming convention goes like this:

✔ Spreadsheet filename

✔ Sheet name (the tab name at the bottom of the spreadsheet)

✔ Column name

✔ Row name

When you're working within a single spreadsheet, the first two items are referenced. They are assumed. The column and row names, however, are, important. Lotus Symphony Spreadsheets uses the naming scheme of `Column_LetterRow_Letter`. So if you're in the top cell of the spreadsheet, the cell address is A1. If you go down three rows and over five columns, the address is E3.

To find out the letter of the column, look to the top of the column. These letters always appear here. Similarly, the row numbers appear to the left of the rows.

You also can reference a cell or group of cells using a special name called named ranges. You learn about named ranges in Chapter 9, "At Home on the Range."

Adding data manually

The easiest way to enter data into a spreadsheet is by typing the data directly into a cell. To do this, click inside the cell and type the data. What you type is up to you. You can enter all of your data into one cell (you'll need to enlarge it, of course), or you can put disparate information into separate cells.

Usually, the data you enter in spreadsheets is used for some kind of analysis or sorting. Table 8-1 shows some information that you may want to add to a spreadsheet, with each distinct piece of data residing in its own cell.

Table 8-1	Information You Can Add to a Spreadsheet	
Manager	**Sales Region**	**Sales Data**
Williams	East	$4,000.000.00
Riley	West	$3,400,000.00
Greggs	North	$5,200,00.00
Nicholson	South	$6,500,000.00

Figure 8-7 shows how this same data can look in a spreadsheet. Notice how the column headings are placed as a header row, which helps you organize your data.

Sometimes, you might enter data that shows up as a series of ###. This means that the data is too large to fit into the cell and that you need to enlarge it to show the entire value. To increase the size of a column, you can double-click the small black line that appears between column letters. This resizes the column so that it is as large as the largest item in that column. You can do the same for resizing rows. Or you can manually resize a column or row by clicking and then dragging the black line between rows and columns.

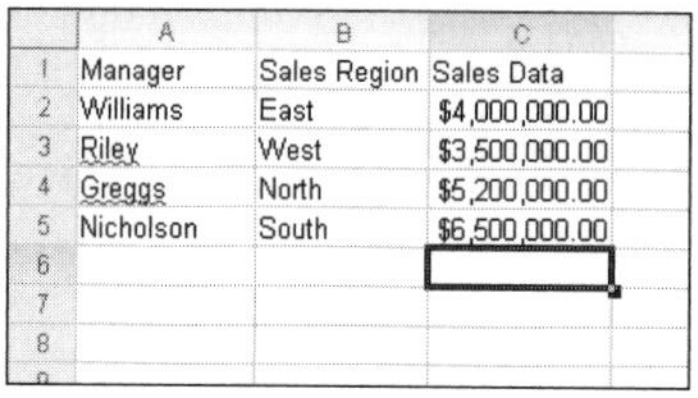

Figure 8-7:
Data
entered in
rows and
columns is
more man-
ageable and
useful as a
data analy-
sis tool.

	A	B	C
1	Manager	Sales Region	Sales Data
2	Williams	East	$4,000,000.00
3	Riley	West	$3,500,000.00
4	Greggs	North	$5,200,000.00
5	Nicholson	South	$6,500,000.00
6			
7			
8			

Specifying type of data you enter

When you enter a piece of information in a Lotus Symphony Spreadsheets, it doesn't know the difference between a number, date, normal word, or some other kind of data. That is, until you specify the type of data you are entering. By default, Lotus Symphony Spreadsheets interprets everything as a number. You might, however, want a value to represent a date, or even a time value.

To change data types, use the following steps:

1. **Enter a value in a cell.**

2. **Right-click the cell and choose Text and Cell Properties.**

   The Text and Cell Properties dialog box appears.

3. **Click the Numbers tab.**

4. **From the Category list, select the data type you want to specify for your data.**

5. **From the Format list, select the format of the data type.**

6. **Click OK.**

Using fills to enter data

As you work with more spreadsheets and more data, you'll find that, many times, data repeats itself or belongs to a series that Lotus Symphony Spreadsheets can repeat or recognize as Lotus Symphony Spreadsheets. For example, the data in Figure 8-8 includes a great deal of repeated data or series-type data (days of the week).

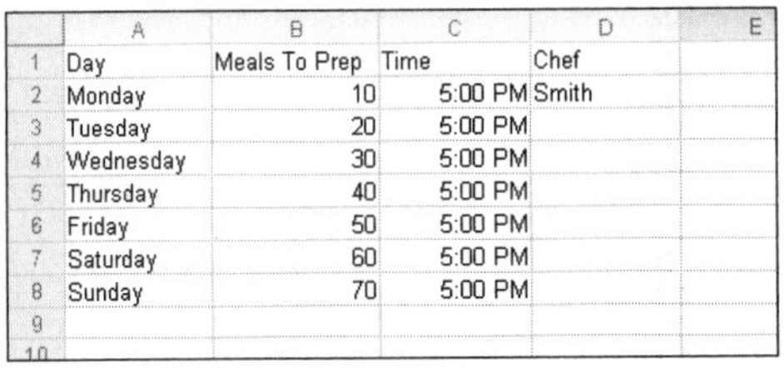

Figure 8-8:
Lotus
Symphony
Spread-
sheets can
enter some
data auto-
matically.

	A	B	C	D	E
1	Day	Meals To Prep	Time	Chef	
2	Monday	10	5:00 PM	Smith	
3	Tuesday	20	5:00 PM		
4	Wednesday	30	5:00 PM		
5	Thursday	40	5:00 PM		
6	Friday	50	5:00 PM		
7	Saturday	60	5:00 PM		
8	Sunday	70	5:00 PM		
9					
10					

Figure 8-8: Lotus Symphony Spreadsheets can enter some data automatically.

Instead of entering all of this data manually (one cell at a time) you can use the cell fill tools. These enable you to select a cell or range of cells and then tell Lotus Symphony Spreadsheets that you want to repeat the data or use a repeated pattern.

To use the fill tools, find a cell you want to repeat and click it. (Don't put your cursor in it.) You'll see an outline around the cell with a small tab in the lower-right corner of it. Click the tab and, still pressing the mouse button, drag to fill the cells. Release the mouse button, and you'll see the data that Lotus Symphony Spreadsheets came up with.

For example, I'll show how you can add a new column, called Chef, to cell D1. Then I show how you can add the name Smith to cell D2. In my sample spreadsheet, she's the chef from Monday to Wednesday. Morris finishes up the week. Use the following steps to do the fill:

1. **Enter** Chef **in cell D1.**
2. **Type** Smith **in cell D2 and press Enter.**
3. **Grab the bottom-right corner of cell D2 and drag down to cell D4.**

   Figure 8-9 shows how Lotus Symphony Spreadsheets highlights the borders of the cells you want to fill.

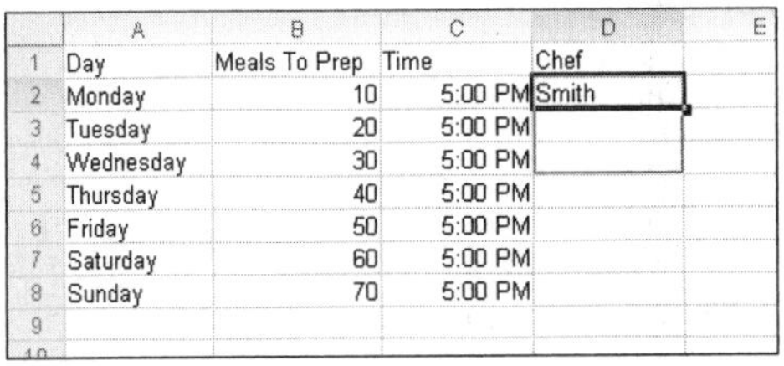

Figure 8-9:
Enter some
data and
then use the
fill tool to fill
in data auto-
matically.

	A	B	C	D	E
1	Day	Meals To Prep	Time	Chef	
2	Monday	10	5:00 PM	Smith	
3	Tuesday	20	5:00 PM		
4	Wednesday	30	5:00 PM		
5	Thursday	40	5:00 PM		
6	Friday	50	5:00 PM		
7	Saturday	60	5:00 PM		
8	Sunday	70	5:00 PM		
9					
10					

Figure 8-9: Enter some data and then use the fill tool to fill in data automatically.

   4. **Release the mouse button.**

   Lotus Symphony Spreadsheets fills each cell.

   5. **Type** Morris **in cell D5.**

   6. **Grab the bottom-right corner of cell D5 and drag down to cell D8.**

   7. **Release the mouse button.**

   The final spreadsheet looks like the one in Figure 8-10.

	A	B	C	D	E
1	Day	Meals To Prep	Time	Chef	
2	Monday	10	5:00 PM	Smith	
3	Tuesday	20	5:00 PM	Smith	
4	Wednesday	30	5:00 PM	Smith	
5	Thursday	40	5:00 PM	Morris	
6	Friday	50	5:00 PM	Morris	
7	Saturday	60	5:00 PM	Morris	
8	Sunday	70	5:00 PM	Morris	
9					
10					
11					

Figure 8-10: Column D is now filled out.

For repeated patterns, such as days of the week, month names, and so on, select at least two of the items in the pattern and then drag down (or up, right, or left, if you want to go those ways). This fills the cells with the rest of the pattern until you stop. With numbers, if you use the fill tool, Lotus Symphony Spreadsheets adds one to the number, or if you select a series (such as 10, 20, and so on) and use the fill, Lotus Symphony Spreadsheets uses that fill pattern to fill the next cells.

Embedding data from other documents

You may not want to type any data into your spreadsheet — especially data you have in another format. With Lotus Symphony Spreadsheets you can copy and paste a great deal of data from one source to your spreadsheet. For example, you may have a list of information in a text file (that you read with Windows Notepad). If so, you can open the document in Notepad, select the data, choose Edit⇨Copy, and the choose Edit⇨Paste in your spreadsheet. The data appears in Lotus Symphony Spreadsheets, and you didn't need to type anything.

Another way to embed data from another source uses the Import Data feature. With this tool, you walk through some steps that enable you to specify the layout of the data before it comes into your spreadsheet.

The following steps show how to use it:

Using Notepad to paste data

Often, data resides in a document, database, spreadsheet, Web page, or other file that you want to pull into your spreadsheets. When you paste that data, the data may look funny, format into the wrong columns and rows, or plunk down in a single cell. For analysis and sorting tasks, these scenarios usually don't work for you. In those cases, use an intermediate application to strip out any funky formatting that the original data has. One great tool for this is Windows Notepad. It's located in the Accessories folder of your Windows program files. Copy and paste your data there and then copy and paste it into Lotus Symphony Spreadsheets. You'll be amazed at how clean the data comes in (usually).

1. **Open a new Spreadsheets spreadsheet.**

2. **Choose Manipulate⇨Import External Data⇨From File.**

   The Import Data from File dialog box appears.

3. **Click Browse.**

   The Insert dialog box appears. You need to find a file that includes data you can import. Some sample data appears on the enclosed CD-ROM at the back of this book.

4. **Select a file that includes data you can import.**

   You may need to change the Files of Type drop-down setting to indicate the type of file you want to import. In this case, I chose the Text CSV file type.

5. **Choose Insert.**

   The Text Import dialog box appears. (See Figure 8-11.) This dialog box guides you through importing the data from the selected file. Notice at the bottom of the dialog box the data appears in nice columns and rows.

Figure 8-11:
Use the Text Import dialog box to set up the parameters for importing the data.

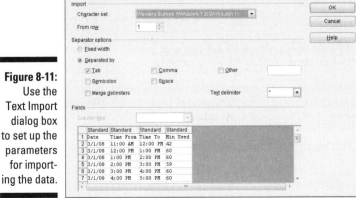

6. **Use the Separator Options, if necessary, to denote if the data uses a different separator than a Tab.**

7. **Click OK.**

   The Import Data from File dialog box appears. (See Figure 8-12.)

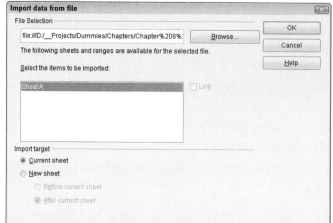

Figure 8-12:
The Import Data from File dialog box.

8. **Select the data name you just imported.**

   It appears in the Select the Items to Import list.

9. **Click OK.**

   Lotus Symphony Spreadsheets imports the data into the spreadsheet.

When computers save raw data to a text file, they need a way to know when one piece of data ends (such as a number) and another piece begins. They use separators, such as commas, tabs, spaces, and similar characters. When you import data into Lotus Symphony Spreadsheets, you need to specify what these separators are.

Navigating the Spreadsheet

When you have some data in a spreadsheet, you can learn a few navigation tricks to help you get around. The following sections describe how to use the mouse and keyboard to navigate your spreadsheets.

Moving around with the mouse

The basic tool for moving around the spreadsheet window is the mouse. You use it for several different navigation tasks, including:

✔ Clicking in cells

✔ Sliding vertical and horizontal scroll bars to see data not currently showing on-screen

✔ Choosing menus and commands

✔ Right-clicking a cell to expose contextual menus and commands

✔ Clicking the spreadsheet tabs to navigate to a new sheet

By default, Lotus Symphony Spreadsheets adds one sheet to your spreadsheet when you create it using the File⇨New command. If you need additional sheets, such as if you want to add related data to a spreadsheet, right-click the A tab at the bottom of the Lotus Symphony Spreadsheets window and choose Insert Sheet. In the Create Sheet dialog box (see Figure 8-13) select the position of the new sheet — before or after the current sheet. Click OK. The new sheet appears in the spreadsheet file as sheet B.

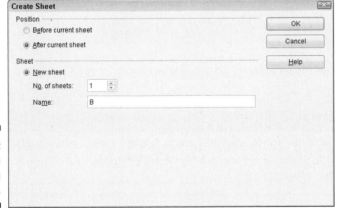

Figure 8-13:
The Create
Sheet dialog
box.

Moving around with the keyboard

You can use the keyboard to navigate a spreadsheet. In fact, many users prefer the keyboard as a navigational tool when they're entering large amounts of data. They like to keep their hands on the keyboard, instead of moving their hand to the mouse each time they need to move to a different cell.

The most common ways to use the keyboard to move around in a spreadsheet are as follows:

- ✔ Press Enter after typing content into a cell. The insertion point moves to the next row.

- ✔ Use the arrow keys (up, down, left, and right) to move around the spreadsheet.

- ✔ Use the Page Up and Page Down keys to navigate up and down one page at a time.

- ✔ Press Tab to navigate within a row, moving from left to right.

- ✔ Press Shift+Tab to navigate within a row, moving from right to left.

Selecting Data

At some point in time, you need to select data in your spreadsheets. Lotus Symphony Spreadsheets makes it possible to select a word or number in a cell, select data in multiple cells, or select all the data in the spreadsheet. The following sections describe these tasks.

Selecting a word or number in a cell

When you need to select a word or number in a cell, you might think "What's the big deal? Just click the cell and choose Edit⇨Copy."

That's one way to do it. And that's a good way if you want to select the entire contents of the cell. Look at cell A11 (which contains the words *Mercury Vapor)* in Figure 8-14 as an example. Say you want to select only the word *Mercury* in that cell. To select just that word, double-click the cell (A11) and then highlight the word you want to select. Choose Edit⇨Copy. Figure 8-15 shows the selected word.

	A	B	C	D
1	**Type**	**Sales**	**Sales Manager**	
2	Incandescent	$4,324.00	Jackson	
3	Halogen	$3,389.00	Monroe	
4	Green 3-Way	$2,198.00	Washington	
5	Fluorescent	$1,300.00	Monroe	
6	Strobe	$6,831.00	Jackson	
7	Black	$7,190.00	Jackson	
8	Spot	$2,539.00	Washington	
9	Auto Lites	$4,983.00	Monroe	
10	Field Lights	$3,253.00	Monroe	
11	Mercury Vapor	$8,215.00	Jackson	
12				
13				

Figure 8-14: A sample spreadsheet for selecting data.

Figure 8-15:
Double-click
and then
highlight
a word,
phrase, or
value to
select it
within a cell.

	A	B	C	D
1	**Type**	**Sales**	**Sales Manager**	
2	Incandescent	$4,324.00	Jackson	
3	Halogen	$3,389.00	Monroe	
4	Green 3-Way	$2,198.00	Washington	
5	Fluorescent	$1,300.00	Monroe	
6	Strobe	$6,831.00	Jackson	
7	Black	$7,190.00	Jackson	
8	Spot	$2,539.00	Washington	
9	Auto Lites	$4,983.00	Monroe	
10	Field Lights	$3,253.00	Monroe	
11	Mercury Vapor	$8,215.00	Jackson	
12				
13				

When you select a cell (even if you simply click it once), the content of that cell appears in the formula. The formula bar appears above the column headings at the top of the spreadsheet. When text or values appear here, you can select them with your mouse. Sometimes, you may find it easier to select data in the formula bar than in a cell, particularly if the cell appears small and you don't want to reformat the cell to a larger size just to grab a copy of a piece of data.

Selecting data in multiple cells

To select data in multiple cells, you have to drag with the mouse over the cells containing the data you want to select.

After you select the cells, copy the data using your favorite method, such as Ctrl+C. You can now paste the data to a different location on the spreadsheet, or into a different spreadsheet, document, or other file.

When you select data in multiple cells this way, the data remains formatted in multiple cells. When you paste that data into a different part of your spreadsheet, for example, the integrity of those cells remains. (If you select five rows of data, five rows of data are pasted back in — instead of squished into one row). Where you may find this different is when you paste the data into a different application, such as a text file. Then the data will be formatted using tabs to separate each cell's data.

Selecting all data

For large copy and paste operations, times when you need to share large amounts of data, or when you want to duplicate a spreadsheet onto another sheet, you can select all the data on your spreadsheet.

To do this, use one of the following methods:

✔ Choose Edit➪Select All.

✔ Press Ctrl+A.

✔ Click the empty gray cell that falls to the left of column A and above row 1.

Your entire spreadsheet is highlighted when you select it all.

Saving Your Spreadsheets

As you create new spreadsheets and modify existing ones, you need to make sure any changes you make are saved to disk. What this means is that you take the information that appears on the monitor and make a permanent copy of it on your hard disk or other drive (such as a network drive or flash media device). You can continue to work on the spreadsheet, but should periodically take the time to save your changes.

Using different file formats

When you use Lotus Symphony Spreadsheets to create or work on files, you have a few options for saving the file. You can save files in the following formats:

✔ Open Document Spreadsheet (`.ods`)

✔ Microsoft Excel (`.xls`)

✔ Adobe Portable Document (`.pdf`)

✔ IBM Spreadsheet (`.sxc`)

✔ Text (`.csv`)

When saving spreadsheets, you also can save them as template files. For Lotus Symphony Spreadsheets templates, you save them as Open Document Spreadsheets Templates with an `.ots` file extension. You also can save files in the IBM Spreadsheet Template format (which uses the `.stc` extension).

Saving in Open Document format

The primary format for saving Lotus Symphony Spreadsheets files, Open Document Spreadsheet format, provides a way for other Open Document-compliant applications to read Lotus Symphony Spreadsheets files. For example, the OpenOffice product, available from OpenOffice.org, supports

Open Document files. Likewise, Sun Microsystems provides Open Document support in its StarOffice product.

By default, when you save a new spreadsheet in Lotus Symphony Spreadsheets, the Open Document format is automatically selected. To save in Open Document format, follow these steps:

1. **Open a new Lotus Symphony Spreadsheets document.**

2. **Enter some data in the spreadsheet cells.**

   The section called "Entering Content," earlier in this chapter, discusses this in more detail, but for now you can type any characters you want. If you don't, the Save command on the File menu (see Step 3) doesn't display.

3. **Choose File⇨Save.**

   The Save As dialog box appears.

4. **Type a name for the file in the File Name field.**

5. **Click Save.**

   The spreadsheet is saved in the .ods file format.

If the Open Document Spreadsheet (*.ods) format doesn't show up as the default file format in the Save As dialog box, you can click the File Type down arrow and select the Open Spreadsheet file format.

Working with Files from Other Spreadsheet Applications

Lotus Symphony Spreadsheets is a great application, but it isn't the only spreadsheets app in the world. You can't rely on just poring through volumes of good data saved in Lotus Symphony Spreadsheets format. Sometimes the data you need to access resides in other spreadsheet formats, such as Lotus 1-2-3, IBM Spreadsheets, Microsoft Excel, or the open source ODS format. As a Lotus Symphony Spreadsheets user, you need to learn how to handle these types of data so that you can incorporate that data into your spreadsheets.

To open a file saved in another spreadsheet format, do the following:

1. **Start Lotus Symphony.**

2. **Open a new blank Lotus Symphony Spreadsheets file.**

3. **Choose File⇨Open⇨File.**

   The Open dialog box appears.

4. **Click the arrow on the File Type button. (It's to the right of the File Name field.)**

   A list of file types that Lotus Symphony supports appears.

5. **Choose Lotus 1-2-3 (*.123), IBM Spreadsheets(.sxc), OpenDocument Spreadsheet (*.ods), or Microsoft Excel 97/2000/XP (*.xls) from the list.**

   A list of files saved in the selected format appears.

6. **Select the file you want to open.**

7. **Click Open.**

   Lotus Symphony Spreadsheets opens the file and displays it in the Lotus Symphony Spreadsheets window.

After you open a third-party file in the Lotus Symphony Spreadsheets window, you should analyze the information that displays. You may find that some of the data (such as charts or tables) doesn't convert exactly like it should (or like you want it to). In these cases, you need to manually fix these problems, or even delete the information and re-create or design a new object for the file. A chart that doesn't display correctly, for example, should probably be removed (if it appears in the imported file at all) and re-created using the Lotus Symphony Chart Setup tool.

Don't expect the Lotus Symphony Spreadsheets import converter to work 100 percent every time you import a file. Some of the items that may pose some problems include:

- ✔ Animated text and characters
- ✔ Bookmarks
- ✔ Comments
- ✔ Complex charts, such as those using arrays and source data stored in other spreadsheet files.
- ✔ Graphics that use file formats not supported by Lotus Symphony Spreadsheets.
- ✔ Hyperlinks
- ✔ Nonstandard cell formatting.
- ✔ Sophisticated macros.
- ✔ Functions and formulas, such as those that include several nested statements.
- ✔ Database links that have been changed or lost because of different computer and network configurations.
- ✔ Embedded objects
- ✔ Pivot tables

Many different types of files store lists of data. You may find that Lotus Symphony Spreadsheets can handle a number of these files without doing a lot of conversion work. However, sometimes you may find it quicker to import a file into a text editor (like Windows Notepad) and clean up the data first before pulling it into a Lotus Symphony Spreadsheets file. What does "cleaning" do? Text editors format information in straight ASCII (American Standard Code for Information Interchange) format, which has no formatting embedded into the file. The only fancy formatting in text files is the *text-wrap* function, which wraps text lines to the next line when its characters get to the right edge of the window. However, you can't add graphics, put borders around text, add bullets or fancy numbers, or insert similar objects. This makes text files great for stripping out everything but the raw data. And sometimes putting data into text files first and then porting over to Lotus Symphony Spreadsheets makes the data easy to work with. You don't have to remove any fancy character formatting or styles just to work with the information.

Working with Word Processing Files

Not only can you use information saved in other spreadsheet files for your Lotus Symphony Spreadsheets data, you can use data stored in some word processing files. For example, some word processing documents include long lists of data, such as a table that includes manufacturing parts.

Lotus Symphony Spreadsheets doesn't support opening word processing files right inside its window. Instead, you can open the file in Lotus Documents (if the file format is one that Lotus Documents supports, of course) or from the original application and then select the data from that window. The data can then be pasted into the Lotus Symphony Spreadsheets file.

The following shows an example of importing data that resides in a word processing document:

1. **Open Lotus Symphony.**

2. **Display the Lotus Symphony Spreadsheets file in which you want to import the data.**

   You can start a new Lotus Symphony Spreadsheets document if you want.

3. **Open the word processing file in Lotus Documents or another word processor.**

4. **Select the data in the word processing file.**

5. **Choose Edit⇨Copy.**

   The selected information copies to the Windows Clipboard so you can paste it into your spreadsheet document.

6. Switch to the Lotus Symphony Spreadsheets file.

7. Choose Edit➪Paste.

The information copied to the Windows Clipboard shows up in your Lotus Symphony Spreadsheets files.

Not all applications include the Edit➪Copy and Copy➪Paste commands to copy data to the Windows Clipboard. With most Windows programs, however, you can use the keyboard combination of Ctrl+C to copy something and Ctrl+V to paste that item. The combination for cutting a selection (which removes it from the original document) is Ctrl+X.

Chapter 9

At Home on the Range

In This Chapter

▶ Using relative and absolute references

▶ Naming ranges

▶ Including named ranges in formulas

*W*hen most of us give directions to someone from out of town who wants to find a local store or restaurant, we usually don't say, "Go to 523 East Main Street." If that person lives out of town, he or she will probably not know how to get to 523 East Main Street. Instead, we give directions using references, such as take a right after the third stop sign, or some such. With Lotus Symphony Spreadsheets, there are times when knowing the specific location of a cell or group of cells can be very useful, but so can using references to point the way to your data. Lotus Spreadsheets enables you to use absolute references and relative references to your data.

Unless you have a photographic memory, trying to remember the specific cells in which data reside in your spreadsheets can be next to impossible. But sometimes you need to know the address of a cell for a calculation you are setting up. One way to get a grip on this problem is by naming a group of cells as a named range. Lotus Symphony Spreadsheets makes it easy to add your own named ranges.

In this chapter, you find out about absolute and relative references, how to use them in formulas, and how to use named ranges in Lotus Symphony Spreadsheets.

Knowing Your References

Lotus Symphony Spreadsheets uses two types of references: relative and absolute. *Relative references* are those that look at the relative position of the cells in respect to a formula. For example, they look for data in a cell that is two cells to the left of itself and three cells down. *Absolute references* refer in formulas to specific cells, such as A1, C288, N45 — and they *always* refer to those cells. Even if you move the formula, those references continue to look for information in those specific cells.

By default, you use relative references when you create formulas, but you can quickly modify this any time you want to put together a formula that requires absolute references. The following two sections describe these types of references and show how to use them.

Be sure you understand the differences between relative and absolute references. You'll appreciate it later when you start working with formulas a great deal, especially those that you copy to different cells, or even to different spreadsheets in a file.

Using relative references

To use relative references, simply enter the cell letters and numbers in a simple formula, such as:

```
=B1+B2+B3
```

Lotus Symphony Spreadsheets automatically treats those cells' references as relative ones.

Here's an example of a formula using a relative reference. In Figure 9-1, a formula (=D2–C2) created in cell E2 finds the difference between the amount in cell D2 and C2. (Notice that the values are all in row 2.) When you copy the formula to a cell in a different row (row 3), the references automatically change to the same columns in the new row, so your formula calculates the correct information. In this instance, when you copy the formula down to cell E3, the formula changes to =D3–C3. How does Lotus Symphony Spreadsheets know you want these cells calculated? It doesn't. It just knows that in your original formula, you instructed it to do the following:

Figure 9-1:
Relative references are the default reference type in Lotus Symphony Spreadsheets.

	A	B	C	D	E
1			Estimated Taxes	Actual Taxes Due	
2		Jan-09	$4,300.00	$4,324.00	=D2-C2
3		Feb-09	$3,200.00	$3,389.00	
4		Mar-09	$2,500.00	$2,198.00	
5		Apr-09	$2,000.00	$1,300.00	
6		May-09	$7,200.00	$6,831.00	
7		June-09	$8,000.00	$7,190.00	
8		July-09	$1,200.00	$2,539.00	
9		Aug-09	$5,100.00	$4,983.00	
10		Sep-09	$3,300.00	$3,253.00	
11		Oct-09	$7,200.00	$6,980.00	
12		Nov-09	$3,000.00	$1,290.00	
13		Dec-09	$3,500.00	$4,598.00	
14	Totals				
15					
16					

TIP

I discuss formulas and *functions* (built-in formulas) in Chapter 12. For this chapter, I use very simple formulas, such as adding or subtracting two values. For more complex formulas, see Chapter 12.

1. Look for the value ($4,324.00) in the cell that is one cell to the left (D2) of the cell that the formula's in.

2. Look for the value ($4,300.00) in the cell that is two cells to the left (C2) of the cell that the formula's in.

3. Subtract the second number ($4,300.00) from the first number ($4,324.00) you found.

4. Display the result ($24.00) in this cell (E2).

When you copy the formula to the next cell, the instructions in the formula (in the preceding list) remain the same. But the cells that are in those positions change (D3 and C3 instead of D2 and C2).

You can test this theory by experimenting with a spreadsheet of your own. Enter some data that resembles the data in Figure 9-2. (If you aren't sure how to get the dollar signs and decimals to show up, don't worry about that for now. Any numbers will do. I tell you how to format Spreadsheets cells for specific types of data in Chapter 8.)

	A	B	C	D	E	F
1			**Estimated Taxes**	**Actual Taxes Due**		
2		Jan-09	$4,300.00	$4,324.00	$24.00	
3		Feb-09	$3,200.00	$3,389.00	=D3-C3	
4		Mar-09	$2,500.00	$2,198.00		
5		Apr-09	$2,000.00	$1,300.00		
6		May-09	$7,200.00	$6,831.00		
7		June-09	$8,000.00	$7,190.00		
8		July-09	$1,200.00	$2,539.00		
9		Aug-09	$5,100.00	$4,983.00		
10		Sep-09	$3,300.00	$3,253.00		
11		Oct-09	$7,200.00	$6,980.00		
12		Nov-09	$3,000.00	$1,290.00		
13		Dec-09	$3,500.00	$4,598.00		
14	**Totals**					
15						
16						

Figure 9-2: Use relative references to copy cell formulas from one cell to the next.

In cell E2 write a formula that adds the values in two cells, such as the following:

```
=D2+D3
```

Copy and paste the formula down one cell and to the right one cell. The results may confuse you. Instead of adding two cells that have data in them, you really are adding up only one cell of data because the formula finds a blank value for the second value.

Using absolute references

The trick to using absolute references, however, is to use a special character to indicate that cell reference as an absolute reference. The special character Lotus Symphony Spreadsheets uses is $. So, to change in the formula =B2–C2 the relative references of B2 and C2 to absolute references, type in the following:

```
=$B$2–$C$2
```

The cell references don't change, regardless of where you copy the formula.

Don't want to type in all of those dollar signs ($) to convert relative references to absolute? You don't have to. Select the information in a cell and press Shift+F4. Lotus Symphony Spreadsheets changes the column and row values to absolute references. Press Shift+F4 again. Lotus Symphony Spreadsheets changes only the row value to absolute reference. Finally, press Shift+F4 a third time. Lotus Symphony Spreadsheets changes only the column value to absolute reference. If you press Shift+F4 for a fourth time, the entire selection changes back to relative references (no dollar signs).

Figure 9-3 shows how an absolute reference looks in a spreadsheet.

	A	B	C	D	E
1			**Estimated Taxes**	**Actual Taxes Due**	
2		Jan-09	$4,300.00	$4,324.00	=$D$2+$C$2
3		Feb-09	$3,200.00	$3,389.00	
4		Mar-09	$2,500.00	$2,198.00	
5		Apr-09	$2,000.00	$1,300.00	
6		May-09	$7,200.00	$6,831.00	
7		June-09	$8,000.00	$7,190.00	
8		July-09	$1,200.00	$2,539.00	
9		Aug-09	$5,100.00	$4,983.00	
10		Sep-09	$3,300.00	$3,253.00	
11		Oct-09	$7,200.00	$6,980.00	
12		Nov-09	$3,000.00	$1,290.00	
13		Dec-09	$3,500.00	$4,598.00	
14	**Totals**				
15					

Figure 9-3: An absolute reference in a Lotus Symphony Spreadsheets file.

When you copy the formula to a different cell, the results remain the same, as shown in Figure 9-4.

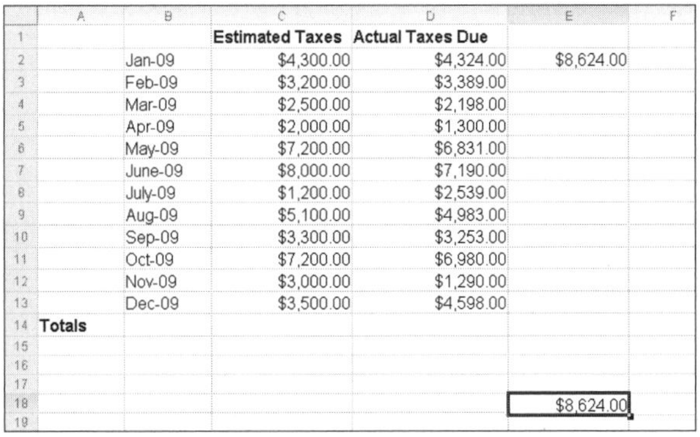

	A	B	C	D	E	F
1			Estimated Taxes	Actual Taxes Due		
2		Jan-09	$4,300.00	$4,324.00	$8,624.00	
3		Feb-09	$3,200.00	$3,389.00		
4		Mar-09	$2,500.00	$2,198.00		
5		Apr-09	$2,000.00	$1,300.00		
6		May-09	$7,200.00	$6,831.00		
7		June-09	$8,000.00	$7,190.00		
8		July-09	$1,200.00	$2,539.00		
9		Aug-09	$5,100.00	$4,983.00		
10		Sep-09	$3,300.00	$3,253.00		
11		Oct-09	$7,200.00	$6,980.00		
12		Nov-09	$3,000.00	$1,290.00		
13		Dec-09	$3,500.00	$4,598.00		
14	Totals					
15						
16						
17						
18					$8,624.00	
19						

Figure 9-4:
Copying
absolute
references.

The value of absolute references

I can hear you now: When would I use an absolute reference? Don't I want the flexibility of moving a formula and letting it automatically update? Sometimes that's great — and very handy for copying formulas for a long list of values. However, you may want to create a formula that uses a value in a cell that you don't want to change. (At least, you may not want to change the location to which that formula points.) For example, you may create a spreadsheet that calculates payments for auto loans. Insert a formula in a cell and base the formula on interest rate, cost of vehicle, and number of payments. The cell in which the formula resides may later change. (For example, you may insert a new column that moves that cell over to the right a little.) But the cells in which the three other values reside won't change. That's when absolute references work great.

Another instance when absolute references work to your advantage is when you reference a cell on a different spreadsheet. Use absolute references to specify a specific cell on a specific spreadsheet. The following formula, for example, returns the value entered in cell D3 on sheet A to a cell on sheet B. (See Figure 9-5.)

```
=A.$D$3
```

Figure 9-5:
Look at the
formula bar
to see the
reference to
sheet A and
the absolute
references
to cell D3 on
that sheet.

B4		√=		=A.$D$3	
	A	B	C	D	
1					
2					
3					
4		$3,389.00			
5					
6					
7					

You can use absolute references and relative references together. For example, $A2 refers to the absolute reference of column A, and a relative reference to row 2. Conversely, A$2 refers to relative reference to column A and an absolute reference to row 2.

Understanding Ranges

When working with data in Lotus Symphony Spreadsheets, you may find it easier to reference a group of cells by a name. These are called *named references.* Instead of referencing a column of cells related to a new product line as C3:C12, use a name that describes that range of cells, such as Lights. Figure 9-6 shows a range of cells that relates to a product line of lights. Assume, for example, that each month you write a report using the values shown in these cells. Instead of entering the range of cells here, you can just reference the entire collection as something easier to remember, such as Lights.

Figure 9-6:
A spread-
sheet with
a range of
values for
different
lighting
products.

	A	B	C	D
1		**Fly By Light, Inc**		
2			March 2010	
3		Incandescent	$4,324.00	
4		Halogen	$3,389.00	
5		Green 3-Way	$2,198.00	
6		Fluorescent	$1,300.00	
7		Strobe	$6,831.00	
8		Black	$7,190.00	
9		Spot	$2,539.00	
10		Auto Lites	$4,983.00	
11		Field Lights	$3,253.00	
12		Mercury Vapor	$6,980.00	
13				

When you want to include the range of values in this sheet, pop in the named range of `Lights` and Lotus Symphony Spreadsheets finds the values for that range and uses them in your calculations. Continue to the next section to find out how to set it up.

Naming a range

To name a range, use the following steps:

1. **Open Lotus Symphony Spreadsheets with a blank spreadsheet.**

2. **Enter your data.**

   If you don't have any data on hand, you can use the following. Enter the values in a column, starting at cell C3.

   $4,324.00

   $3,389.00

   $2,198.00

   $1,300.00

   $6,831.00

   $7,190.00

   $2,539.00

   $4,983.00

   $3,253.00

   $6,980.00

3. **Select the entire range of cells.**

4. **Choose Create⇨Names⇨Define.**

   The Define Range Names dialog box appears. (See Figure 9-7.)

5. **Type a name in the Name field.**

   When creating names for your named ranges, get in the habit of using names that begin with a letter and have no other symbols or spaces except for periods and the underscore. For names like `lights and cameras`, use a name like `lights_and_cameras`. These types of names tend to work better in formulas and import into Microsoft Excel with few hassles if you decide to export your Lotus Symphony Spreadsheets file into Excel.

Figure 9-7:
The Define
Range
Names dia-
log box.

6. Click the Add button.

The new name appears in the list of named ranges.

If you need to select another range of cells to name, you don't need to close the Define Range Names dialog box. Type the name of the new range and enter the range values in the Assigned To field. Or if you don't know the range, click the Shrink button, which shrinks the dialog box so you can see more of the spreadsheet. Make your selection and click the Maximize button to show the full dialog box again, but with your new range selected.

7. Click OK to save your new name.

When the Define Range Names dialog box was open, you may have noticed a few options at the bottom of the window. The following list describes these options:

- **Print range** specifies the name range as a print range.

- **Filter** specifies that the named range can be used in a Special Filter created from the Manipulate menu.

- **Repeat column** specifies the named range as a column that repeats.

- **Repeat row** specifies the named range as a row that repeats.

Named ranges are used in filters (for Special Filters), as print ranges (which define the area on a spreadsheet that prints), and in formulas. Chapter 12 discusses setting up filters, and Chapter 10 explains how to print your spreadsheets.

Using named ranges in formulas

In this section, you look at using named ranges in formulas.

When you set up formulas (see Chapter 12), you can use specific cells or a range of cells. You also can use named ranges. Using named ranges in formulas makes it easier to read your formulas; that is, naming the cell range can make it easier to discern what that part of the formula returns.

Look at a simple formula:

```
=SUM(C3:C6)
```

This formula adds the values displayed in cells C3, C4, C5, and C6. In Figure 9-8, I added the formula to cell C7. Instead of using that formula, however, I decided to create a named range for that formula and call it `Quarterly_Results`. That name is easier to surmise what it's summing, as opposed to just `C3:C6`. We then can plug in that named range in other parts of our spreadsheets and it uses the same criteria for calculating returns.

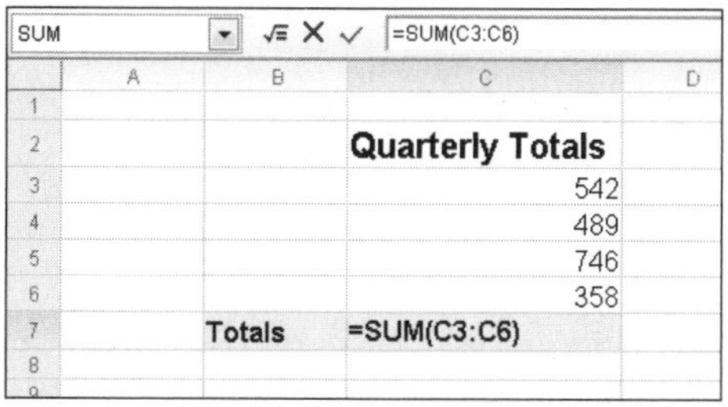

Figure 9-8: Creating a formula to use in a named range.

Figure 9-9 shows the selection I made on which to base the new named range. I highlighted the cells that appear in the formula along with the cell that contains the formula. I followed the steps in the preceding "Naming a range" section to assign the name to the selected range.

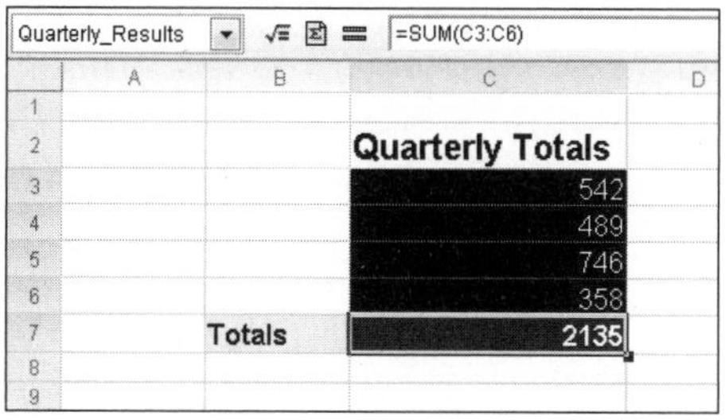

Figure 9-9: The named range includes the selected information.

I then can plug the named range, `Quarterly_Results`, into the formula instead of the original cell range (`C3:C6`). Use the following steps to do this:

1. **Click inside cell C7.**

2. **Click inside the formula bar.**

3. **Type** `=SUM(` **and choose Create⇨Names⇨Insert.**

    The Insert Name dialog box appears.

4. **Select Quarterly_Results.**

5. **Choose OK.**

6. **Type) at the end of the formula.**

7. **Press Enter.**

In the formula bar (which appears above row A), the named range appears in the formulas. (See Figure 9-10.)

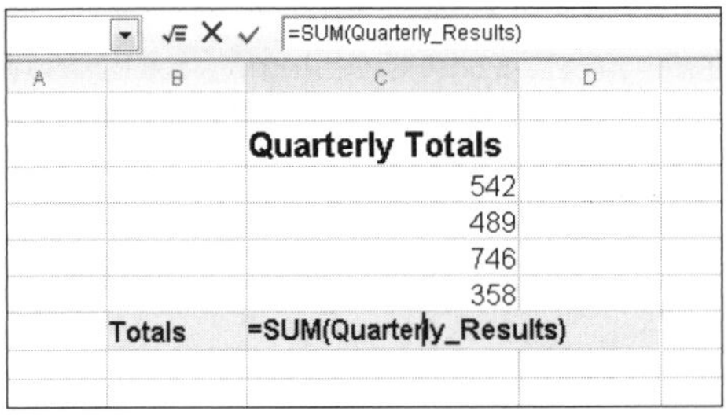

Figure 9-10:
The named range appears in the formula now.

	√≡ ✗ ✓	=SUM(Quarterly_Results)
A	B	C	D
		Quarterly Totals	
		542	
		489	
		746	
		358	
	Totals	=SUM(Quarterly_Results)	

Chapter 10

Printing Spreadsheets

. . . .

In This Chapter

▶ Understanding Print Preview

▶ Dealing with page breaks

▶ Setting up pages for printing

▶ Modifying printer options

. . . .

*O*ne of the most satisfying aspects of working a spreadsheet comes at the end of all that work: You can print your spreadsheet and show it off to all of your esteemed colleagues. They'll marvel at the concise rows and columns and your mixture of serious boldfaced headings with colorful but professional charts. You'll be humbled.

Or, like so many of us, you print your spreadsheet and realize that you forgot to add the correct formatting or page numbers to each page. If you're really inexperienced at printing spreadsheets, you may wonder why you just printed off fifty pages — when your data takes up only two of them.

In this chapter, you're led through the process of printing your Lotus Symphony Spreadsheets files. I show how you can use the Print Preview option to review what your spreadsheet looks like prior to printing it. I cover setting up different printing options, such as adding a page number to each page, printing only certain sections of the spreadsheet, and setting up a multipage spreadsheet to print.

Understanding How Lotus Spreadsheet Prints

Spreadsheets aren't like word processing documents. With a document, you pretty much know how it will print. First, you look at the page count — if it says five pages, that's how many you expect to print. Second, unless you specifically select a portion of it to print, you expect the full document to print. Finally, you expect word processing documents to print so that all the text you see on the screen appears within the margins (as long as you keep the margins set to the appropriate width for your printer and paper).

With spreadsheets, these expectations go out the window. Especially if you're bold enough to hit the Print button after you work in your spreadsheet for awhile. What prints is anybody's guess. Let's review our expectations and how they align with printing spreadsheets:

- ✔ **Page count.** Sure, Lotus Symphony Spreadsheets prints the number of pages you create. But how do you know the correct number? Most experienced users rely on the Print Preview feature to view the number of pages that will eventually print. You can do that, too. If it's too many pages, you can edit the content or modify the layout some to squeeze your data into as few pages as you can.

- ✔ **What actually prints.** The number of rows and columns you can have in a spreadsheet is fairly large. Unless you specify the number of rows and columns you want to print, Lotus Symphony Spreadsheets may print every possible column and row in the file. You may not want that.

- ✔ **Onscreen data doesn't fit on one page.** Spreadsheets are primarily designed for you to view on-screen. That's where your data lives — at least someplace on a computer — and that's where you can manipulate it using the Lotus Symphony Spreadsheets tools. So when you view a spreadsheet, the columns can go off the screen edge on the right for many screens. Similarly, the rows can flow many screens to the south (that is, the bottom of the screen). But when you go to print the spreadsheet, you need to think in terms of the paper sizes that your printer uses. For most people, that means outputting at $8^1/_2$ inches by 11 inches (landscape view) or 11 inches by $8^1/_2$ inches (portrait view).

Using Print Preview

As you work in a spreadsheet that you plan to print eventually, take a few moments every so often to view the spreadsheet in Print Preview. (See Figure 10-1.) This gives you an idea of how Lotus Symphony Spreadsheets prints your spreadsheet. If you don't like what you see, you can modify the spreadsheet before you get too close to finishing it. Sometimes if the design proves too cumbersome for a nice hard copy at the end, you may have to scrap the design and go with something else. However, doing that early can save a lot of time and aggravation in the end.

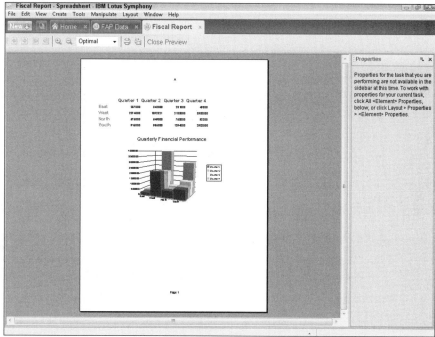

Figure 10-1:
An example of a spreadsheet in Print Preview mode.

To use the Print Preview feature, use these steps:

1. Start Lotus Symphony Spreadsheets and open a spreadsheet.

2. Choose File⇨Print Preview.

Your spreadsheet displays in the Print Preview window. (See Figure 10-2.) Notice that you can see the page numbers for each page here.

When you are in Print Preview mode, that's all you can do. You can preview what the printout will look like, but you can't do any editing or changing of the data itself. You're really looking at a picture of your spreadsheet. So if you find a mistake on your spreadsheet, click the Close Preview button and make your changes in the normal spreadsheet window.

As you view your spreadsheet in Print Preview, you have a few display and navigation options from which to choose:

✔ **Previous Page button:** Click to move to a previous page, such as from page 3 to page 2.

✔ **Next Page button:** Click to move through each page in your spreadsheet.

✔ **First Page button:** Click to return to the first page of the spreadsheet. You remain in Print Preview.

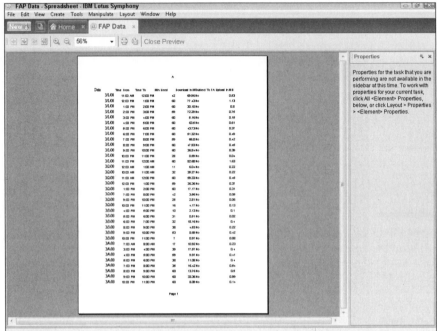

Figure 10-2:
Print
Preview
lets you
know if your
columns of
data print
on one page
or multiple
ones.

✔ **Last Page button:** Click to jump to the last page of the Print Preview.

✔ **Zoom In button:** Click this button to increase the magnification of the Print Preview.

✔ **Zoom Out button:** Click this button to decrease the magnification of the Print Preview.

✔ **Zoom drop-down box:** Select a zoom setting or type one in to increase or decrease magnification of the Print Preview. When you type a zoom value, enter the value (make it less than 400), type %, and the press Enter.

✔ **Print button:** Click this button to send your spreadsheet to the printer. The Print dialog box appears, which you learn more about in the "Printing an entire spreadsheet" section, later in this chapter.

✔ **Print Preview Options button:** Click this button to display the Print Preview Options dialog box. (See Figure 10-3.) This dialog box includes different settings for the Print Preview tool, such as setting page margins and print format (landscape versus portrait). Click Cancel to close this dialog box.

✔ **Close Preview button:** Click this button to close the Print Preview window and to return to the spreadsheet window.

Figure 10-3:
The Print
Preview
Options
dialog box.

The Next Page button on the Print Preview window doesn't display if your spreadsheet doesn't have more than one page. Also, when you reach the last page of your spreadsheet in Print Preview, the Next Page button becomes grayed out (unavailable) until you move to a previous page.

When you're finished looking at the Print Preview of your spreadsheet, click Close Preview. The next section discusses printing your spreadsheet.

Printing an entire spreadsheet

In the Print Preview window, you can see how your spreadsheet will look when printed. If it doesn't suit your needs, make sure you make any changes to the spreadsheet so that your print job looks the way you want it.

When your spreadsheet becomes ready to print, use the following steps to print the entire file:

1. Choose File⇨Print.

The Print dialog box appears. (See Figure 10-4.)

Figure 10-4:
The Print
dialog box
controls
several
factors of
your print
job, such
as printer
device and
print range.

2. Make any changes to the printer settings.

In the "Setting Up Print Options" section, later in this chapter, I discuss some of these options.

3. Click OK.

Your spreadsheet prints to the selected printer.

Viewing and removing unwanted page breaks

If, after you print a spreadsheet or view it in Print Preview, you notice there are some unwanted page breaks in the spreadsheet, take them out. To do this, find the page breaks in your spreadsheet and move them if they're breaking where blank pages are displayed. Sometimes blanks appear if you move your data around and forget to remove empty cells.

To see where page breaks appear in your spreadsheets, choose File⇨Page Breaks. A preview window appears, displaying where the page breaks occur in your spreadsheet, like the ones in Figure 10-5. Page breaks appear as heavy dark blue lines.

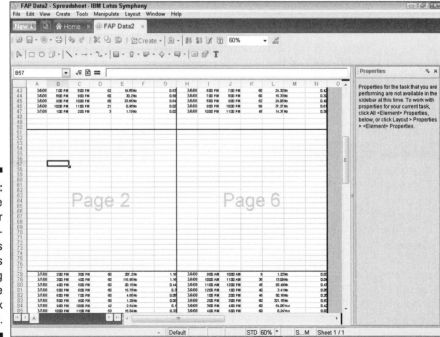

Figure 10-5:
You can see where your spread-sheet's page breaks occur using the Page Break command.

Those large page numbers you see in the middle of each page while viewing your spreadsheet in Page Break view are only temporary. They don't appear on your spreadsheet when you print the file. They just appear here to help you know exactly which page is which.

In the example shown in Figure 10-5, page 3 appears blank. You don't really want page 3 to print as a blank page, so you must remove the blank cells within it. Choose File➪Page Break again to return to the spreadsheet editing window. Select those rows that have blank cells in them, right-click, and choose Delete Cells. The cells disappear and the content originally appearing at the end of the spreadsheet moves up.

As a way to double-check your modifications, run the Page Break and Print Preview tools again before printing your spreadsheet. You may save some time by doing this now, not to mention printer paper and toner, if you discover something that doesn't look right. Change it now and then print the spreadsheet.

Another way to suppress printing blank pages uses the Suppress Output of Empty Pages command located on the Print Options dialog box. Those settings are discussed in the upcoming section called "Modifying Lotus Symphony Spreadsheets Printer Options."

Printing non-Lotus Symphony Spreadsheets spreadsheets

To print spreadsheets saved in formats other than Lotus Spreadsheet format (.ods), use the instructions found in Chapter 13 to import and convert the spreadsheet. Save the spreadsheet in Open Document Spreadsheet format and then follow the information in this chapter to print the spreadsheet.

Setting Up Print Options

While the earlier part of this chapter tells you how to do some printing tasks in Lotus Symphony Spreadsheets, this part tells you a little more about some printing options. The main areas shown in the following sections include the page setup options and printer options.

Configuring page setup options

As a general rule, the more detail about a spreadsheet that you can put on a printout of the spreadsheet the better. That is, if you can include header and footer information, page numbers, and similar information, it will be easier in the future to identify the spreadsheet and its related file (if you include the filename in the footer, for example).

To begin working with these features, you use the Page Setup command found on the File menu. When you choose that command, the Page Properties dialog box appears. (See Figure 10-6.)

Figure 10-6: The Page Properties dialog box includes several options for setting up spread-sheets before you print them.

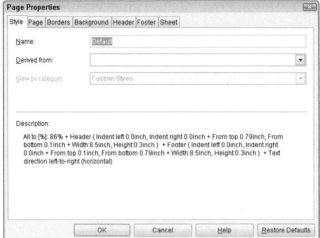

Click the Page tab. On this tab, you can find the options discussed in Table 10-1.

Table 10-1	Page Tab Options
Option	*Description*
Orientation	Choose between Landscape or Portrait layout of your spread-sheet. Portrait is the default and when printed on a standard sheet of paper prints at 8½-inches wide by 11-inches tall. Landscape swings the layout 90 degrees clockwise so that the page is 11-inches wide by 8½-inches tall. A little picture to the right of the options displays an example of the orientation.
Format	Enables you to select the paper type set up in your printer. The default is Letter, but you also have choices of Legal, Tabloid, A1, and more. The option you choose here must be supported by the printer you print to.
Width	Lets you set the width of the paper you select in the Format drop-down list.
Height	Lets you set height of the paper you select in the Format drop-down list.

Option	Description
Margins	Set the left, right, top, and bottom margins here. Many printers have to have at least some white space between the edge of the paper and the first character printed. For example, the printer I usually print to has a .75-inch requirement, so the margins are set up for .79 inches. I could set this to .75 inches, but that was the default setting and it seems to work fine — so why bother?
Layout Settings: Page Layout	Provides the options for applying styles to your files. You can set this up so that styles apply to right (even-numbered) and left (odd-numbered) pages, only the left or right, or both.
Layout Settings: Format	Enables you to set the format that the page numbers use when printed. By default, standard numbering is used, but you also can use Roman numerals or upper or lowercase letters.
Layout Settings: Table Alignment	Specifies how content in cells is aligned when printed. For example, you can align content vertically, horizontally, or both. Watch the example graphic at the top of the dialog box to see how these options affect the cell layout.

After you set the Page tab options, click OK to activate them now. To continue setting up other Page Setup options, keep the Page Properties dialog box open.

Next, look at the Header and Footer tabs. The *header* of a spreadsheet includes the area at the top of each page that is not part of the actual data area. *Footers* are similar, but they're at the bottom of the page. Headers and footers include common information for your spreadsheet that prints on every page or every other page, depending on your preference.

You set up header and footer information similarly, so the following steps show how to set up header values on the Header tab. You can use the same method for the Footer tab.

1. **Click the Header tab on the Page Properties dialog box.**

   The Header tab appears.

2. **Select the Header On check box.**

3. **Select the Same Content Left/Right check box.**

   This places the header information on both the odd and even numbered pages.

4. **Click the Edit button.**

   The Header (Page Style: Default) dialog box appears. (See Figure 10-7.) In this dialog box, you set up the content that you want to appear on the header (or footer if you're using the Footer tab).

Figure 10-7:
Use the
Header
(Page Style:
Default)
dialog box
to set up
the informa-
tion that
you want
displayed as
your header.

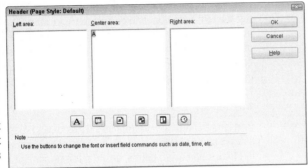

5. **Click inside the Left Area box.**

   The information you add to the Left Area box appears on the left third of the header.

6. **Click a field button, such as the Date button.**

   Today's date appears, which appears in the header area.

   Notice inside the Center area box is the letter A. This denotes the name of the spreadsheet. You can leave it there, if you want the spreadsheet name to appear in the header area.

7. **Click the Right Area box.**

8. **Click the Time button.**

   The current time appears.

9. **Click OK to save your settings.**

10. **Click the Header tab and add the following items to the header:**

    • *Left Area:* Type the path name of the file, such as C:\My Documents\spreadsheet.ods.

    • *Center Area.* Keep the Page 1 item there. Click to the right of the 1 and press the spacebar to create a space. Type the word **of** and then press the spacebar. Click the Pages button. When printed, the header will say "Page 1 of 5," for example.

11. **Click OK.**

12. **Click OK to close the Page Properties dialog box.**

You can test your Page Setup options by using the Page Preview tool again. When you display the spreadsheet in Page Preview, you may need to use the zoom tools to get a close-up view of the header and footer items.

Modifying Lotus Symphony Spreadsheets printer options

The Print dialog box provides another set of options for controlling your print settings. You can, for example, specify the printer to which you want to print, as well as a print range.

To set Print dialog box options, use the following steps:

1. **Choose File⇨Print.**

   The Print dialog box appears. (Refer to Figure 10-4.)

2. **From the Name drop-down box, select a printer to which to print.**

3. **In the Print range area, you can choose from the following:**

   - *All* prints all pages in your spreadsheet.

   - *Pages* enables you to specify a subset of pages to print, such as 1-4.

   - *Selection* prints only the area you previously selected, such as a range of cells.

4. **In the Copies area, specify the number of copies of each page you want to print.**

   For example, if you want two copies of each page, set this value to 2.

5. **Click the Options button.**

   The Print Options dialog box appears.

6. **To instruct Lotus Symphony Spreadsheets to print only selected sheets in a workbook, select Print Only Selected Sheets.**

7. **To keep Lotus Symphony Spreadsheets from printing any blank pages in your spreadsheets, select Suppress Output of Empty Pages.**

8. **Click OK.**

9. **Click OK again.**

   Your spreadsheet prints using the settings you've selected.

Because your printer settings are based on the type of printer you select from the Name drop-down list, all of your printer settings will change after you select a new printer from the Print dialog box. Be sure to check over your settings before sending a large print job to the printer. In fact, you may want to print just a few pages using the Print Range options to test how your spreadsheet prints to the newly selected printer.

Chapter 11

Adding Spice to Your Spreadsheets

. . . .

In This Chapter

▶ Creating charts

▶ Adding backgrounds

▶ Changing border colors and sizes

▶ Adding graphics

▶ Dealing with spreadsheet applications

. . . .

*L*et's face it. Spreadsheet information can be boring. It's usually just a series of data — rows and columns of numbers and characters — stored in one place. Even so, Lotus Symphony Spreadsheets provides formatting options to help you dress up your spreadsheets.

Some formatting options you use not only improve the looks of a spreadsheet, but also make some spreadsheets more functional for you and other users. For example, you can set up a spreadsheet that uses a blue background color to denote data that should be updated manually by an end-user, and red background for data that should remain untouched.

Another way to dress up your information involves creating charts to present data in a graphical format. You can create different kinds of charts, such as bar charts, pie charts, line graphs, and radar charts using the Chart Style tool.

Finally, different formatting options allow you to create your own spreadsheet applications that you can deploy and distribute to other users. With some spreadsheet applications, you may want to include macros to automate redundant or complex steps and calculations.

This chapter introduces you to many of the formatting options you can use to format and embellish your spreadsheets and spreadsheet applications.

Adding Charts

Charts provide a way for you to turn raw data into graphical formats. This makes presenting and analyzing data easy because it allows users to see patterns and trends in the data. Figures 11-1 and 11-2 show the same data, one in standard data columns and rows, the other in chart format. Which one would you rather analyze while sitting in a stuffy board room? For me, I would rather take a quick look at a chart to give an analysis of the data being presented.

Figure 11-1:
Some raw data as viewed in Lotus Symphony Spread-sheets standard rows and columns.

	Type	Sales
	Fly By Light, Inc	
	March 2010	
	Type	Sales
	Incandescent	$4,324.00
	Halogen	$3,389.00
	Green 3-Way	$2,198.00
	Fluorescent	$1,300.00
	Strobe	$6,831.00
	Black	$7,190.00
	Spot	$2,539.00
	Auto Lites	$4,983.00
	Field Lights	$3,253.00
	Mercury Vapor	$6,980.00

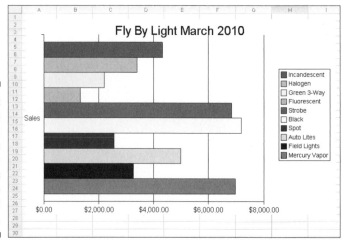

Figure 11-2:
The same data shown in Figure 11-2, this time displayed as a chart.

Charts are easy to create in Lotus Symphony Spreadsheets. As long as your source data makes sense — that is, your columns and rows are set up properly — you can insert new charts in just a matter of a few wizard steps. In addition to creating charts easily, you can have Lotus Symphony Spreadsheets update charts automatically when you update the raw data for that chart. I tell you how you can do that in the sections that follow.

What are *graphs?* You sometime may hear or read references to spreadsheet graphs. Graphs are really the same thing as charts.

Creating charts in your spreadsheets

You create charts by selecting data in your spreadsheet and then picking the type of chart you want to use. Lotus Symphony Spreadsheets comes with a number of different chart types from which to choose. You can choose from the following types:

- ✔ Lines
- ✔ Area
- ✔ Columns
- ✔ Bars
- ✔ Pies
- ✔ XY Charts
- ✔ Radar
- ✔ Stock Chart

Charts arrange data using the x and y Cartesian coordinate system. The *x-axis* runs horizontally and the *y-axis* runs vertically. By default, the data that appears in the first column you select becomes the x-axis data. Data in the second column becomes the y-axis data.

Charts come in two different dimensions:

- ✔ **2D, or two dimensional,** charts are "flat" — that is, you see both the x- and y-axis views as if on a flat sheet of paper.

- ✔ **3D, or three dimensional,** adds depth to each of the x- and y-axis views by adding the z-axis. The 3D view can provide a more professional look to your charts, but you should use it for charts that don't have a lot of data across the x-axis. Large charts in 3D view can become difficult to separate out each data series.

As you enter data in a spreadsheet in which you want to insert a chart, use the following guidelines:

- ✔ **Have in mind the type of chart you want to use.** You may want to hand draw an example of the chart you want to use, placing the x- and y-axis details so you can enter the raw data in that manner.

✔ **Enter data into columns.** If your data has names, put those in the left column (column A, for example). Then put the data for that name in the column to the right of it (column B, for example). This makes it easier for the Chart Setup wizard to line up your data correctly.

✔ **Make sure there are no blank columns or rows in your data.** By default, the Chart Setup wizard includes all the cells you select prior to running the wizard. You can modify the chart later to remove any blanks, but it's easier to not have them to begin with.

The following steps show how to create a chart based on the data shown in Figure 11-1.

1. **Select the data you want to chart.**

   Figure 11-3 shows the data I'll place in the chart. Notice that I selected the label row — it contains Type and Sales. Lotus Symphony Spreadsheets adds these labels to the chart.

	A	B	C	D
1		**Fly By Light, Inc**		
2			March 2010	
3		**Type**	**Sales**	
4		Incandescent	$4,324.00	
5		Halogen	$3,389.00	
6		Green 3-Way	$2,198.00	
7		Fluorescent	$1,300.00	
8		Strobe	$6,831.00	
9		Black	$7,190.00	
10		Spot	$2,539.00	
11		Auto Lites	$4,983.00	
12		Field Lights	$3,253.00	
13		Mercury Vapor	$6,980.00	
14				
15				
16				

Figure 11-3: Select the data you want to chart.

2. **Choose Create⇨Chart Setup.**

   The Chart Setup wizard appears.

3. **Select the First Row as Label check box.**

   This places the data in the top row as labels for your data.

4. **Select the First Column as Label check box.**

   This places the data in the first column as a label for your data.

   Be default, the Chart Setup wizard creates the new graph on the selected worksheet, which is A in this case. You can select to place it on another worksheet by selecting an option from the Chart Results in Worksheet drop-down list. You can select any worksheet in your spreadsheet or choose to create a new worksheet on which to place the chart.

5. Click Next.

The second screen of the Chart Setup wizard appears. (See Figure 11-4.)

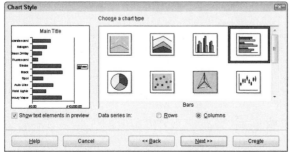

6. Select the Show Text Elements in Preview check box.

This option enables you to look at a preview of the chart as you build it.

7. Select Bars from the Choose a Chart Type list.

This option arranges the data so that the x- and y-axis data are switched. I do that here because my column A data includes words that are long and display better in the y-axis.

8. Click Next.

The third screen of the Chart Setup wizard appears.

9. Keep the default options selected on this screen.

10. Click Next.

The fourth screen of the Chart Setup wizard appears.

11. Select the Chart Title check box.

12. In the text box beside Chart Title, type a name to appear above the chart.

13. Select the X Axis check box under the Axis Titles area.

14. Type a name for the x-axis.

15. Select the Y Axis check box under the Axis titles area.

16. Type a name for the y-axis.

17. Click Create.

Lotus Symphony Spreadsheets creates the new chart and adds it to the worksheet specified on the first screen of the Chart Setup wizard. Figure 11-5 shows the new chart we just created.

Figure 11-5:
Our new chart added to worksheet A.

By default, the chart appears on the worksheet from which you select the data for the chart.

Editing charts

After you create a chart in your spreadsheet, you can edit it. Some of the edits you can make include:

- ✔ Resizing the chart
- ✔ Moving the chart
- ✔ Changing the chart type
- ✔ Updating data in the chart
- ✔ Editing chart labels

One of the first things you may want to do when a chart appears on your worksheet is to resize it. By default, the size of the chart usually appears kind of small, even for those with good eyesight. To resize the chart, do the following:

1. **Click the chart to show the resizing handles around the entire chart.**

   You can turn off the Properties sidebar to get more room on your worksheet area by clicking the close button on the top right of the sidebar.

2. **Grab one of the resizing handles and drag the side of the chart to a new position.**

3. **Release the resizing handle.**

Lotus Symphony Spreadsheets resizes the chart, making it larger.

Grab a corner of the chart to resize the chart in two different directions at the same time. For example, grab the lower-right corner handle and drag it to the lower-left corner of the worksheet. Lotus Symphony Spreadsheets resizes the chart, moving the right side of the chart and the bottom of the chart simultaneously. This method has the added benefit of keeping the chart size in proportion so your charts don't get a warped look to them.

4. **Continue resizing the chart as needed to make it the size you desire.**

You can also move charts to different areas on your worksheet or to a different worksheet entirely. To move a chart, do the following:

1. **Click the chart to show the resizing handles.**

2. **Click inside the chart and hold down the left mouse button.**

Notice that the mouse pointer changes to a four-sided arrow when the pointer appears within the boundary of the chart. This shows you that you can move the chart in any direction.

3. **Move the chart to another place on the worksheet.**

4. **Release the mouse button.**

You can also move charts to other worksheets in your spreadsheet file, or to other documents (such as a Lotus Symphony Documents document). Using the copy and paste method provides an easy way to move your charts. To do this, select your chart and choose Edit⇨Copy (or press Ctrl+C) to copy the chart to the Windows Clipboard area. Move to the new spot on your worksheet, display a different worksheet, or open a document in which to paste the chart. Place the insertion point where you want the chart to appear and choose Edit⇨Paste (or press Ctrl+V). The chart appears at the insertion point.

You can remove a chart from your worksheet by selecting the worksheet and pressing Delete. You also can right-click the chart and choose Cut from the context menu that appears.

Modifying the look and feel of charts

As you get more familiar with charts, you'll find that most charts need a little tweaking after you initially create them. The best way to do this requires you to experiment with different types of charts. Some of the tweaks you may want to try include the following:

✔ Updating data

✔ Changing label and title formatting

✔ Adding a border around the chart

To update data in your chart, simply change the data in the original spreadsheet. For example, my sample chart shows a product named Mercury Vapor. If I want to change the sales results from $6980.00 to $8215.00, I can do this by clicking inside cell C13, changing the data, and pressing Enter. The data in the chart changes as well. Figure 11-6 shows this.

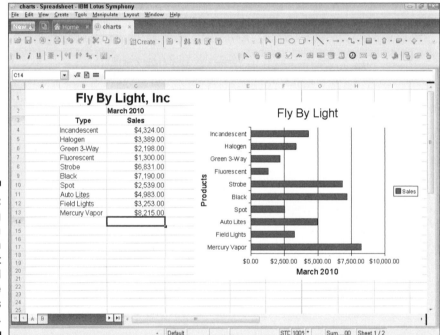

Figure 11-6: Updating the data on which a chart is based updates the chart as well.

When you copy and paste a chart from Lotus Symphony Spreadsheets to Lotus Symphony Documents, the data doesn't stay *linked*. This means that you can't update the original data source in Lotus Symphony Spreadsheets and have it update the embedded chart in Lotus Symphony Documents. You can use the Edit⇨Paste Special command to embed the chart originally and then update the data in Lotus Symphony Documents by double-clicking the chart to activate it. Then right-click the chart in your document, choose Chart Data, and modify the data in the Chart Data window. (See Figure 11-7.) Click the Apply to Chart button to store your changes in the chart. Click Close when finished modifying the data.

Figure 11-7:
You can
manually
update
charts
embedded
in Lotus
Symphony
Documents
using the
Chart Data
window.

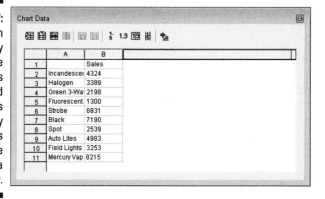

When you want to change label and title formatting, do the following:

1. **Double-click the chart in Lotus Symphony Spreadsheets.**

2. **Right-click anywhere inside the chart and choose Titles➪Main Title (or the title you want to modify).**

   The Title dialog box appears. (See Figure 11-8.)

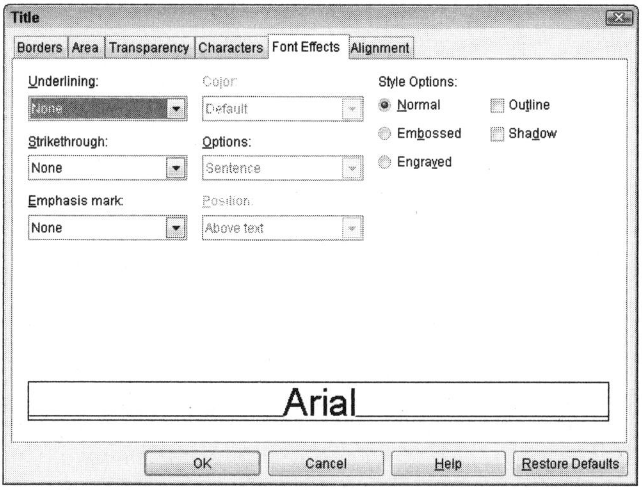

Figure 11-8:
The Title
dialog box
enables you
to modify
the format-
ting for your
chart titles.

3. **Use the options on the various tabs to modify the title formatting.**

   For example, I make the following changes to the title:

   • On the Fonts tab, set the Style Options area to Shadow.

   • On the Characters tab, set the Font Color to Red.

- On the Characters tab, change the Font Size setting to 36.

- On the Area tab, select Color and then select a color for the background. I chose black.

4. Click OK to apply your formatting changes to the chart.

Another modification you may want to perform includes adding a border around your chart. To do this, follow these steps:

1. Double-click the chart.

2. Right-click and choose Chart Area.

The Chart Area dialog box appears. (See Figure 11-9.)

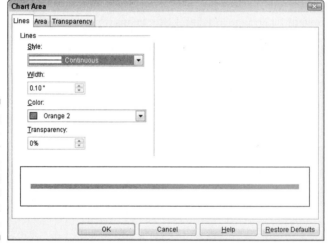

Figure 11-9:
Add a border to your charts using the Lines tab on the Chart Area dialog box.

3. Click the Lines tab.

4. Select a border style from the Style drop-down list.

5. Select a width for the border from the Width drop-down list.

6. Select a color for the border from the Color drop-down list.

7. Click OK.

The chart appears with a border around it.

Other formatting options are available for charts. You can, for example, choose the Chart Wall option from the right-click menu to add a wall around the chart data area. Also, you can set the font characteristics for characters displaying on the x- and y-axis. To do this, choose Axis⇨All Axis from the right-click menu. Modify the Character and Font Effects tabs and click OK. As mentioned previously, spend some time modifying different chart settings to get familiar with the types of changes you can make.

Changing chart types and styles

After you put a chart into your spreadsheet, you may realize you want a different type of chart. You may, for example, decide that a pie chart would work better for the information you're displaying. Or you may choose a 3D chart type for your worksheet.

Lotus Symphony Spreadsheets makes it easy to change from one chart type to another without going through the entire process of re-creating the chart. To change chart types, do the following:

1. **Double-click the chart you want to change.**

2. **Right-click and choose Chart Type.**

   The Chart Type dialog box appears, as shown in Figure 11-10.

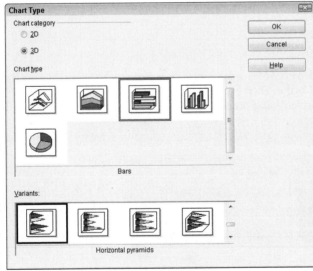

Figure 11-10: You can choose a different chart type for your charts.

3. **Select a different chart type.**

   Click the 3D radio button to see 3D chart types.

Notice that not all the chart types are available when you open the Chart Type dialog box. That's because Lotus Symphony Spreadsheets displays additional chart types (or variations of a type) when you click a type in the Chart Type area. When you do this, variations (also called *chart styles*) appear in the Variants area at the bottom of the dialog box. You can then click one of those variations to use as your new chart type.

4. Click OK to apply your changes, as shown in Figure 11-11.

Figure 11-11: Lotus Symphony Spreadsheets changes the chart type to the new one you selected from the Chart Types dialog box.

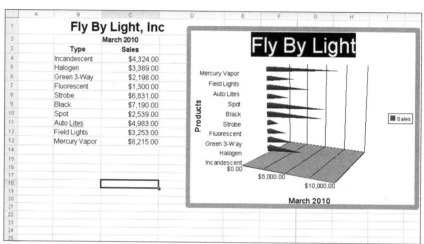

If you like the chart type for your chart but want to modify just the style, you can do so. Double-click the chart and right-click. Choose Chart Style to open the Chart Style dialog box. (See Figure 11-12.) Choose a new style and then click Create.

Figure 11-12: You can change just the chart style if you want.

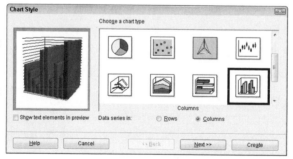

Adding Backgrounds to Spreadsheets

Another way to dress up your spreadsheets includes adding backgrounds to them. You can apply backgrounds to specific cells or an entire worksheet. This can add color to different areas on your spreadsheets to help users locate important or required data inputs. You also may want to add backgrounds to color-code different worksheets in a spreadsheet file. This enables you to tell users to use a specific colored worksheet for a specific type of data.

You can add background graphics to your spreadsheets as well. This enables you to add watermarks to your worksheets, or even company logos that display in the background.

One way to include an image in the background of your worksheet requires you to use the Page Setup tool. Choose File⇨Page Setup. On the Background tab, choose Color or Graphic from the Background Type drop-down list. If you choose Color, choose a color from the Color grid on the tab. If you choose Graphic, select Browse to specify the graphic to use. Click OK when you're finished. Colored backgrounds don't display unless you view your spreadsheet in File⇨Print Preview mode. If you choose a graphic, however, that shows up when you view your spreadsheet in normal view.

The following steps show how to add background colors to selected cells:

1. **Select the cells to which you want to add a background color.**

   You can select one or many cells in a worksheet. For my example, I selected just the cells that include data.

2. **Choose Layout⇨Properties⇨Text and Cell Properties.**

   The Text and Cell Properties dialog box appears.

3. **Click the Appearance tab.**

4. **Click the Cell Color drop-down list.**

5. **Choose a color, such as Turquoise 3.**

6. **Click OK to apply the background to your selected cells.**

To add a background graphic to your spreadsheet, perform the following steps:

1. **Choose Create⇨Graphic from File.**

   The Create Graphics dialog box appears.

2. **Select a graphic.**

3. Choose Open.

Lotus Symphony Spreadsheets inserts the graphic into your worksheet.

4. Size the graphic to the size you want it to appear in the background.

5. Right-click the graphic and choose Arrange⇨To Background.

As shown in the example in Figure 11-13, the image appears in the background of the worksheet.

Figure 11-13:
A worksheet
with a
background
image
added.

To learn more about inserting graphics into your spreadsheets, see the section called "Inserting Graphics into Your Spreadsheets," later in this chapter.

Modifying Border Colors and Sizes

Lotus Symphony Spreadsheets enables you to modify the color and size of your cell borders. For example, some spreadsheets use a border color of red to indicate totals for a calculation. You can also use border colors to help format an entire row or column of data.

You can adjust border sizes to be thicker or thinner, depending on the type of design you want to achieve. Thick borders surrounding key information on your worksheet can help draw attention to the information when users read the data. Also, using a thicker border around some elements, such as instructions for filling out the worksheet, helps differentiate these cells from the ones where users need to enter data.

To modify cell border colors and sizes, use these steps:

1. **Select a cell you want to modify.**

   You also can select multiple cells to modify.

2. **Right-click and choose Text and Cell Properties.**

   The Text and Cell Properties dialog box appears.

3. **Click the Borders tab.**

4. **Choose a border type from the Line Arrangement area.**

   For example, choose the All Border option to create a border around the entire cell.

5. **Choose a border style from the Style list.**

6. **Choose a color for the border from the Color list.**

7. **Choose OK to apply your changes.**

If you want to repeat the same border and color formatting to multiple cells, use the Duplicate Formatting tool on the Main toolbar.

Inserting Graphics into Your Spreadsheets

You can add graphics to your Lotus Symphony Spreadsheets files to add some life to otherwise dry raw data, illustrate information in your worksheets, display a logo for your company or department, or display product information. There are a number of other uses for graphics as well.

After you get a graphic into your worksheet, you can modify the position and size of the graphic, rotate the graphic, as well as perform other tasks on it. The following sections describe some basics of working with graphics.

Embedding graphics for some pizzazz

To embed graphics into your Lotus Symphony Spreadsheets files, perform the following steps:

1. **Choose Create⇨Graphic from File.**

   The Create Graphics dialog box appears.

2. **Select a graphic.**

Ready-to-add graphics

Lotus Symphony comes packaged with several graphics you can use in your spreadsheets. You can find these files in a subfolder where you installed Lotus Symphony, which may be difficult to find as you navigate through the Create Graphics dialog box. The following shows the default path for these graphics:

```
C:\Program Files\IBM\Lotus\
     Symphony\Framework\Shared\
     Eclipse\Plugins\com.ibm.
     productivity.tools.gallery.
     common_3.0.1.20080229-1700.
```

You may want to create a shortcut to this folder to make it easy to find each time you need to access it for graphics.

3. **Choose OK.**

   Lotus Symphony Spreadsheets inserts the graphic into your spreadsheet. Figure 11-14 shows an example of a graphic inserted into Lotus Symphony Spreadsheets.

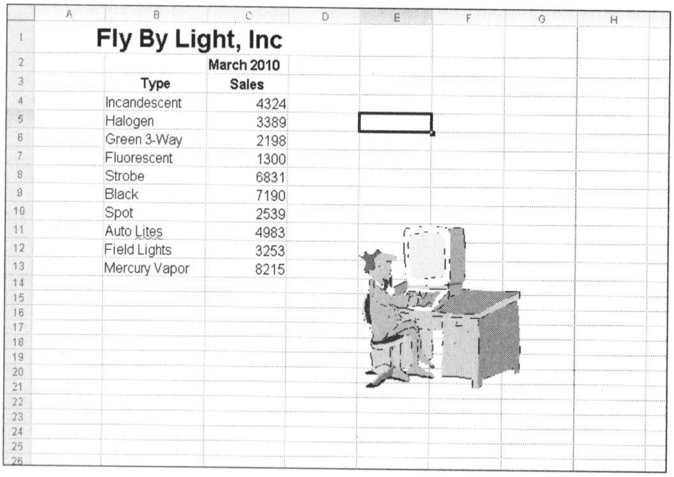

Figure 11-14: You can embed graphics into your spreadsheets, such as the sample one shown here.

	A	B	C	D	E	F	G	H
1		**Fly By Light, Inc**						
2			March 2010					
3		Type	Sales					
4		Incandescent	4324					
5		Halogen	3389					
6		Green 3-Way	2198					
7		Fluorescent	1300					
8		Strobe	6831					
9		Black	7190					
10		Spot	2539					
11		Auto Lites	4983					
12		Field Lights	3253					
13		Mercury Vapor	8215					

The included images with Lotus Symphony use the Windows Metafile Format, or WMF. In order to view a sample of these, use an image editor or viewer such as Microsoft Windows Paint, Microsoft Office Picture Viewer, Adobe Photoshop, or others. Windows doesn't provide a thumbnail view of these types of images by default.

Modifying position and size of graphics

After you insert (or embed) a graphic into your spreadsheet, you can modify its position and size.

To move a graphic on the spreadsheet, click the graphic and then click and hold down the left mouse button. The cursor changes to the four-sided arrow. Drag the image to another location on the spreadsheet and release the mouse button.

You use the resizing handles to size the graphic. Click the image you want to resize to display the resizing handles. Drag a resizing handle (or the corner to resize the image in two directions) to resize the graphic.

If you resize the graphic too much in one direction, such as horizontally, you may notice the graphic can look warped. This means the proportions are different from the original file and can look a little funny. To ensure you resize an image and keep its original proportions, hold down the Shift key while you resize the graphic.

Rotating a graphic

You can rotate graphics you embed in Lotus Symphony Spreadsheets, which can help you align a graphic along the edge of a column of data, correct an image that should be rotated (such as a photograph that has been inadvertently rotated), or add a little fun to your worksheets.

To rotate a graphic, do the following:

1. **Select a graphic on your spreadsheet.**
2. **Right-click and choose Flip.**
3. **Choose the direction you'd like to rotate the graphic.**
    - *Vertically:* Rotates the graphic 180 degrees from top to bottom.
    - *Horizontally:* Rotates the graphic 180 degrees from right to left.

Changing a graphic's color and brightness

Sometimes the graphics you embed into Lotus Symphony Spreadsheets need a little tweaking to change the graphic's colors or brightness. Lotus Symphony Spreadsheets provides some tools for changing these properties. You can use the Graphics tab of the Graphic Properties dialog box to make these changes.

Don't expect to be able to modify specific portions of an image using the Graphics tab of the Graphic Properties dialog box. These controls enable you to apply changes to the entire graphic, not specific places on the graphic. For example, if you want to change the color of just the desk in the graphic shown in Figure 11-15, you can't do it with the Lotus Symphony Spreadsheets tools. You need to use an image editing program for that task.

To change colors and brightness for a graphic, do the following:

1. **Right-click a graphic in your spreadsheet.**

2. **Choose Graphic Properties.**

   The Graphic Properties dialog box appears.

3. **Click the Graphics tab, as shown in Figure 11-15.**

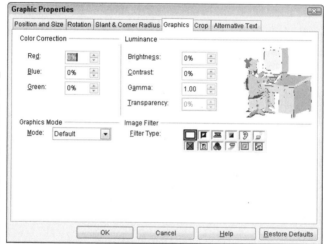

Figure 11-15: Adjust the color and brightness of graphics in your Lotus Symphony Spreadsheets files.

4. **Adjust the Color Correction settings (Red, Blue, and Green) to change the color of the selected graphic.**

5. **Change the Brightness setting under Luminance to change how bright or dark the graphic appears on the worksheet.**

6. **Choose OK after you make your changes.**

The changes you make to a graphic in a worksheet don't change the properties of the original graphics file. That means the next time you insert that graphic, the original colors and brightness will appear again.

Cropping graphics down to size

Some graphics include stuff you may not want appearing in your spread-sheet. For example, if you need a graphic of a car, a graphic that has a person standing next to a car has more information than you need. In a case like this, you don't need to cut out that person from the original graphic file. Instead, use the cropping tool to crop out what you don't want to show.

To use the cropping feature, use the following steps:

1. **Right-click a graphic in your spreadsheet.**

2. **Choose Graphic Properties.**

   The Graphic Properties dialog box appears.

3. **Click the Crop tab.**

4. **Use the Left, Right, Top, and Bottom settings to crop the graphic to your liking.**

5. **Click OK to apply your changes.**

Creating Spreadsheet Applications

Spreadsheet applications are spreadsheet files created to meet certain data collection and analysis needs, usually for a departmental or organizational need. They are simply a spreadsheet file a user or group of users puts together to collect and analyze data. A spreadsheet application can be a single worksheet that displays information needed for a department or organization, but usually spreadsheet applications are several worksheets grouped into one file to which multiple users contribute. For example, a company may require the accounting department to fill out specific information about monies spent on employee benefits for a quarter, while the human resources department is required to fill out sections of the spreadsheet application that deals with employee positions and the benefits each employee signs up for. A manager or vice president can then see the filled out information (perhaps through a printout or page sent to a Lotus Symphony Documents document) that combines all the data into an executive summary.

The term *spreadsheet application* doesn't refer to a specific tool or feature in Lotus Symphony Spreadsheets. It's simply a spreadsheet file that includes several different aspects of the features and tools you can use in Lotus Symphony Spreadsheets. Think of them as the culmination of the different skills you learn in Lotus Symphony Spreadsheets, all of which you put into a single file you send to others for completing.

Making the application look good

If you are responsible for putting together a spreadsheet application in Lotus Symphony Spreadsheets, here are a few things to keep in mind:

✔ **Have a clear goal for your application.** You may want to put these goals in a list (use Lotus Symphony Spreadsheets for this!) so you can keep track of them. Expand on them as you work on the application.

✔ **Test and retest the application before deploying it.** Make sure you test the application before sending it to other users. You may also want to ask another user (or group of users) to help you test the application. This way, they can point out areas that don't work on their systems or areas of the spreadsheet that are confusing.

✔ **Ensure your calculations and formulas are correct.** Chapter 12 discusses formulas and functions. You should evaluate each calculation that you put in your application to ensure that it's giving you the correct results.

Many of us aren't experts on formulas that are used in different disciplines. If you work for a firm that specializes in real estate, for example, your expertise may lie in the area of creating and testing spreadsheet usage, but it may not be in the area of calculating mortgages. If this is the case, ask the mortgage expert in your office or lending institution to look over your calculations. You don't want to be wrong when the application becomes a live document out in the office.

✔ **Create good documentation for the entire application.** Add help items throughout to guide users on each page and each piece of information you require. Finally, provide specific information on what users should do when finished. For example, should they save the file (File➪Save) or is this done automatically for them? Should they save the file to a specific folder or network location? Should they keep a copy for themselves? Can they make a copy? Do they need to route the spreadsheet via e-mail?

Figure 11-16 shows the opening worksheet of a sample spreadsheet application. This application is included on the enclosed CD-ROM for you to view and use.

Distributing the application

Usually, spreadsheet applications are distributed to other users within a company or organization. Sometimes, applications can be generated by larger institutions, such as a federal or state agency, and the application can be sent to regional or local companies or organizations. In most cases, the files are sent via e-mail or downloaded from a centralized Web site.

Figure 11-16:
Spread-
sheet
applications
usually have
an opening
worksheet
that
describes
the applica-
tion and
points users
to where to
begin.

In some cases, the files are compressed to reduce their file sizes. You can achieve this in Windows XP or Windows Vista by using the Send To⇨ Compressed Folder command from a Windows Explorer window.

Some spreadsheet applications include highly sensitive and confidential information. For example, many include Social Security numbers, phone numbers, banking and financial information, and similar data. To ensure the information remains secure, follow the procedures for securing and releasing confidential information that your company adheres to. You may need to ask your human resource or information technology directors for complete details on this in your company.

Another way to distribute spreadsheet applications includes saving them to disk media, such as:

✔ CD-R

✔ DVD-R

✔ Flash drives

✔ Portable hard drives

Use the method best suited for your needs and your company.

Automating repetitive tasks with macros

Using Lotus Spreadsheet macros provides one way to ensure repetitive tasks are completed in your stand-alone spreadsheets and spreadsheet applications. *Macros* are mini-programs that you create that perform tasks automatically in your spreadsheets. An example of a macro you might use is one that automatically formats a range of cells after a user inputs specific data.

To create a macro, use the following steps:

1. **Open the spreadsheet in which you want to create a macro.**

   Make sure the spreadsheet has been saved to a filename you can remember.

2. **Choose Tools⇨Macros⇨Record Macro.**

   The Record Macro window appears.

3. **Perform a task you want to record as a macro.**

   As an example, highlight about a dozen cells in the spreadsheet. Change the color of the cells' background to orange. That will be the task that your new macro will perform.

4. **Click Stop Recording.**

   The Macro dialog box appears. (See Figure 11-17.) The name of your spreadsheet automatically appears in the Save Macro In box of the Macro dialog box.

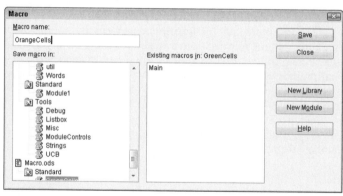

Figure 11-17:
Use the Macro dialog box to name and store your new macro.

5. **Type a name for the macro in the Macro Name box.**

   I use the name `OrangeCells` in this example.

Macro names cannot include spaces, so use the camelback naming convention (a mixed-case spelling in which each word starts with an uppercase letter), such as OrangeCells, or use a hyphen (-) or underscore (_) in the name to separate words.

6. **Select the folder that is named after the document.**

   In my example, the folder's name is `Macro.ods`.

7. **Click the Save button.**

8. **Click Yes if prompted to overwrite the Main macro.**

9. **Choose File⇨Save to save your document with the new macro.**

After you create a macro, you need to close the spreadsheet and then reopen it before you can run the macro.

When I saved the new macro, it was in the `Macro.ods` file. But I need to reopen that spreadsheet, and then I can run the macro from that spreadsheet. In my case, however, I also should change the background colors of the cells back to white (or something besides orange). That way, when I run the macro, I can actually see the results.

To run a macro, do the following:

1. **Open the spreadsheet in which you stored the macro.**

2. **Choose Tools⇨Macros⇨Macros.**

   The Macro dialog box appears.

3. **Select the macro from the Macro From list.**

4. **Choose Run.**

   The macro executes, performing the procedure you recorded earlier.

As the macro executes, you won't see the menus and dialog boxes that you may have selected during the macro recording process. Instead, the macro executes the commands at the Lotus Symphony application level, bypassing the user-interface items.

Chapter 12

Making Calculations

In This Chapter

▶ Working with formulas

▶ Understanding operators

▶ Using dates and times in formulas

▶ Using the Solve Equations tool

▶ Using functions

▶ Adding and modifying DataPilot tables

Spreadsheets are not only good for making lists and charts, but they're also fantastic at calculations. Businesses seem to live and die by the spreadsheet, and calculations and analysis of their results can mean approval of new projects, hiring of new employees, expansion of existing product lines, and so much more. With Lotus Symphony Spreadsheets, you can create calculations ranging from simple (averaging a short list of values, for example) to complex (such as actuarial formulas for global risk analysis).

You can create your own formulas to make calculations meet your needs. You also can use Lotus Symphony Spreadsheets functions to help you create your calculations. *Functions* are built-in formulas for performing many common (and some not-so-common) calculations. For example, the FVAL function allows you to calculate the future value of an investment.

This chapter shows you how to add calculations to your spreadsheet, as well as how to use formulas and functions. You also see how you can use Lotus Symphony Spreadsheets DataPilots to analyze your results. And finally, DataPilots enable you to turn your seemingly static data into dynamic information based on different summaries you want to create.

Adding Formulas to Spreadsheets

Use formulas and functions to create calculations in your spreadsheets. For basic calculations, a little practice should allow you to get expert enough to enter them manually.

Understanding formulas

At its basic level, a *formula* performs a calculation based on values stored in cells, commands, and references. Figure 12-1, for example, shows one of the most basic formulas known to humankind.

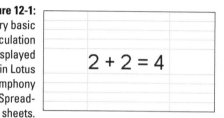

Figure 12-1: A very basic calculation displayed in Lotus Symphony Spread-sheets.

$$2 + 2 = 4$$

This formula takes the first number, adds it to the second number, and displays the result. In my example, I put the entire formula and data inside of one cell. But Lotus Symphony Spreadsheets provides a way to enter single data entries into separate cells. In Figure 12-2, you see the following three cells:

Figure 12-2: A very basic calculation placing values and results in cells.

2   2   4

- C14 includes the value 2
- D14 includes the value 2
- E14 includes the value 4

Although we use an example of summing two numbers here, Lotus Symphony Spreadsheets actually provides a built-in function for summing numbers. It is called SUM. In fact, spreadsheet users run this function so often that it has its own button on the Formula bar.

To create the simple example formula in Lotus Symphony Spreadsheets that automatically generates a result, use the following syntax:

```
=C14+D14
```

Place that formula in cell E14, but only the result of the calculation appears. To see the formula, click the cell in which the result appears and look in the Formula bar, as shown in Figure 12-3. To enter your formula, click the cell and begin the formula with the equal sign. Lotus Symphony Spreadsheets automatically fills in the Formula bar as you type the formula.

Figure 12-3:
The basic calculation showing the formula in the Formula bar.

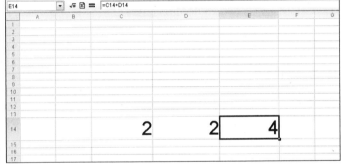

As you can see, you don't need to insert actual values into the formula, just the cell references. The formula does the rest. This way, you can swap out the actual values in cells C14 and D14 and the formula handles them just as easily. After you enter the formula, press Enter to see the results.

When working with formulas, Lotus Symphony Spreadsheets handles the cell references as relative references. (See Chapter 9 for information about relative and absolute references.) That means Lotus Symphony Spreadsheets interprets the sample formula as: "Take the value in the cell two places to the left of this cell (the one in which the formula currently resides) and add it to the value in the cell one place to the left of this cell (the one in which the formula currently resides). Display the result here." That lets users copy the formula to other cells that have the same kind of data set up. You could, for instance, have a list of numbers in columns C and D from rows 1 to 15. Drag your formula into each row in the E column down to row 15. Results for each formula appear in the column E cells.

There may be times that you want formulas to use absolute references. As I discuss in Chapter 9 place the dollar sign character ($) in front of each cell reference, such as =$C$14+$D$14.

Modifying formulas

Lotus Symphony Spreadsheets makes it easy to modify your formula. To do this, follow these steps:

1. **Click inside the cell that has the formula.**

2. **Click inside the Formula bar.**

3. **Modify the formula.**

4. **Press Enter or click the Accept button (the green check mark on the Formula bar).**

   The formula updates and the displays the new results.

You can turn on a feature in Lotus Symphony Spreadsheets that enables you to see formulas instead of results in the actual cells. This can help you locate the cells in which your formulas reside. To turn on this feature, Choose File➪Preferences➪IBM Lotus Symphony➪Lotus Symphony Spreadsheets➪View. Select Formula in the Display section and click OK.

Working with operators

Along with the values that you enter in a formula, you also have to put in operators. *Operators* are the symbols and special words that denote what type of calculations that Lotus Symphony Spreadsheets should perform.

You may also hear the term *operands* when working with spreadsheet programs. Operands are the numbers or cell references in a formula.

Table 12-1 lists Lotus Symphony Spreadsheets operators.

Table 12-1	Lotus Spreadsheet Operators	
Operator	*Description*	*Example*
+	Adds two numbers.	A2+R433
–	Subtracts a number from another number.	B23–A12
*	Multiplies two numbers.	B2*B3
/	Divides one number from another number.	E12/G8
"	Encloses a string.	"Product 1"
^	Assigns an exponent to the value.	F2^2
=	Assigns values as equal.	A2=B5
&	Concatenates two values.	G1&E3

Operator	Description	Example
<	Compares a value to see if it is less than another value.	A3<R3
>	Compares a value to see if it is more than another value.	A3>R3
=<	Compares a value to see if it is less than or equal to another value.	A3=<R3
=>	Compares a value to see if it is more than or equal to another value.	A3=>R3

Along with the operators, you also need to become familiar with the order of operation that spreadsheets use. The following lists the order of operation:

1. Items in parentheses

2. Values with exponentiation

3. Applying positive or negative

4. Multiplication or division

5. Addition or subtraction

6. Calculation from left to right

Calculating with dates and times

Lotus Symphony Spreadsheets handles calculations that include dates and times in a special way. Dates and times are stored in Lotus Symphony Spreadsheets as serial values, but are displayed as normal-looking date or time formats in the spreadsheet. For example, the date 04/19/2008 displays as 4/19/2008; however, the computer stores the value as 39557.

Because of this, you can create calculations on dates using serial values and then have Lotus Symphony Spreadsheets display the results in a format that you can easily comprehend.

You need to make sure your cells are formatted properly to see serial values or dates. To format a cell, right-click the cell and choose Text and Cell Properties. The Text and Cell Properties dialog box appears. On the Numbers tab, set Category to Date (or Time) and then set Format to the display format you prefer (such as 12/31/99). To see dates and times in serial value format, set Category to Number and Format to General.

To see how this works, do the following example. It calculates the number of days between two dates, a date in the future and today's date (the actual date you are doing this formula).

1. **Enter the following formula into cell B4:**

   ```
   ="12/31/2010"-NOW()
   ```

   The formula calculates the number of days (represented by the NOW() function) and subtracts it from a date in the future, 12/31/2010.

2. **Press Enter.**

3. **Format the cell as General.**

   The answer appears.

REMEMBER

In Step 1 of the preceding example, you use a built-in date function called NOW(). It uses the current date for calculations you perform. You learn more about functions in the "Working with Functions" section, later in this chapter.

Filtering calculations

After you run calculations in your spreadsheets, you may want to see only certain rows and columns of the returned data. You can achieve this by using filters, such as the Instant Filter function. The Instant Filter function enables you to see only those rows that have identical information in the column you're filtering.

Filters don't remove data from your spreadsheets. Rather, the data that you filter out is merely hidden from view.

For example, in Figure 12-4, I have a list of products based on product name, sales data, and sales manager responsible for that line of products. If I want to see the data for just one of the sales persons, Jackson, I can do this quickly by setting up an Instant Filter and then doing the calculations. Here's how:

Figure 12-4: Sample data to which I can apply an Instant Filter.

Fly By Light, Inc		
March 2010		
Type	Sales	Sales Manager
Incandescent	$4,324.00	Jackson
Halogen	$3,389.00	Monroe
Green 3-Way	$2,198.00	Washington
Fluorescent	$1,300.00	Monroe
Strobe	$6,831.00	Jackson
Black	$7,190.00	Jackson
Spot	$2,539.00	Washington
Auto Lites	$4,983.00	Monroe
Field Lights	$3,253.00	Monroe
Mercury Vapor	$8,215.00	Jackson

1. **Set up a spreadsheet similar to the one in Figure 12-4.**

   You can use any data you want; just have two or more cells in a column with identical data, such as the Sales Manager column in Figure 12-4.

2. **Select the cells with data you want to filter. Be sure to include the column heading row.**

   In my example, I select rows 6 through 16 in columns C, D, and E.

3. **Choose Manipulate⇨Filters⇨Instant Filter.**

   The Instant Filter drop-down arrows appear on each column of the filtered area.

4. **Click the Instant Filter button on the heading of the column you want to filter.**

   I'm filtering sales manager names, so I click the Instant Filter button on the Sales Manager cell.

   A drop-down appears with the names of each unique item in this column.

5. **From the drop-down list, choose the item you'd like to display data for.**

   I choose Jackson from the drop-down list.

   Only those rows of data that include Jackson in the Sales Manager column appear. Figure 12-5 shows the filtered data.

Figure 12-5:
The sample data with an Instant Filter of Jackson applied.

Fly By Light, Inc			
	March 2010		
Type		Sales	Sales Manager
Incandescent		$4,324.00	Jackson
Strobe		$6,831.00	Jackson
Black		$7,190.00	Jackson
Mercury Vapor		$8,215.00	Jackson

When you open the drop-down menu for an Instant Filter item, such as the Sales Manager column in the preceding example, there are other filtering items from which to choose. For example, you can use the All option to display all the data in your column. This is the same as if you didn't apply a filter at all. The Standard Filter option displays the Standard Filter dialog box. In this dialog box, you can set up your own filters, using operators, field names, conditions, and values.

When you use the Instant Filter, or any other filter, you should remove any filters before deleting data. If you don't, you may delete data filtered out (not showing) but within the range of your selection for deletion. For example, if you filter on Washington to delete only his data, you need to select each row individually by selecting one row, holding down the Ctrl key, and selecting another row. Continue this process until all his rows are selected. Then delete the selection. If you don't use the Ctrl key to select individual rows, but instead select the filtered view by using the mouse and bounding box (the normal way to select several contiguous items), and then delete the items, you'll also delete any rows that fall within that range but are currently hidden by the filter.

You can turn off the Instant Filter by choosing the selection on which the Instant Filter activated. Then choose Manipulate➪Filter➪Instant Filter. Lotus Symphony Spreadsheets removes the filter.

Working with the Solve Equations tool

Lotus Symphony Spreadsheets provides the Solve Equations tool, which enables you to calculate a value based on a value you specify in the formula. Let's say you set up an equation to find the payment on a vehicle you plan to purchase. Using trial and error, you then want to adjust the Monthly Payment area to get your payment down to one that you can afford. You want to keep the initial purchase price and the interest rate items the same. The Number of Months, however, need to change. The Solve Equation tool provides an excellent analysis option for quickly calculating this value.

To get started, you can use the data shown in Figure 12-6 for an example. Or create a table with the following column headings, from left to right: Purchase Price, Interest Rate, Number of Months, and Monthly Payment. Enter the appropriate values in the first three columns, and enter the following formula (which appears in cell E5 in Figure 12-6) in the Monthly Payment column:

```
=B5*(C5/12)/(1-(1+C5/12)^-D5)
```

The formula calculates the monthly payment based on the current data in the table.

Figure 12-6: Sample data for calculating car payments.

	A	B	C	D	E	F
1						
2						
3						
4		Purchase Price	Interest Rate	Number of Months	Monthly Payment	
5		36000.00	0.06	48.00	845.46	
6						
7						

Use the following steps to learn how to use the Solve Equation tool, which enables you to solve an equation based on the result you want. In my example, I choose a lower monthly payment and use the Solve Equation tool to calculate the number of months required for that loan.

The formatting for each of the cells in this example uses two decimal places. You may want to change your sample spreadsheet to use that same formatting as well.

1. **Click in the cell with the formula.**

   In my case, that's cell E5.

2. **Choose Tools⇨Solve Equations.**

   The Solve Equation dialog box appears. (See Figure 12-7.)

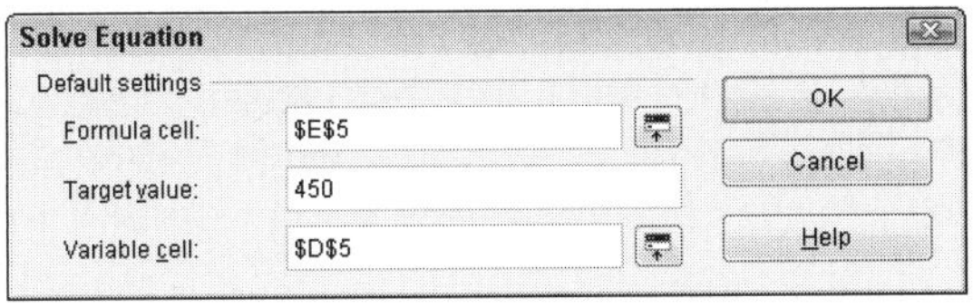

Figure 12-7:
The Solve
Equation
dialog box.

Solve Equation

Default settings

Formula cell: $E$5   OK

Target value: 450   Cancel

Variable cell: $D$5   Help

3. **Click in the Variable Cell box.**

   In this cell, I need to enter the data I want to change based on the monthly payment I want to make.

4. **Click in the cell that contains the Number of Months value.**

   On my worksheet, that's cell D5. The cell name D5 appears in the Variable Cell box. This is the data I want to change based on the monthly payment I want to make.

5. **In the Solve Equation dialog box, enter a value in the Target Value box. This value represents the monthly payment amount you would like.**

   For example, enter 450.

6. **Click OK.**

   The Lotus Symphony Spreadsheets screen appears with the calculated results. Notice that the value displays in this dialog box. (See Figure 12-8.) This amount will display in the Number of Months column inside of cell D5.

7. **Click Yes.**

   The value returns to the Number of Months column.

Figure 12-8:
A screen
appears
showing the
calculated
results of
the Solve
Equation.

Our example shows that my contract would be for over 102 months (8.5 years), which I'm sure most lending institutions would not go for. So you could run the Solve Equations again and use a larger monthly payment for the Target Value box value to calculate a new Number of Months value. Or you could use the Purchase Price in the Variable Cell box and then specify a monthly payment you would like to make based on interest rate and number of months. This calculates the total amount of money you'll be able to spend based on the interest rate and length of the loan. (Be sure to manually change the number of months to a normal value, such as 48 or 66, for instance.)

Working with Functions

As I've mentioned before, Lotus Symphony Spreadsheets includes over 150 pre-built formulas called *functions*. Functions perform specific calculations so you don't have to write your own functions when you need to calculate some data.

Table 12-2 lists just a few of the common functions available.

Table 12-2	Common Spreadsheet Functions
Function Name	*Description*
ACCRINT	Calculates accrued interest for an interest-bearing security.
ARABI	Returns a Roman numeral value.
COUNT	Returns the count of numbers in an argument list.
DATE	Returns the internal value of the date given.
DOLLAR	Changes a number to a dollar amount.
IPMT	Calculates compounded interest.
LEN	Returns the length of a string of text.

Function Name	Description
LOOKUP	Returns the value from a range or selection.
PI	Returns the value of PI.
REPT	Repeats a string of text.
SUM	Adds a list of values together.
T	Changes a value to text.

See Appendix B for more information about the different functions available with Lotus Symphony. You also can use the Lotus Symphony Help to learn more about functions. To find this information, choose Help➪Help Contents and enter *Functions* in the Search field. Click Go to conduct your search.

Choosing functions

To use a function in your spreadsheet, enter the function's name in the formula toolbar followed by any required and optional *parameters*. Parameters are the values that make up the function, so you calculate for the results you desire.

If you don't know the name of the function or don't know how to set up the proper parameters for a function, use the Choose Function dialog box. This dialog box lists each function, the parameters for each, and enables you to walk through the building process of setting up the function using the Instant Pilot.

Some functions include parameters that aren't required, called *optional parameters*. When you set up a function that allows for optional parameters, the Function Instant Pilot (similar to Windows Wizards) of the Choose Function dialog box displays them in normal text. Required parameters are listed in bolded text.

For example, when you use the SUM function, you enter the following:

```
=SUM(range of cells to calculate)
```

To illustrate how to choose functions using the Function Instant Pilot of the Choose Function feature, follow these steps to use the SUM function:

1. **Open a spreadsheet that contains a list with values you can sum.**

   Figure 12-9, for example, includes a list that I use as sample data.

2. **Select the cell in which you want the results to show after you create the function.**

3. Choose Create⇨Choose Function.

The Function Instant Pilot starts and displays the Choose Function dialog box.

	A	B	C	D	E	F	G
4			Fly By Light, Inc				
5				March 2010			
6			Type	Sales	Sales Manager		
7			Incandescent	$4,324.00	Jackson		
8			Halogen	$3,389.00	Monroe		
9			Green 3-Way	$2,198.00	Washington		
10			Fluorescent	$1,300.00	Monroe		
11			Strobe	$6,831.00	Jackson		
12			Black	$7,190.00	Jackson		
13			Spot	$2,539.00	Washington		
14			Auto Lites	$4,983.00	Monroe		
15			Field Lights	$3,253.00	Monroe		
16			Mercury Vapor	$8,215.00	Jackson		
17							
18							
19							
20							
21							
22							

Figure 12-9: Using the SUM function in a spreadsheet.

4. Select the SUM function on the Functions tab.

5. Click Next.

6. Enter the range of cells for the function in the number1 field. (See Figure 12-10.)

To select the cells interactively — that is, click on the cell in the live spreadsheet — click the Shrink button on the right side of the number1 field. Select the cells and then click the Maximum button to return to the Function Instant Pilot.

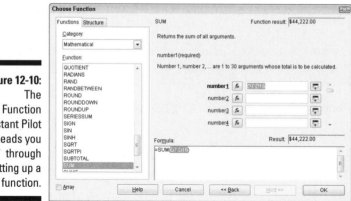

Figure 12-10: The Function Instant Pilot leads you through setting up a function.

7. Click OK.

For some functions, you may need to click the Next button to continue setting up the function parameters. For the SUM function, however, I just want to sum up a column of values, so my work is done here.

The spreadsheet displays the results of the calculation in the cell you specified in Step 2. (See Figure 12-11.)

	A	B	C	D	E	F	G
4			**Fly By Light, Inc**				
5			March 2010				
6			**Type**	**Sales**	**Sales Manager**		
7			Incandescent	$4,324.00	Jackson		
8			Halogen	$3,389.00	Monroe		
9			Green 3-Way	$2,198.00	Washington		
10			Fluorescent	$1,300.00	Monroe		
11			Strobe	$6,831.00	Jackson		
12			Black	$7,190.00	Jackson		
13			Spot	$2,539.00	Washington		
14			Auto Lites	$4,983.00	Monroe		
15			Field Lights	$3,253.00	Monroe		
16			Mercury Vapor	$8,215.00	Jackson		
17				$44,222.00			
18							
19							
20							

Figure 12-11: The results of the SUM function.

While on the Functions tab of the Choose Function dialog box, you can filter the functions into different predefined categories to help you find the function you want to use. To do this, choose an item from the Category drop-down list. For example, to find functions related to financial calculations, choose the Financial category.

Modifying functions

Although you can't modify the actual formulas used by a function, you can modify the parameters you enter for a function. To do this, you can modify the formula in the Formula bar, or you can return to the Function Instant Pilot to do your modifications.

To return to the Function Instant Pilot for changes to your formula, do the following:

1. Click in the cell that contains the formula.

2. Click the Choose Function button on the Formula bar.

The Choose Function dialog box appears, with the Structure tab showing.

3. **Modify the parameters of the function.**

4. **Click Next (if necessary).**

5. **Click OK to save your changes and to apply the modified function to your spreadsheet.**

Using nested functions

Nested functions are those that appear inside of another function.

In my example in the "Choosing Functions" section, I show how you can calculate the sum of the data stored in the Sales column of a monthly sales totals spreadsheet. To get an idea of how nested functions work, assume that the spreadsheet has another cell (G7) that contains a total of sales from a previous quarter. If I want to sum the Sales column and then add that sum to the value found in cell G7, my formula will look like the following:

```
=SUM(G7;SUM(D7:D16))
```

When nesting functions, be sure to keep track of your parentheses. You must make sure you have an equal number of open and closed parenthetical marks (and), to ensure that your calculations work. Also, be sure the marks are in the correct positions to ensure your calculations perform as expected.

Working with DataPilots

DataPilots enable you to summarize data in different ways to view patterns in data. You take a set of data in one table (a list) and then manipulate it based on summaries you want to view.

Besides setting up the original spreadsheet, one of the most important facets of DataPilots is knowing what questions you want to ask about your data. For example, you may look at your data and want to know how many units you sold in a given territory, when those units were shipped, and similar questions. Without DataPilots, you can filter and sort for this type of information, but you have to do that manually or set up macros to handle that analysis. After you get comfortable with DataPilots, you can use them for your data analysis.

Setting up DataPilot tables

To use DataPilots, make sure you store your data in columns and rows. Figure 12-12 shows some sample data to use for running DataPilot analyses. After you get your starting data set up, save the spreadsheet.

Figure 12-12:
Start your
DataPilots
with a
spread-
sheet of
data neatly
organized
in columns
and rows.

	A	B	C	D	E	F	G
1	Territory	Shirt Style	Unit Ship Date	Units Shipped	Retail Price	Cost of Goods	
2	East	Cotton T	04/03/2010	20	12.00	5.87	
3	East	Sport	04/03/2010	25	14.00	6.32	
4	East	Collar	04/03/2010	45	22.00	9.47	
5	East	Cotton T	04/04/2010	56	12.00	5.87	
6	East	Sport	04/04/2010	78	14.00	6.32	
7	East	Collar	04/04/2010	28	22.00	9.47	
8	West	Cotton T	04/03/2010	33	12.00	5.87	
9	West	Sport	04/03/2010	88	14.00	6.32	
10	West	Collar	04/03/2010	79	22.00	9.47	
11	West	Cotton T	04/04/2010	55	12.00	5.87	
12	West	Sport	04/04/2010	46	14.00	6.32	
13	West	Collar	04/04/2010	33	22.00	9.47	
14							
15							

To set up a DataPilot based on this data, perform the following:

1. **Click inside the data.**

2. **Choose Manipulate⇨DataPilot⇨Start.**

   The Data Pilot dialog box appears. A grid showing Row, Column, and Data areas appears. Next to these areas are buttons for each column from your spreadsheet.

3. **Click a column button and right-click.**

   Before you right-click a button, click it first. It seems to work better when you do this. Otherwise, your previously selected column is moved to a different area on the DataPilot table.

4. **Click a place on the DataPilot table to add the selected column.**

5. **Repeat until each area includes the data you want to analyze.**

   In my example, I use the following setup:

   - *Row:* Shirt Style

   - *Column:* Territory

   - *Data:* Units Shipped

   You can change the type of calculation performed in the Data area. For example, the default one used when I specified the Units Shipped column for that area was the SUM function. You can see this by looking at the label of that area. It is named Sum-Units Shipped. To change this function, click Options and then click User-Defined to specify your own function. Click OK to return to the Data Pilot dialog box.

6. **Click the More button.**

   The bottom part of the Data Pilot dialog box expands.

7. Choose New Sheet from the Result To drop-down list.

This specifies Lotus Symphony Spreadsheets to place the DataPilot table onto a new blank worksheet in your spreadsheet file.

8. Click OK.

The DataPilot table appears on a new tab, as shown in Figure 12-13.

Figure 12-13:
A new DataPilot table on a new worksheet tab.

	A	B	C	D	E
1	Filter				
2					
3	Sum - Units S	Territory			
4	Shirt Style	East	West	Total Result	
5	Collar	72	112	184	
6	Cotton T	76	88	164	
7	Sport	103	134	237	
8	Total Result	251	334	585	
9					
10					
11					
12					

After you create a DataPilot table, you can modify it, analyze its data, or output the data. The following sections describe each of these actions.

Filtering DataPilot data

With the DataPilot table, you can filter data to show only that information you want to analyze or verify predictions you might have made about the data.

To filter the data, do the following:

1. Click the Filter button on the DataPilot table.

The Filter dialog box appears.

2. Select a field from the Field Name drop-down list.

This is the field you want to filter by.

3. Select a filter condition from the Condition drop-down list.

4. Specify a value in the Value field.

You also can click the drop-down list to select Not Empty or Empty.

5. Click OK.

The filter conditions are applied to the DataPilot table. (See Figure 12-14.)

	A	B	C	D	E
1	Filter				
2					
3	Sum - Units S	Territory			
4	Shirt Style	East	West	Total Result	
5	Sport	103	134	237	
6	Total Result	103	134	237	
7					
8					
9					

My sample data represents a small amount of data. In most real-life scenarios, the data that shows in the DataPilot tables can get rather large. That's why it's handy to use the Filter feature to view only the data you want to analyze.

Modifying DataPilot tables

You can update the data on the DataPilot table by modifying the original data source. In my sample case, I need to return to the A tab, make changes to the data, and then refresh the DataPilot table. To refresh the data, click the DataPilot tab (called DataPilot_A_1 in my example), right-click the DataPilot table, and choose Refresh. The table refreshes using the data I changed on the original data source table.

Outputting DataPilot data

You can output DataPilot data much like you can output data that you don't add to DataPilots. To print a DataPilot table, click the tab on which the DataPilot resides, choose Print, and then click OK.

You might also want to send your DataPilot information to other users via e-mail or save the data to a shared Web or network location. The easiest way to do this is using the PDF export feature. To do this, follow these steps:

1. **Choose File⇨Export.**

   The Export dialog box appears.

2. **Enter a new name in the File Name field, if desired.**

3. **Click Save.**

   The PDF Options dialog box appears.

4. **Choose Selection to choose only the DataPilot table tab.**

5. **Click Export.**

   Lotus Symphony Spreadsheets exports the data to a PDF file.

Part IV
Using IBM Lotus Symphony Presentations — the Presentation Application

In this part . . .

*T*he really fun part of working with IBM Lotus Symphony is the part when you can turn it off and go home. But when you have to stay late at work and actually get something done, read this part of the book. It's about creating slide shows you can show to your cubicle mates. (You do have to share your cubicle with four other people, right?) You should also read about Image Animations. Trust me. You'll want to.

Chapter 13

Creating a Presentation

. . . .

In This Chapter

▶ Opening Lotus Symphony Presentations

▶ Moving around the program

▶ Typing and formatting text on a page

▶ Looking at pages up close, far away, and in high contrast

▶ Using grids, rulers, and autocorrect

▶ Adding, modifying, and moving tables

▶ Saving presentations

. . . .

*O*ver the years, presentation software has become one of the most popular types of software for all types of users, from corporate executives to legal defense teams to home users creating simple slide shows for home entertainment. Lotus Symphony Presentations enables you to create digital slide shows for presentations and Web sites. You can use Presentations for meetings, entertainment, church functions, fund-raising events, and more.

To become familiar with how to create your own presentations, this chapter discusses starting Lotus Symphony Presentations, creating a Lotus Symphony Presentations file, navigating a presentation, and viewing the pages you create. I also cover adding content to your pages, using the Lotus Symphony Presentations tools, incorporating tables into your presentations, and saving presentations.

Starting Lotus Symphony Presentations

To get started using Lotus Symphony Presentations, you first need to start Lotus Symphony Presentations from the IBM Lotus Symphony Home tab or from a shortcut link to a previously saved Lotus Presentation file. When you start Lotus Symphony Presentations from the Lotus Symphony Home tab, a new blank presentations page appears. You can add content to it, such as text, graphics, animations, and other objects, and then save the file to the Open Document Presentation format, or `.odp`.

You may be familiar with another presentation program, Microsoft Office PowerPoint. That application is similar to Lotus Symphony Presentations in that you create slides to play back in a slide show or digital presentation. One thing to keep in mind as you work through Lotus Symphony Presentations is that the term *slides* in PowerPoint is analogous to the term *pages* in Lotus Symphony Presentations.

To start Lotus Symphony Presentations, do the following:

1. **Choose Start➪Programs➪IBM Lotus Symphony.**

   The Lotus Symphony main window appears, with the Home tab showing.

2. **Click Create a New Presentation.**

   A new blank presentation page appears, as shown in Figure 13-1.

3. **Add content to your new presentation.**

   The section "Adding Information to Your Pages" later in this chapter details how to add content to your pages.

You also can start a new presentation by choosing File➪New➪Presentation from the Lotus Symphony window. This creates a blank presentation page, on which you can add your own information. Finally, you can choose the New button on the Lotus Symphony main window and choose Lotus Symphony Presentations. A new blank page appears.

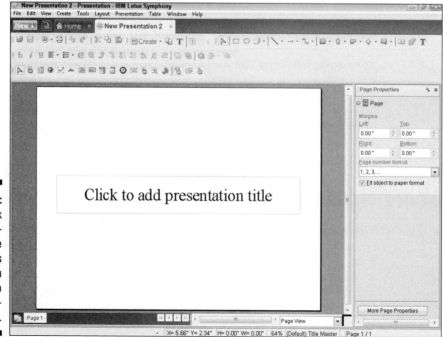

Figure 13-1: A new blank presentations page appears when you create a new presentation.

Even though Lotus Symphony supports the Open Document Presentations format, sometimes it doesn't open files saved in the `.odp` file format if that file was created in another open source program that includes features not yet approved by the OpenSource specification. You may need to convert the file to a different format, such as to a Microsoft Office PowerPoint format (`.pps`) using a different application and then importing that file into Lotus Symphony Presentations.

Creating a presentation from another presentation

Not only can you open a presentation from a shortcut icon on your system, but you also can save that file to a different filename or location, duplicating that presentation. You can then modify the duplicate presentation so that your original stays intact. This is a good idea if the original includes information you want to use for a new presentation, but you still want to keep the original as a different presentation.

After you open the original presentation, do the following to create a duplicate presentation from it:

1. Choose File⇨Save As.

The Save As dialog box appears, as shown in Figure 13-2.

2. Enter a new filename in the File Name box.

3. Click Save.

Lotus Symphony Presentations saves the file to a different name.

Creating a presentation using a template

Lotus Symphony Presentations enables you to create presentations using templates. *Templates* are files that include predefined elements, such as boilerplate text, graphics, and styles. They enable users to work in a presentation file without starting from a blank page. Some templates include only a single page, requiring users to add new pages to fill out the presentations. Other templates might have several pages included and the user just needs to fill out specific information about the new presentation he or she wants to create.

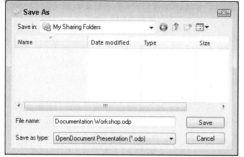

Figure 13-2:
Use the
Save As
dialog box
to create a
copy of an
existing
presentation.

You can find Lotus Symphony Presentations templates on the Web, such as at the IBM Lotus Symphony Web site and other sites. To learn more about Web sites devoted to Lotus Symphony, read Chapter 20.

To get started using a Lotus Symphony Presentations template, do the following:

1. **Start Lotus Symphony.**

2. **Choose File⇨New⇨From Template⇨Presentation.**

   The New from Template dialog box appears. The Template Organizer option on the left enables you to view and manage the templates you have installed on your system.

3. **Select a template from the Templates list.**

   If you don't have templates showing in your Templates list, see the paragraphs following these steps to find out about the Template Organizer.

4. **Click OK.**

   Lotus Symphony Presentations opens the template. Figure 13-3, for example, shows what the Festive.otp template looks like. On your screen, if you choose the Festive.otp template, the grayish blobs you seen in the figure are actually blue, red, mustard, and teal in color.

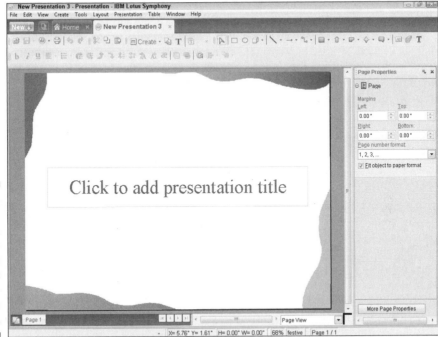

Figure 13-3:
Some
templates
provide
colorful
backgrounds
and enter-
taining
designs.

5. Choose File⇨Save.

The Save dialog box appears.

You can't overwrite template files when you open them in this manner. You can edit them, but I don't cover that topic in this book. Suffice it to say that when you open a new presentation based on a template, the new presentation needs its own name.

6. Type a name for the new file.

7. Click Save.

Lotus Symphony Presentations saves the new file as an Open Document Presentation file (.otp).

All three Lotus Symphony applications can use the Template Organizer. However, to open a template in Lotus Symphony Presentations, the file extension for the template must be .otp. To understand more about the Template Organizer and how to set up templates in it, read Chapter 5. That chapter devotes attention to Lotus Documents, but the principles of the Template Organizer that you find there apply to Lotus Symphony Presentations as well.

You can now add your own content to the presentation. The next time you want to use the template again, it appears just as it did this time (unless someone has modified it, of course), with boilerplate content and design elements.

If you want to use a template but you don't want to see any of the predefined content, click the Create Presentation Based on Page Designs Only option before you leave the New from Template dialog box. This option tells Lotus Symphony Presentations that you want to use the page design (colors, graphics, styles, and so forth) from the template, but not any of the content. The default option uses content and design.

Navigating a Presentation

When you first open a blank presentation, Lotus Symphony Presentations displays a page with an area denoted as Click to Add Presentation Title. This displays on a *title page,* one of the types of pages that you can add to your presentations. You can click this text and add your own title for your presentation.

Learn about more types of presentation pages later in this chapter in the "Adding new pages using Instant Layouts" section.

When you open a presentation, you'll need to know some basic procedures for navigating the Lotus Presentations environment and separate pages. The following sections describe these procedures.

Moving around with the mouse

The primary way for getting around a presentation is by using a mouse. Lotus Symphony Presentations provides common tools, menus, buttons, and other features that you're probably familiar with if you have experience with other Windows programs.

Aside from the common mouse techniques, you should also know how to navigate from one page to the next when you have presentations with multiple pages. To do this, you click the page tab at the bottom of the window in which a page appears. Figure 13-4 shows multiple page tabs at the bottom of the window. When you click the Page 5 tab, for instance, that page displays.

To the right of the tabs are VCR-type controls (or iPod-type controls, for those of you in the younger crowd) for moving to each page in succession, as follows:

 ✔ Click the right arrow to move forward one page at a time.

 ✔ Click the left arrow to move backward one page at a time.

 ✔ Click the fast-forward arrow to move to the last page in the presentation.

 ✔ Click the rewind arrow to move to the first page in the presentation.

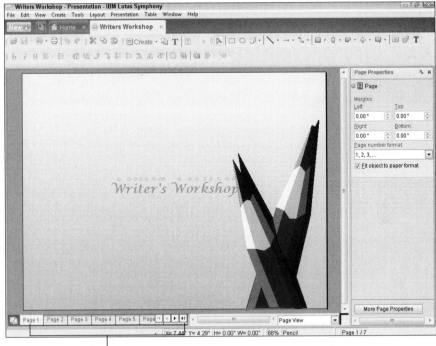

Figure 13-4:
Use the
page tabs
to navigate
from one
page to the
next.

Tabs

Any time you are working on a page or other object while in Lotus Symphony Presentations, think of the right-click menu. This menu, sometimes referred to as the *context menu,* provides menu choices related to the item you right-click on. For example, if you right-click a graphic on a page, a long list of menu choices appears relating to tasks you can perform on that graphic.

Moving around with the keyboard

Another way to move around your presentation file uses keyboard controls. There are several keyboard shortcuts you can use to navigate your presentations, including the following:

- ✔ F2 enables you to edit text.
- ✔ F5 or F9 starts a slide show.
- ✔ Shift+F5 starts a slide show from the current page.
- ✔ Esc ends a slide show.
- ✔ Enter or Page Down takes you to the next page during a slide show.
- ✔ Backspace or Page Up returns you to the previous page during a slide show.

✔ Page Down displays the next page while in editing mode.

✔ Page Up displays the previous page while in editing mode.

✔ F7 starts the Spell Check tool.

✔ Ctrl+F9 shows the outline view of your presentation.

Lotus Symphony Presentations includes several more keyboard shortcuts. To learn more about them, open the Lotus Symphony Presentations Help tool (choose Help➪Help Contents) and navigate to the Keyboard Navigation for IBM Lotus Symphony Presentations topic. You can find it in the Lotus Symphony Presentations folder.

Jumping to a specific page

Finally, as you start to work on several pages in your presentations, you may need to quickly jump to a specific page. Of course, you've already learned one way — click the page tab at the bottom of the page. However, the list of page tabs may not show all the pages in your presentation. To jump to a specific page, use the Navigator. The following steps tell how to use this tool:

1. **Open a presentation that has several pages.**

2. **Choose Edit➪Navigator.**

   The Navigator opens, as shown in Figure 13-5.

3. **Double-click the page number you want to view.**

   The page you select appears as the active page.

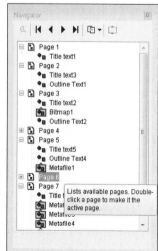

Figure 13-5: Use the Navigator to jump to a specific page in your presentation.

When you use the Navigator, you can keep it open as you work on your pages. Because it initially opens as a fairly large window, feel free to resize the window and reposition to the side so it keeps out of your way while you work. Figure 13-5, for instance, shows the Navigator resized and moved to the right side of the window.

Adding Information to Your Pages

When you create a new blank presentation, or when you want to add new content to an existing page, you need to know how to add information to your pages. One of the most basic tasks in Lotus Symphony Presentations involves adding text, which the following section shows how to do. You also find out how to add bulleted and numbered lists, format your text with styles, and view the master page.

Also, you learn how to insert new pages into your presentation. You want to do this any time your presentation discusses a new topic that warrants its own page. You may also want to do this for pages that display graphics, illustrations, tables, or any other type of content that's too large for other pages in your presentation.

Although you don't want to make your presentation so large (that is, use a high number of pages) that it disinterests your audience, you should have enough pages that your individual pages aren't too cluttered. Your presentations may be shown on digital projectors or other mediums, so keep in mind that some viewers may have difficulty reading smaller font sizes. Keep font sizes large (a font size of 22 or above usually suffices for large venues) so that your audience members can read every word without the assistance of binoculars.

Inserting text

To add text to your pages, you first must insert a text box. Then you add the text inside that box. You can move the text box, resize it, style text within it, and change color properties of it.

As you learn in the next section, some of the new pages that you can add include text boxes by default. However, you may want to insert an additional text box on a page or start with a blank page and add text boxes and other objects manually.

The following shows how to insert a text box and text into a page:

1. **On a presentation page, click the Text Box button on the Main toolbar.**

   (The Text Box button also can appear on other toolbars, such as the Drawing toolbar).

   The mouse pointer displays as a crosshairs pointer.

2. **Draw a rectangular box where you want the text to appear.**

   A rectangular text box appears on your screen. The insertion point appears inside the text box.

3. **Type your text.**

   As you type text, the text box enlarges to accommodate the text you enter.

Text boxes resize vertically. That is, as your text flows to a different line, the text box grows vertically. If you want to make the text box wider, add your text and then use the resizing handles to stretch the box horizontally (to the right or to the left).

Adding new pages using Instant Layouts

Lotus Symphony Presentations provides several different types of pages that you can add to your presentations. You use the Instant Layout feature to select predefined page setups to help you create the type of page you want for your presentation.

Each type of Instant Layout page (except for the blank page option) provides areas that have been predefined for different types of objects. Boilerplate text appears on the new page, giving you some guidance on what you should add next. For example, when you insert the Title Only page, the boilerplate text Click To Add Presentation Title appears. Do what the boilerplate explains to insert text, graphics, and other objects onto your pages.

To add a new page to your presentations, do the following:

1. **Open a presentation.**

2. **Choose Create⇨New Page.**

   The Create New Page dialog box appears. (See Figure 13-6.)

3. **Select a page from the Select an Instant Layout area.**

4. **Click OK.**

   The new page appears in the presentation.

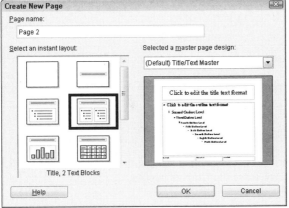

Figure 13-6:
The Create
New Page
dialog box
displays
new pages
you can add
to your
presentations.

If you don't replace the boilerplate information on Instant Layout pages, don't worry. That information doesn't appear when you play your slide show or when you print the pages.

You don't have to use only the type of object displayed on the page type when you add it to your presentation. For example, if you add a page that shows the table object, you can add a text box, graphic, or other object. In fact, you don't even have to add a table to that page. You can delete the container for that object and put anything you like there. The page types just provide a quick template for different types of pages you can set up.

Table 13-1 describes the types of Instant Layout pages Lotus Symphony Presentations enables you to add to your presentation files:

Table 13-1	Instant Layout Page Types
Page Name	**Description**
Blank Page	Displays an empty page.
Title Only	Displays a title page, with the title heading centered horizontally and vertically.
Title, Text	Displays a title heading at the top of the page and a text box below it.
Title, 2 Text Boxes	Displays a title heading at the top of the page and two text boxes below it.
Title, Chart	Displays a title heading at the top of the page and a chart button to create a chart on your page.
Title, Table	Displays a title heading at the top of the page and a table button to create a table on your page.

(continued)

Table 13-1 *(continued)*

Page Name	Description
Title, Clipart, Text	Displays a title heading at the top of the page, a button for inserting clip art, and a text box.
Title, Text, Chart	Displays a title heading at the top of the page, a text box, and a chart button to create a chart in your page.
Title, Text, Clipart	Displays a title heading at the top of the page, a text box, and a button for inserting clip art.
Title, Chart, Text	Displays a title heading at the top of the page, a chart button to create a chart in your page, and a text box.

Figure 13-6 shows the Create New Page dialog box. Each Instant Layout page appears on the left side under the Select an Instant Layout area. A sample of the page appears in this area. When you click an Instant Layout, you can see a larger version of the sample. For example, the one selected in Figure 13-6 is the Title, 2 Text Blocks Instant Layout.

Adding a bulleted or numbered list to a page

When you present information on your presentation pages, you should consider putting the information in lists. Lists help you present information in an ordered way. Also, lists make your text easier to read.

Lists can be bulleted or numbered. The following is a bulleted list:

- Bullet item 1
- Bullet item 2
- Bullet item 3

As you add bulleted items to your pages, Lotus Symphony Presentations styles them the same for each level. A level equates to the number of times you indent (tab over) to the bulleted item. The outermost level, which has no manual tabs added, is the First Outline Level. Tab over once and the item becomes a Second Outline Level item. The lowest default level is the Ninth Outline Level.

By default, when you add a new page that includes a text box to your presentation, the text enters as a bulleted list item. Simply start adding your text, press Enter for a new line, and a new bulleted item appears on the following line.

Numbered lists are ordered and include a number to the left of the text. As you add a new numbered list item, Lotus Symphony Presentations automatically increments the list. Figure 13-7 shows an example of a numbered list.

The following list (it's a bulleted list, by the way) explains how to set up each type of list:

- To format text as a bulleted list, click the down arrow on the Bullets toolbar button. Click the Bullet item on the drop-down list.

- To format text as a numbered list, click the down arrow on the Bullets toolbar button. Click the Numbering item on the drop-down list.

When you choose the bullet or numbered toolbar button, Lotus Symphony Presentations remembers the last one you selected. So if the icon shows the bullets, you can click it directly to format your text with bullets. If not, the numbers appear.

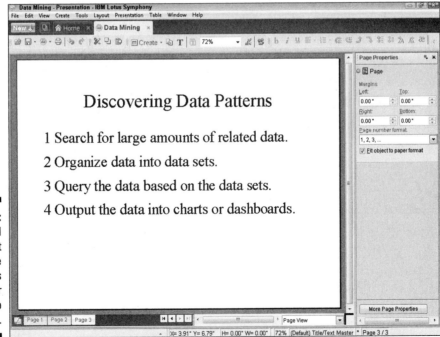

Figure 13-7: Numbered lists let you create procedures and other step-by-step discussions.

Formatting text with styles

Lotus Symphony Presentations includes several paragraph styles that you can add to your pages. Styles let you use identical formatting features for similar types of information. For example, all your main content items can be styled using one style, while all your subtopics can be styled another.

To see a list of the styles provided by Lotus Symphony Presentations, choose Layout⇨Style List or press F11. The Style List appears, as shown in Figure 13-8.

You may need to select Presentation Styles from the Style Type drop-down list to see the list of styles you can use with your presentations. Of course, if you insert graphics in your pages, you can use the Graphics Styles list to apply styles to them.

To apply a style to selected text or paragraph, click the style from the Style area and click Apply. The text changes to reflect the formatting associated with the style you choose.

You can modify styles to match the type of formatting you want in your presentations. To modify a style, select one from the Style List and click Modify. On the dialog box for that style, such as Outline 1, select the formatting options you want to change. Click OK when you finish modifying the style.

You also can create your own styles. You can create them from text you've already formatted (which is a good way to see how your style will actually look!) or create a style by choosing different formatting options.

Figure 13-8: The Style List includes Presentation Styles for your presentation pages.

Because it's the easiest way, I show how to create your own styles from a selection of text. Use the following steps:

1. **Open a presentation page and format a paragraph of text using the following parameters:**

   • Font: Arial

   • Font Size: 34

   • Font Color: Orange

2. **Select the paragraph.**

3. **Right-click and choose Create Style from Selection.**

   The Create Style dialog box appears.

4. **Type a name for the new style.**

   I use the name Orange Arial for my style.

5. **Click OK to save your new style.**

   The style appears in the Style List dialog box. It appears in the list of styles when you choose the Graphics Styles option from the Style Type drop-down list.

Viewing Your Pages

Lotus Symphony Presentations provides several ways to view your pages as you work on them. Of course, your finished presentation most likely will be displayed on a monitor or projector using the Screen Show tools. As you create your presentation, you may want to view pages in different ways, including the following:

- ✔ **Page View displays pages in the default editing view.** I use Page View for most of this chapter's discussion.

- ✔ **Outline View displays page information in outline format.** Figure 13-9, for example, shows an example of this view. When you click a page that includes a graphic, that graphic displays in a small window for your review.

- ✔ **Page Sorter View shows a thumbnail of each page so you can view the order of them and rearrange the slide show quickly.** Figure 13-10 shows an example of the Page Sorter view.

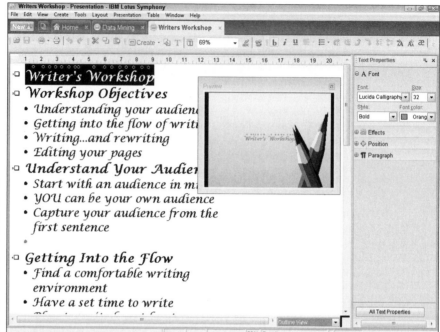

Figure 13-9:
Outline view lets you view your pages' content without other formatting showing.

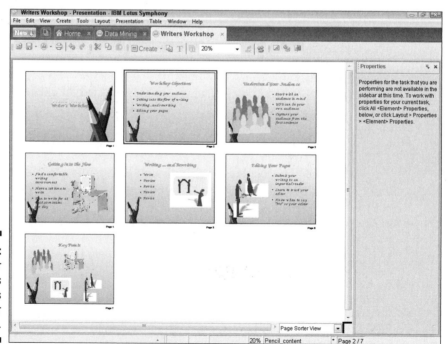

Figure 13-10:
Page Sorter View shows thumbnails of your pages.

✔ **Notes View displays notes (see Figure 13-11) that you can add to accompany your presentation.** These notes don't display during the slide show, but you can display them on your computer monitor during the slide show for your reference. As you work on your presentation, however, use the Notes View to fill out discussion points you want to address with the audience. Notes are great places to put references to other resources, such as books and Internet sites.

For information on preparing for and playing back your slide shows, read Chapter 18.

To change to different views, choose View➪Page and select from one of the menu choices. Or you can click the Page View toolbar list that appears at the bottom of the Lotus Presentations window. When you click this menu, the four page-editing views appear.

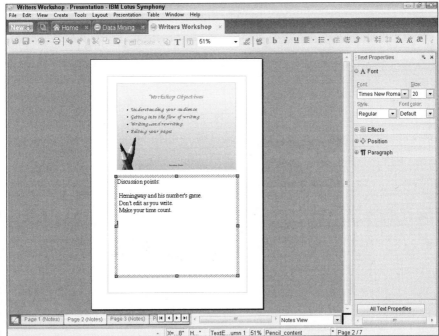

Figure 13-11: Use the Notes View to view and edit your slide show notes.

Setting zoom options

To help you see the details of a page or an object on a page, you can use the zoom option. The zoom option also enables you to zoom out on your page so you can see more of the page, but with less detail.

To use zoom, do the following:

1. **Choose View➪Zoom.**

   The Zoom dialog box appears.

2. **Choose a zoom setting. Use the Variable setting to set your own zoom factor.**

3. **Click OK.**

Another way to change zoom settings is by using the Zoom toolbar drop-down list. It appears on the Main toolbar and includes the zoom settings found in the Zoom dialog box. To specify a variable zoom, type in the percentage amount you want to zoom (a lower percentage zooms out from the page) and press Enter.

Changing display quality

Lotus Symphony Presentations provides settings for you to view your slide show pages in black and white, grayscale, and high contrast. You may want to do this for testing how well your pages look when printed on standard black-and-white printers, or if you need to meet accessibility standards for your presentations. Some audience members may need to view your slide show in these types of display qualities.

To set display quality, do the following:

1. **Open a presentation.**

2. **Choose View➪Display Quality.**

3. **Choose from one of the following:**
   - Color
   - Grayscale
   - Black and White
   - High Contrast

   Your presentation pages display in the display quality you choose.

To return to color, choose View➪Display Quality➪Color.

Using Lotus Symphony Presentations Tools

Lotus Symphony Presentations includes tools to help you set up your presentation pages to make them as professional and error-free as possible. These tools include:

✔ The Guideline Grid

✔ Rulers

✔ Instant Corrections

The following sections discuss these tools in more detail.

Displaying the Guideline Grid

Sometimes you need to position a text box, graphic, or other object precisely on a page. You might, for instance, want to line up a series of images on your page. To help with this task, turn on the Guideline Grid. The Guideline Grid displays a set of square grids over the entire presentation page. These grids help you line up objects and text horizontally and vertically.

For real precision, you can turn on the Snap feature. This moves any item you place on the page precisely on the nearest grid. You don't have to worry about eyeballing the placement. Simply move the object close to the grid where you want to place it, release the mouse, and the object snaps to that grid. There are times, however, when the object snaps to a grid you didn't intend. In those cases, move the object again, this time closer to the target grid.

To turn on and set the Guideline Grid, do the following:

1. **Open a presentation.**

2. **Choose View⇨Guideline Grid.**

   The Guideline Grid dialog box appears, as shown in Figure 13-12.

3. **Select Visible Grid.**

Figure 13-12: The Guideline Grid dialog box.

Guideline Grid

☑ Visible grid	☑ Snap to grid
Grid color:	Snap range:
■ Light red ▾	5 Pixels

Grid spacing
Horizontal:	0.50"
Vertical:	0.50"	☐ Proportional spacing

Grid subdivision
Horizontal:	1	point(s)
Vertical:	1	point(s)

[OK] [Cancel] [Help]

4. Choose a color from the Grid Color drop-down list.

My example uses the color red, for example.

5. Select Snap to Grid.

6. Click OK.

The Guideline Grid displays on the current presentation. (See Figure 13-13.) In this example, the camera graphic has been selected to show the way the object outline can be lined up with the Guideline Grids.

If you open another presentation, the Guideline Grid doesn't display. Repeat these steps to turn it on for each presentation.

Another tool you may want to use is the Guide when Moving tool. This tool displays when you move an object (such as a graphic) and displays a large gridline up the object horizontally and vertically as you move the object. To turn on this tool, choose View⇨Guide when Moving. Repeat the steps to turn it off.

To turn off the Guideline Grid, choose View⇨Guideline Grid and deselect the Visible Grid option. Click OK.

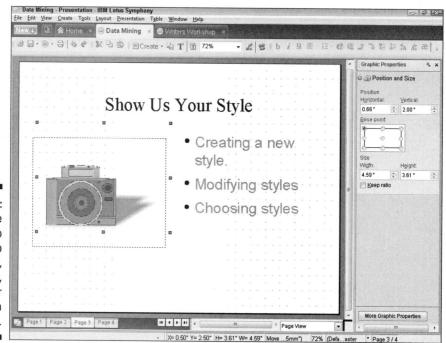

Figure 13-13:
Guideline Grids help you line up graphics, text boxes, and other objects on your pages.

Turning on rulers

Lotus Symphony Presentations enables you to turn on and off the layout rulers. Rulers appear at the top and left of the page window. They enable you to place items on the pages at precise locations, set up tab stops, and see measurements of margins and spacing between objects.

To turn on the rulers, choose View⇨Rulers. Figure 13-14 shows the rulers in the sample presentation. When you click an object — in this case, the text box on the right side of the page — the ruler shows you where the indents and tabs are for that object. Notice the rulers display a shaded section aligning with the indents of the selected text box. Also, the tabs for that object appear on the top ruler (horizontal) as small icons. (Look at about the 4½–inch mark for one of these tab icons.)

Figure 13-14: Rulers help you line up your text and objects, as well as configure indents and tab settings.

Turning on (or off) snap lines

Lotus Symphony Presentations includes snap lines to help you position objects and text on your pages. The snap lines display as vertical and horizontal lines that you can drag from the rulers. To display snap lines, make sure you have the rulers turned on (see previous section), choose View⇨Snap Lines⇨Snap Lines Visible and then choose View⇨Snap Lines⇨Snap Lines to Front to see the snap lines on top of your current slide.

Next, click on a ruler, say the top horizontal ruler, and then drag down to your slide. A snap line appears. You can do the same with the vertical ruler. Also you can add multiple vertical and horizontal snap lines to help you align objects on your page.

Snap lines do not display when you print your pages or when you play back your presentation as a presentation.

Setting up Instant Corrections

With Instant Corrections, Lotus Symphony Presentations automatically changes the spelling and capitalization of common words. Many words have common misspellings, and Instant Corrections can find those words as you type them and correct them automatically for you. For example, if you type **accomodate** in Lotus Symphony, Instant Corrections recognizes that you're trying to type *accommodate* and fills in the correct letters for you. Or if you type **differances** when you really mean *differences,* Instant Corrections catches and corrects your error. By default, Lotus Symphony Presentations includes a long list of these Instant Corrections, and you can add to them.

Another mistake Instant Corrections picks up on includes those times you inadvertently type two capital letters at the beginning of a word, or use lowercase spelling to start off a new sentence. Instant Corrections changes these common mistakes to their proper capitalizations.

In addition to single words, Lotus Symphony changes short phrases, abbreviations, and symbols as well. You can enter the standard copyright symbol, for example, by quickly typing **(C)**. This tells Instant Corrections to change it to ©.

Just like the Spell Check tool, Instant Corrections doesn't understand the context in which a word, phrase, or symbol is used. It may change an entry that you want to be untouched. Be sure to reread your pages to ensure nothing gets automatically changed that shouldn't be. For example, sometimes you may enter **(C)** and don't want it changed to the copyright symbol. In these cases, press the undo button on the Lotus Symphony Presentations toolbar until the original entry returns.

To set up Instant Corrections, choose Tools⇨Instant Corrections. The Instant Corrections dialog box appears. (See Figure 13-15.) The dialog box includes four tabs, as explained below:

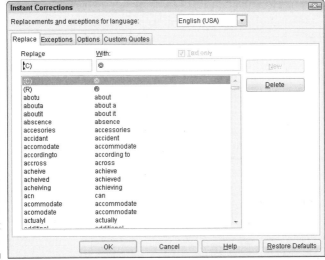

Figure 13-15:
Instant
Corrections
auto-
matically
replaces
commonly
misspelled
words with
their correct
spellings.

✔ **Replace:** Use this tab to set up new words, symbols, or phrases you want monitored by Instant Corrections. You type the entry into the Replace field and then enter the replacement word or phrase in the With field. Click the New button to add it to the list. You also can delete a combination by selecting it and then clicking Delete. Click the Restore Defaults to return the list to its original settings.

✔ **Exceptions:** Use this tab to set up exception rules for Instant Corrections. For example, if you want abbreviations or words to remain unchanged (such as abbreviations that use two initial capital letters), specify them on this tab.

✔ **Options:** Use this tab to set the Instant Corrections options, such as correcting two initial caps (two uppercase letters), using the Replace tab settings, and more.

✔ **Custom Quotes:** Use this tab to set how quotation marks are modified by Instant Corrections. By default, quotation marks are changed to use a more stylized font than just straight up and down. Sometimes this can pose problems for different programs, especially, if you plan to export the presentation and import it into another program.

Choose OK to save any settings.

Adding Tables to Pages

Tables enable you to set up text and other objects in cells to help you display information in a structured way. Lotus Symphony Presentations includes a table creation tool, editor, and drawer to help you insert and modify tables in your presentations. The following sections describe how to work with tables in your pages.

Inserting a table

When you create a table, you need to specify the number of rows and columns to include in the table. Rows appear horizontally in a table, and columns appear vertically. The intersection of rows and columns makes up cells in which objects — text, graphics, and hyperlinks — are inserted.

When you create a new page and select the Title, Table page, Lotus Symphony Presentations displays a page like the one shown in Figure 13-16. To create your table here, double-click inside the table area to display the Create Table dialog box. You can then complete Steps 2-5 in the list that follows to create your table.

To insert a table on your page, follow these steps:

1. **Open a presentation and create a new page.**

   You can insert tables on any page, so you can create any type of page for the sample.

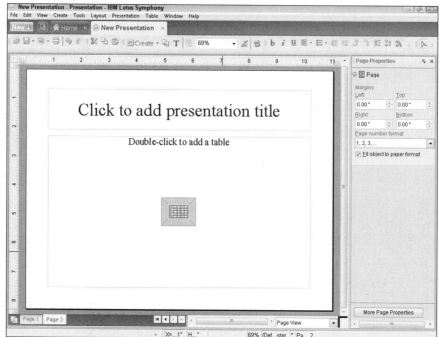

Figure 13-16:
The Title, Table page that includes a control for launching the Create Table dialog box.

2. **Choose Table⇨Create Table.**

   The Create Table dialog box appears.

3. **Enter the number of rows in the Rows field.**

   I use five rows in my example.

4. **Enter the number of columns in the Columns field.**

   I use three columns in my example.

5. **Click OK.**

   A new table appears in the current page.

To add text to a cell, click inside and begin typing. You also can click inside a cell and choose Create⇨Graphic from File to insert a graphic into a cell. As you add content to the cells, they grow vertically (downward) to accommodate the content.

Another way to create a table involves using the Freehand table tool. Choose Table⇨Freehand Table. This turns the mouse pointer into a pen pointer. Click and draw a rectangle the size of the table you want to include. Then use the pen to draw vertical and horizontal lines with the table borders to create the rows and columns. When finished, click outside the table to turn the mouse pointer back into the normal pointer setting. You then can add content, modify the table, move the table, and change cell properties.

Modifying a table

Once you get a table inserted into your page, you may want to modify its properties. The Table menu includes a number of commands to let you change table settings. Table 13-2 describes each command.

Table 13-2   Lotus Symphony Presentations Table Commands

Command	Description
Freehand Table	Enables you to draw a new table by freehand, or modify an existing one. You can, for instance, use this command to draw new columns or rows in an existing table.
Erase Table	Enables you to erase a table or part of a table.
Create Table	Create a new table.
Insert Rows Before	Enables you to insert a new row above the currently selected row.

(continued)

Table 13-2 *(continued)*

Command	Description
Insert Rows After	Enables you to insert a new row below the currently selected row.
Insert Columns Before	Enables you to insert a new column to the left of the currently selected column.
Insert Columns After	Enables you to insert a new column to the right of the currently selected column.
Delete Selected Rows	Enables you to remove a row you have selected.
Delete Selected Columns	Enables you to remove a column you have selected.
Merge Cells	Enables you to combine cells that you have selected.
Split Cell Horizontally	Enables you to divide a selected cell into two rows.
Split Cell Vertically	Enables you to divide a selected cell into two columns.
Select	Provides commands for selecting columns, rows, and the entire table when your cursor resides inside a cell.
Properties	Displays the Table Properties dialog box. (See Figure 13-17.)

The Table Properties dialog box includes several commands for fine-tuning the look of your overall table, including the borders, backgrounds, and text alignment. For example, to set a background for a cell, do the following:

1. **Click inside a cell.**
2. **Choose Table⇨Table Properties.**
3. **Click the Background tab.**
4. **Select a Color from the color box.**
5. **Select Cell from the For Selected drop-down list.**
6. **Click OK.**

The selected color appears as the background of the selected cell.

Another common modification you may want to do includes changing row or column sizes. To do this with the mouse, click the border that you want to move and drag it to the right or left (for a column), or up or down (for a row).

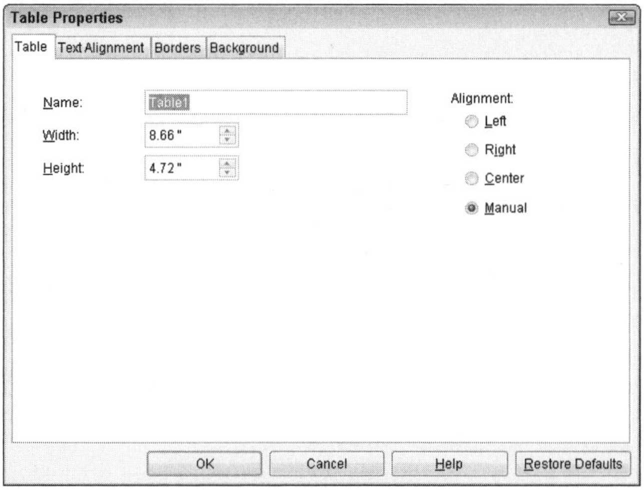

Figure 13-17:
The Table
Properties
dialog box.

Moving a table

To move a table from one page to another, select the entire table. Do this by clicking inside the table. The table becomes active and a selection box surrounds the table. Click the selection box. Small green selection handles appear, indicating that the table is selected.

Another way to select a table uses the Table menu. Click inside the table. Choose Table⇨Select⇨Table. The entire table becomes selected.

Choose Edit⇨Cut to cut the table from this page and to place it into the Windows Clipboard area. Switch to another page and choose Edit⇨Paste to insert the table.

You may need to move the table on the page by grabbing the selection box around the table and dragging the table to its new location on the page.

Saving Your Presentation

After you work on your presentation and get a page started, you may want to take a few moments to save it. You should also get in the habit of saving any time you think of it or whenever you make a number of changes to your presentation. When you save the presentation, you place a file of it on your hard drive or similar device (such as a shared network drive or flash media device).

To save your presentation, do the following:

1. **Choose File⇨Save.**

   The Save As dialog box appears.

2. **Type a filename in the File Name box.**

3. **Select a drive and folder location.**

4. **Choose Save.**

   The presentation file saves to the location specified. Also notice that the name of the file shows up on the Presentation tab.

To close your presentation, save it and then choose File⇨Close. This closes your presentation, but it keeps Lotus Symphony open. The Home tab appears. To exit from Lotus Symphony, choose File⇨Exit.

Chapter 14

Modifying a Presentation

· ·

In This Chapter

▶ Selecting page orientation and layout

▶ Adjusting page margins and changing backgrounds

▶ Moving and removing pages

▶ Creating a consistent look and feel with Master Page designs

· ·

*T*here will come a time when even the best of presentations will need a little (or a lot) of work. You might, for instance, need to change the page margins of your presentation to take into account a new screen ratio or printer size. You may also want to use a different page format — portrait instead of landscape — for your pages.

Reordering the pages in your presentation is another common page modification task. After you get all of your information in your presentation, for example, you may decide that page four belongs later in the presentation. No problem. Lotus Symphony Presentations lets you quickly reorganize your pages to your liking.

Finally, you can alter the Master Pages. Master Pages provide the basic look-and-feel for all your pages in a presentation. A Master Page can have boilerplate information that you want displayed on all pages, such as page numbers, dates, background images, and the like.

In Chapter 13, you see how to create a new presentation, add pages, navigate pages, and modify some of your presentation properties. This chapter discusses modifying page layout properties, page order, and the Master Page design.

Working with Page Properties

With Lotus Symphony Presentations, you can change the content of the information you display on a page. You also can change the page layout, margins, background, and format for your pages. The following sections discuss these points.

Changing page orientation and format

By default, presentations use a standard page format size for each slide show page of $8\frac{1}{2}$ by 11 inches. This also happens to be a standard-size sheet of printer or copier paper. Presentations also have a page orientation of Landscape, which reverses the dimensions, displaying the page wider than taller. With Lotus Symphony Presentations, you can change the orientation and format of your presentation.

If you plan to show your slide show on a standard digital projector and screen, be sure to test your presentation to ensure that any page format changes you make display properly. Sometimes, projectors can show only pages or slides created in the standard $8\frac{1}{2}$-by-11 format or similar ratio.

Lotus Symphony Presentations includes a number of different sizes from which you can choose, including the following:

- ✔ Letter
- ✔ Legal
- ✔ User
- ✔ DL
- ✔ Page
- ✔ Screen

With the User format, you can define the page dimensions you need for the page layout. For example, if you have a custom-size screen or other output (such as for a small mobile device) you can adjust the height and width settings to the desired sizes.

To change page format settings for a presentation, do the following:

1. **Open a presentation.**

2. **Choose File⇨Page Setup.**

   The Page Properties dialog box appears. (See Figure 14-1.)

   You also can right-click a page and choose Page Properties to display the Page Properties dialog box.

3. **Click the Page tab.**

4. **Choose Portrait or Landscape.**

   The default setting is Landscape.

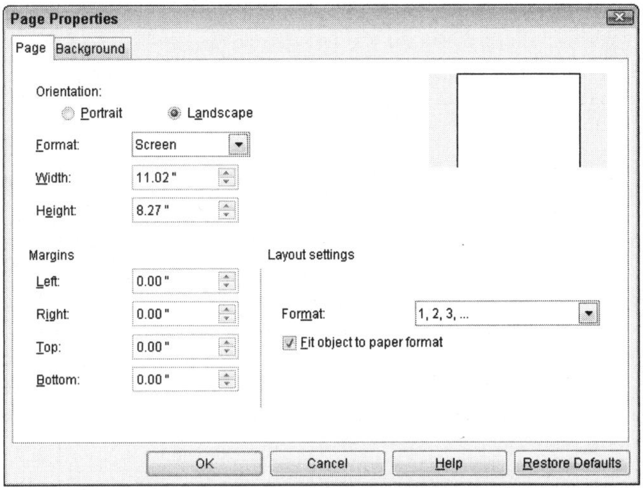

Page Properties

Page | Background

Orientation:
○ Portrait   ● Landscape

Format: Screen ▾

Width: 11.02 "

Height: 8.27 "

Margins

Left: 0.00 "

Right: 0.00 "

Top: 0.00 "

Bottom: 0.00 "

Layout settings

Format: 1, 2, 3, ... ▾

☑ Fit object to paper format

OK   Cancel   Help   Restore Defaults

Figure 14-1:
You can modify the page layout of your presentations.

5. **From the Format drop-down list, select a different page layout, such as Page.**

   Notice how the small sample screen on the top right of the Page tab changes to display a sample view of the new page layout. If you choose the User option, continue to Step 6. Otherwise, skip to Step 8 to continue.

6. **Change the Width setting to match how wide you want the pages to be.**

7. **Change the Height setting to match how tall you want the pages to be.**

8. **Click OK.**

   The new page format and orientation settings take effect for the current presentation.

Some of the page format settings define margins that are outside the margins set by your default printer. For example, a standard printer usually uses an 8$\frac{1}{2}$-by-11-inch sheet of paper. The margin is usually half an inch around the entire page (top, bottom, and two sides) for word processing documents, but it can extend to the edge for presentation pages you show on-screen. (If you print the pages, you may have different margin settings built-in to your specific printer.) When you select an option from the Layout drop-down list that changes the paper size to be larger than your standard printer settings, you're presented with a warning that the margins for the chosen format are outside the print range. Click Yes to continue or No to close the warning box and return to the Page tab to make another choice.

A number of other page layout options are available, including A0, A1, B4, and so on. You can see the dimensions for each of these options when you select them on the Page Layout tab. Look in the Width and Height fields for these dimensions.

You can look at how your final page will appear on-screen or on a projector by choosing File⇨Print Preview. Or set the zoom setting to Entire Page by choosing View⇨Zoom, selecting Entire Page, and clicking OK.

Using a different page layout

With the Page Layout properties, Lotus Symphony Presentations enables you to change the numbering format for your pages, as well as set an option for resizing *drawing objects* on your pages.

Drawing objects include the objects you can create using the Drawing toolbar options. For example, you can use 3D Quickshape to create three-dimensional cubes, cones, and other objects. You learn more about drawing objects in Chapter 15.

On the Page tab of the Page Properties dialog box, you can select choices from within the Format drop-down list below the Layout settings area. This list includes settings for changing the numbering format your pages use to creating numbered lists. By default, Lotus Symphony Presentations uses a format for 1., 2., 3., and so on.

Another page layout setting you can make includes setting whether drawing objects adjust to the size of the paper you choose. The Format setting you set in the "Changing Page Orientation and Format" section earlier specifies the paper size. The Fit Object to Paper Format option resizes any drawing objects to fit the paper you select.

Select the Fit Object to Paper Format check box on the Page tab of the Page Properties dialog box to set this option. By default, Lotus Symphony Presentations turns it on.

Modifying page margins

Page margins specify how far from the edge of the paper text and other objects can start to appear. For most presentations, the margins can be set all the way to the edges of the page. Lotus Symphony Presentations enables you to do this because most presentations display on-screen or via a digital projector. There are no margin restrictions like there are for printing documents to a printer.

With that being said, there are some times when you want to set up presentation pages so that margins are set. To set margins, you use the Page tab of the Page Properties dialog box. Use the following steps:

1. **Open a presentation.**

2. **Choose File➪Page Setup.**

   The Page Properties dialog box appears (refer to Figure 14-1).

3. **Under Margins, set the Left, Right, Top, and Bottom settings to 0.50 inches.**

   The small preview window on the Page tab shows an example of how the new margins will look in comparison to the page edges.

4. **Click OK.**

   A ¹/₂-inch margin appears around the edge of the page. (See Figure 14-2.)

To set a margin for every presentation, modify the Master Page design to include the margin setting you desire. The section "Working with Master Page Designs" discusses how to modify the Master Page.

Selecting a page background

By default, Lotus Symphony Presentations includes pages that have a plain white background. You can change a page to include a background color, design, graphic, or cross-hatching. You also can specify that a background be used for the entire slide show, not just one page of it.

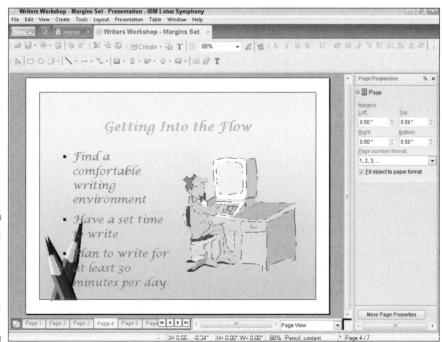

Figure 14-2:
A margin around a presentation page appears as white.

You can also edit Master Pages to include background colors. You can find out more about this in the "Working with Master Page Designs" section later in this chapter.

To change a page's background, do the following:

1. **Open a presentation.**

2. **Choose Layout⇨Background Fill.**

   The Background Fill dialog box appears. (See Figure 14-3.) It includes the following tabs:

   - *Background:* Enables you to specify what type of background you want to use: Color, Gradient, Hatching, or Bitmap. The following four tabs let you specify options for the choice you make.

   - *Colors:* Enables you to set a color for your background. You can select a color from the Color table area or choose a color name from the Color drop-down list.

   - *Gradients:* Enables you to set a gradient color scheme for your background. *Gradients* are just what the name implies — colors that change from one color to another in degrees of gradation.

   - *Hatching:* Enables you to set hatching schemes for your backgrounds. Hatchings are shadings comprising parallel lines or crossing lines (like a cross-hatch design).

   - *Bitmaps:* Enables you to specify a graphic file that you select from a list or import from your system. You also can create a bitmap of your own using the Pattern Editor on the Bitmaps tab. Use the background and foreground color pallets to draw a bitmap, click Add, and enter a new name for the design.

Figure 14-3: The Background Fill dialog box provides several tabs for setting up page backgrounds.

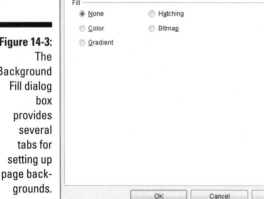

3. **Click the Bitmaps tab.**

   In this example, I use a bitmap image to set as the background.

4. **Choose an image in the image list.**

   For my example, I chose the Wall image.

5. **Click OK.**

   The Page Settings window appears, asking if you want to set the image for all pages in your presentation.

6. **Click Yes.**

   The image appears as the background fill on your pages. (See Figure 14-4.)

Keep in mind your background color when you add text and graphics to your pages. If you set your background to a dark color, use a contrasting color for your text font, such as white, yellow, or light blue. Conversely, use darker font colors for text added to light backgrounds. Also, use graphics that include contrasting or complementing colors. A dark graphic on a black or dark-blue background may be difficult to see.

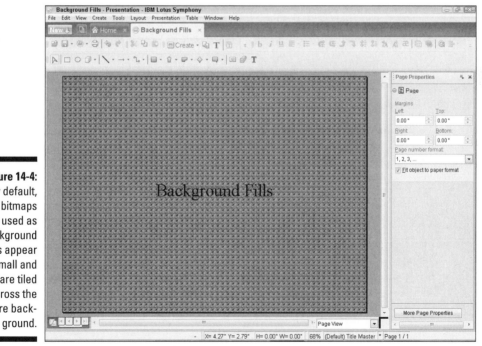

Figure 14-4:
By default, bitmaps used as background fills appear small and are tiled across the entire background.

Creating your own background schemes

On the Colors, Gradients, Hatching, and Bitmaps tabs of the Background Fill dialog box, you can create your own background schemes. To do this, click the Edit button, select the color you want as a background, click OK, enter a new name in the Name field, and click Add. That name appears in the list of choices on the tab on which you created the background scheme. Later if you want to remove that scheme, select it and then choose Delete. Click Yes to confirm the deletion.

Changing Page Order

If you need to reorder your presentation, Lotus Symphony Presentations provides a few different ways to accomplish this task. You can, for instance, use the Page Sorter view to see a thumbnail of your pages and drag pages to different places in the presentation.

There are two quick ways to move pages around in your presentations. The first uses the Page tabs at the bottom of the page window. To do this, follow these steps:

1. **Display a presentation that has multiple pages.**

2. **Click a tab at the bottom of the page window.**

3. **Drag the tab to another place in the order of the pages.**

   As you drag the page, a small set of arrows appears, letting you see where in the order of pages your page will appear. When you drop it on top of a another page's tab, the page you're moving moves to the left of the page you drop it on.

4. **Release the mouse button.**

   Lotus Symphony Presentations moves the page to the new position.

Although the previous method is quick, you may need to see a page's content to know which page you should move or what the page order should be. You can use the Slide Sorter view for this reason. Choose View➪Page➪Page Sorter View. The Page Sorter view appears. (As shown in Figure 14-5.) You now can see a small version of each page in your presentation. These small versions are called *thumbnails*.

To move a page, grab it and drag and drop it to another place in the presentation. When you select a page, a black border appears around that page (refer to Figure 14-5) indicating that it's selected. As soon as you drag and then drop the page, Lotus Symphony Presentations rearranges the pages so that no gaps are left where the page you moved originally was positioned.

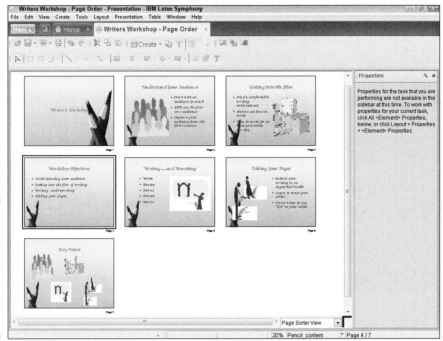

Figure 14-5:
The Slide
Sorter View
provides
you with a
thumbnail
view of your
pages.

You can quickly see the full-size version of a page by double-clicking it in Slide Sorter view. Lotus Symphony Presentations changes to regular Page view, with the selected page displayed.

Removing a Page

You may want to remove a page from your presentation at some point. To do this, you can delete it. To delete a page, do one of the following:

✔ Display the page you want to delete. Choose Edit➪Delete Page. A message appears, asking if you're sure you want to delete the page. Click Yes.

✔ Right-click a page's tab. Choose Delete Page. A message appears, asking if you're sure you want to delete the page. Click Yes.

✔ In Page Sorter View (refer to Figure 14-4), select the page you want to delete and press Delete. A confirmation message appears. Click Yes.

After you delete a page, you can undo the deletion by choosing Edit➪Undo. However, for those times you need to delete a large quantity of pages, you may want to first choose File➪Save As and create a copy of the current presentation by entering a new file name for the file. Then if, after you make a hefty amount of changes you decide you want a particular page back, you can copy and paste that page from your duplicate (and original) file.

Working with Master Page Designs

Each page in Lotus Symphony Presentations uses a Master Page design to define the text formatting style for the text elements on that page. The **Master Page** controls the following:

- Background design
- Title style
- Outline style

Viewing the Master Page design

You can use the Master Page design set by the Instant Layout pages, create your own Master Page, or modify a Master Page. You may want to do this if you want to incorporate your company's or organization's logo or color-scheme into the background. You may also want to have a different title style for your pages.

To see a page's Master Page, open the page and choose View⇨Master⇨Page Master View. (See Figure 14-6.)

Modifying the Master Page design

Lotus Symphony Presentations enables you to modify the design of a Master Page. You might, for instance, want to change the footer to include page numbers, dates, and other information.

When you modify a Master Page, you may want to save the file to a different name first. This way, you retain the original formatting if you ever want to return to it. To save it as a different file, choose File⇨Save As. Enter a new file-name and click Save.

To modify a Master Page, do the following:

1. **Open a presentation that includes three or more pages.**
2. **Select a page other than the first page.**

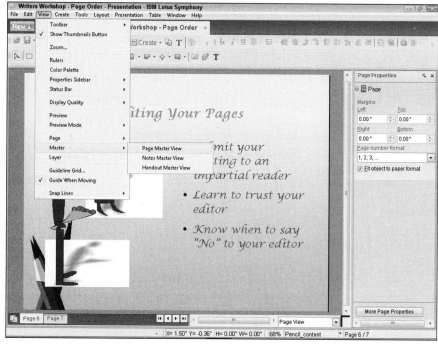

Figure 14-6:
Use the
Page
Master
View
command
to open
a page's
master
page
design.

3. Choose View⇨Master⇨Page Master View.

The Master Page view for the page appears. Any changes you make to this Master Page affects all the pages other than the first page (if that first page is a Title Only page). Also, in some cases, such as when your page doesn't include objects (graphics, headers, or footers), the page may not look any different than it does when you have the Master Page view turned off. In Figure 14-7, you can see outlines for the footer information, as well as the graphics in the upper corners of the page.

4. Modify the Master Page.

For my example, I change the footer information and the background color.

5. Add a new text box at the bottom of the page in the footer area.

You can cover the middle number field with the text box. The number field will not show in the page view.

6. Type Presentation By: *Your Name* **in the text box of the footer and select the appropriate font size.**

My footer says *Presentation By: Rob Tidrow,* and I selected font size 12 to fit the text box.

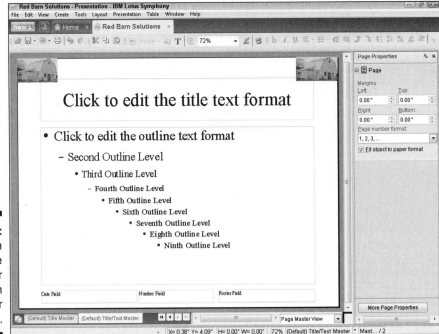

Figure 14-7:
You can
modify the
Master
Page design
of your
pages.

7. **Right-click the page and choose Page Properties.**

   The Page Properties dialog box appears.

8. **Click the Background tab.**

9. **Select the Color radio button.**

10. **Click a color in the color grid.**

11. **Click OK.**

    The background color changes.

The Master Page controls how each subsequent page looks. Changes you make to the first page, however, change only the look of Title Only pages. This is because you may not want some information to appear on the Title page (the opening page) of your presentation. For example, most title pages don't have page numbers showing. Also, you may want to include your name or company logo on the bulk of your pages, but your opening page could have a larger image of the logo.

When you finish working on the Master Page, choose View⇨Page⇨Page View to return to the normal view. From here, you can see the types of changes that you've made to your Master Page.

Creating a new Master Page design

You can create new Master Pages using the Create Master Page tool. You can use this tool when you're viewing a page in the Page Master view.

To use this tool, do the following:

1. **Choose View⇨Master⇨Page Master View.**

   The Master Page view appears.

2. **Choose Create⇨New Master Page.**

   The Create Master Page dialog box appears.

3. **Enter a new name in the Master Page Name field.**

4. **Select the type of Master Page layout from the Layout drop-down list.**

5. **Click OK.**

   A new Master Page appears, based on the type of layout you chose in Step 4.

6. **Modify the Master Page design as necessary.**

7. **Save the new design.**

To create a copy of a Master Page, open that page in Page Master view and choose Create⇨Duplicate Master Page. Lotus Symphony Presentations creates a duplicate of the Master Page.

Chapter 15

Making Presentations Picture-Perfect

In This Chapter

▶ Knowing when to use graphics

▶ Inserting, moving, and resizing graphics

▶ Using the Eyedropper tool to swap colors

▶ Creating and working with drawing objects

One reason presentations are so powerful and appealing is because viewers relate to the graphical nature of presentations. Most good presentations incorporate pictures, animations, and other eye-candy for the audience to view. As you've probably already noticed, Lotus Symphony Presentations enables you to create graphical and entertaining slide shows.

In this chapter, you find out about inserting, moving, and manipulating graphics, using the eyedropper to change colors in a graphic, and adding and modifying drawing objects.

Working with Graphics in Your Presentations

Graphics can provide information in presentations that straight text sometimes can't provide. For example, a flow chart that illustrates a process can be much more effective and informative than a paragraph of text. You can also use graphics to break up a page, making it easier to read. Figures 15-1 and 15-2 illustrate this point. In the first figure, the page includes only text, while the second one includes a graphic. Which one would you rather look at during a day-long seminar?

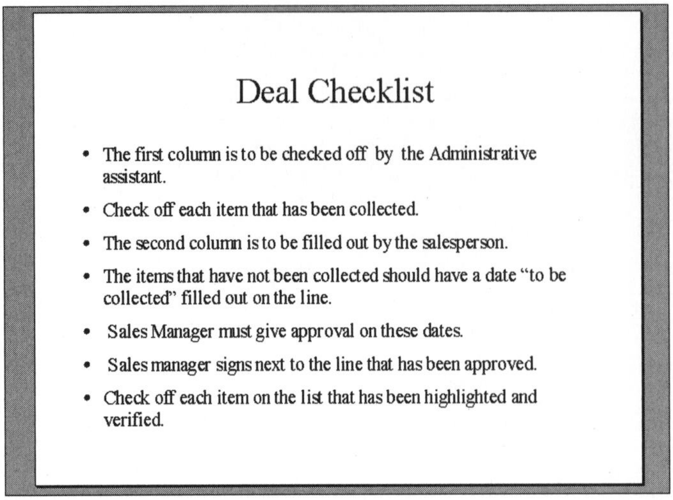

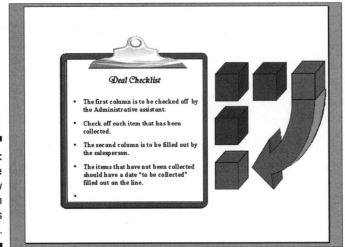

Figure 15-1:
Showing a
slide show
page using
no graphics.

Figure 15-2:
The same
slide show
page with
graphics
added.

Understanding when to use graphics

With presentations, you don't want to go overboard on using graphics. Too
many graphics in a slide show can be just as bad as a presentation devoid of
any illustrations. The following are some guidelines on using graphics in your
presentations:

✔ **Create a theme.** Find a type of graphic that you like and use similar ones
throughout the presentation.

✔ **Use graphics sparingly.** If you find that your page includes more graphics than text, look for ways to trim out some graphics.

✔ **Add graphics-only pages for long presentations.** For presentations that are lengthy and require you and the audience to take a break, add a graphic on a page where the break should occur. This provides a reminder to you to take a break and allows your audience a little breather as well.

✔ **Use company or industry logos.** For presentations relating to your company or an industry, look for photos, clip art, and other graphics that relate to these areas.

If you need a source of graphics for your presentations, don't forget to look inside your own company, school, church, volunteer organization, or similar place. For example, if you volunteer time for a youth organization, ask the organization's management team or board if they can provide you with a set of images they use for their literature and marketing pieces. There are also online places to download graphics, such as Clipart.com (at `www.clipart.com`) and Barry's Clip Art (at `www.barrysclipart.com`). Some companies and organizations require employees and volunteers to use company-approved graphics in all of their public presentations. Some companies like to tie in presentations and other documents with the company Web site, as well.

Inserting a graphic on a page

When you find a page on which to insert a graphic, and in some cases this could be every page, you need to create the graphic on the page. To insert a graphic, use the following steps:

Lotus Symphony Presentations uses the term *create* when you insert a graphic. Don't let this throw you. You don't have to actually create the image file as you go to insert it into your presentation.

1. **Open a presentation.**

2. **Switch to the page on which you want to insert the graphic.**

3. **Choose Create⇨Graphic from File.**

   The Create Graphics dialog box appears, as shown in Figure 15-3.

4. **Locate a folder that includes graphics.**

5. **Select a graphic.**

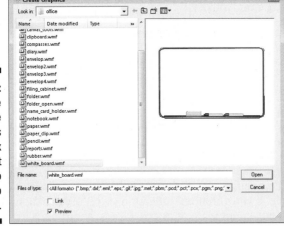

Figure 15-3:
Use the
Create
Graphics
dialog box
to select
graphics to
insert into
your pages.

6. **Click the Preview option.**

   A preview of the graphic appears on the right side of the Create Graphics dialog box.

7. **Click Open.**

   The graphic displays on the selected page.

When you create a new page using a Master Page with the Clipart object, you can double-click the graphics box that reads Double-Click to add graphics to display the Create Graphics dialog box.

You can move, resize, and perform minor modifications on the graphic once you have it in your presentation. You learn about these features in the following sections.

Moving a graphic

After you insert a graphic on your pages, you may want to move it to a different location on the page. To do this, select the graphic and drag it to a new location.

When you move a graphic, you may inadvertently place it on top of another object on the page. Or you may want to achieve an effect like the one shown with the text on the clipboard image shown in Figure 15-2. To determine which object displays on top of another one, use the Arrange tool. To use the

Arrange tool, right-click a graphic or other object and choose Arrange. The following options are available:

- ✔ **Bring to Front:** Displays the selected item on top of any other objects in the stack of objects.

- ✔ **Bring Forward:** Moves the object up one layer in the stack of objects. For example, if you have three objects on top of each other and you Bring Forward the bottom object, it appears as the second object in the stack.

- ✔ **Send Backward:** Moves the object down one layer in the stack of objects.

- ✔ **Send to Back:** Moves the object to the bottom of the stack of objects.

- ✔ **In Front of Object:** Moves the object to the top of the stack.

- ✔ **Behind Object:** Moves the object behind the object below it.

Resizing a graphic

When you select a graphic, handles appear around the graphic, which enable you to resize it.

To resize a graphic, select it and then grab one of its resizing handles. Drag the handle to enlarge or shrink the object. Release when you get the size you desire.

By dragging an image's corner handles, you can enlarge or shrink the image while maintaining its original aspect ratio. That means that if you have an image that's 6 inches by 4 inches and you shrink it by half, the final size is 3 inches by 2 inches. Some images can appear distorted if you don't maintain their aspect ratios.

Removing a graphic

When you no longer need a graphic that you've inserted into your presentation, you can remove it. When you remove the graphic from a page, you're removing it only from this page. You aren't removing it from another page or presentation, nor are you deleting the graphic file from your system.

To remove a graphic, select it on your page and press Delete. Lotus Symphony Presentations removes the graphic from the page.

Sometimes, you may accidentally delete the wrong graphic when you have several layered on each other. To ensure you get the right graphic to delete, you may want to split apart your stack of objects. What I do is grab the top-most object and move it to another place on the page. I do this until I find the object I want to delete and then delete it. You can right-click the top object, if it isn't the one you want to delete, and choose Arrange⇨Send to Back.

Locating new graphics

You may want to find your own graphics to use in Lotus Symphony Presentations. There are a number of different software packages and Web sites that provide image files for you to use in your presentations. The following lists some places you may want to check out:

Clipart.Com at www.clipart.com

ClipartConnection.com at www.clipartconnection.com

Stock Art at www.stockart.com

Vintage Stock Art at www.vintagestockart.com

Be aware of copyright issues with graphics. Some image software and Web site services include proper usage instructions and licensing information that you should read before using graphics in Lotus Symphony Presentations. Some companies, for example, specify that their copyright logo remains on the image if you use it in a presentation.

Also, look on the IBM Lotus Symphony Web site (click the site address on the Home tab of Lotus Symphony) for clip art and other images that you can download to use with your presentations and other files.

Working with the Eyedropper

Lotus Symphony Presentations includes the Eyedropper tool for modifying the color of the graphics you insert into your pages. The Eyedropper lets you select a color on an image and then replace that color with another one. For example, you may want to insert an image, but it has the wrong color scheme for your presentation. Or you may want to change the color to match your company's or organization's colors. You can do that by using the Eyedropper (as long as the image isn't too complex).

The Eyedropper works best on graphics that have distinct areas of color. That is, the graphic should be not so complex (*simple* might be the best term) and have areas of color that are distinct from one another, such as separated by black borders or outlines. For high-end graphics retouching, the Eyedropper may not satisfy you. Look for stand-alone programs such as Adobe Photoshop and Corel Draw for high-end features.

To use the Eyedropper, do the following:

1. **Display a presentation page with a graphic you want to modify.**

2. **Choose Tools⇨Eyedropper.**

    The Eyedropper dialog box appears. (See Figure 15-4.)

Figure 15-4:
Use the
Eyedropper
to change
colors in
your
graphics.

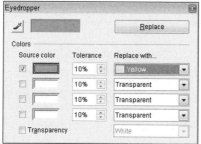

3. **Move the Eyedropper dialog box to the side so you can see your graphic.**

4. **Click the Eyedropper button on the Eyedropper dialog box.**

    This activates the eyedropper so you can pick an image's color that you want to change.

5. **Click a color in the graphic that you want to change.**

    In my example, I change the blue of the book cover to yellow. I click the blue portion, and that color appears in the top box of the Source Color list.

6. **Select a new color from the Replace With drop-down list.**

7. **Click Replace.**

    The Eyedropper tool replaces the old color with the new one.

8. **Click the close button to close the Eyedropper dialog box.**

When you have the Eyedropper dialog box open, you can select up to four different colors to modify. To select additional colors to change, click the check box next to a Source Color box. Then use the Eyedropper to select a color in the graphic.

Creating Drawing Objects

Lotus Symphony Presentations enables you to create drawing objects in your pages. This includes lines, circles, basic shapes, and so forth. You can access the drawing objects from the Drawing toolbar. Table 15-1 lists the types of objects you can create in your presentations.

If you don't see the Drawing toolbar on your screen, turn it on. Do this by choosing View⇨Toolbar⇨Drawing.

Table 15-1	Lotus Symphony Presentations Drawing Objects
Object	*Description*
Rectangle Quickshape	Draws a perfect rectangle on your page.
Ellipse Quickshape	Draws a perfect ellipse on your page.
3D Quickshape	Draws various shapes in three dimensions, such as a pyramid, torus, and half sphere.
Lines	Draws various lines and connected lines, such as polygon shapes, freeforms, and curves.
Arrows	Draws various arrows on your pages, such as double-sided arrows and arrows that start with circles.
Connectors	Draws connectors you can use to connect two shapes together or when using the Flow Chart objects.
Basic Shapes	Draws shapes, such as trapezoids, rounded rectangles, and cubes.
Block Arrows	Draws block arrows, such as chevron, notched arrow to the right, and circular.
Flow Charts	Draws standard flow chart symbols, such as process, magnetic disc, and symbols.
Stars and Symbols	Draws stars, symbols, brackets, scrolls, and more.
Callouts	Draws callouts you can insert text in, such as oval callout and rectangular callout.
Fontwork	Enables you to add graphical text using the Fontwork tool.
Extrusion	Enables you to change the geometry and area of your inserted drawing objects.

To add a drawing object to a page, do the following:

1. **Open a page where you want to draw the object.**

2. **Click a drawing object icon on the Drawing toolbar.**

   The mouse pointer changes to a plus sign, indicating that you are in drawing mode.

3. **Hold down the left mouse button and drag to draw the object on your page.**

   A wire mesh (an outline of the object) view appears, showing the size of the object. (See Figure 15-5.)

4. **Release the mouse button when the object reaches the size you want.**

   Lotus Symphony Presentations draws the object on the page.

You can resize a drawing object by clicking it and grabbing the resizing handles. Move the mouse to enlarge or shrink the object. You also can rotate the object by grabbing the resizing handles located on the corners of the object and moving the mouse. It will rotate the object.

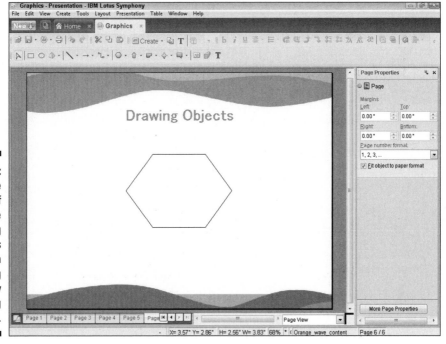

Figure 15-5:
A wire mesh of the drawing object aids you in creating new drawing objects.

Chapter 16

Animating for a Purpose

. . . .

In This Chapter

▶ Considering the guidelines for cool and practical animations

▶ Moving from page to page in style

▶ Building and modifying an animation

. . . .

After you add content to your presentations, you may want to take some time to add some special effects to your pages. Lotus Symphony Presentations enables you to add animations, page transitions, and image animation settings to your presentations.

You can use page transitions to automatically play back your slide show or provide different effects when you manually change pages. For example, you can use a fade transition when moving from one page to the next. You also can set animation effects on individual objects in your pages. For example, you may want a series of graphics to display one at a time during a slide show.

This chapter looks at Lotus Symphony Presentations animations features, using page transitions in your presentations, and using image animations on your pages.

Understanding Lotus Symphony Presentations Animations

Animations can help add a professional touch to your presentation if you employ them correctly. You can add transitions between all of your slide show pages, put in animations for each object in your page, or have transitions only on selected pages.

You also can create animated GIF images to use in your presentations. These images let you apply animation features to a group of GIF images, creating a video of sorts.

Before you start creating animations for your presentations, read the following general rules for using animations:

- ✔ **Don't overuse animations.** Every page doesn't need a five-second transition to the next page. After a few pages, your audience will grow tired of them. After a few more pages, your audience may grumble. And finally, they may become so annoyed that they dread your next transition and become interested in something else — such as the copy of the newspaper they picked up in the lobby.

- ✔ **Practice your presentations in real time.** When you rehearse your presentations, do it in real time. That is, don't skip over parts thinking "Okay, this is the part where the really cool animations come in." Watch and time those animations in rehearsal to ensure that they work correctly and that they aren't too long.

- ✔ **Ensure your computer has enough power for the animations.** When presentations get lengthy and have a large number of graphics and other objects, the file size can get rather large. When you add page transitions and other animations, you may find that the computer you use to play back the slide show may not be powerful enough. Don't wait until you're on stage to figure out this embarrassing situation. Take the time to practice the slide show on the computer you plan to use for the slide show.

Using Page Transitions

A page transition applies a special effect to a page as you display that page. The effects include:

- ✔ Cross-fading
- ✔ Fly In
- ✔ Uncover
- ✔ Fade
- ✔ Open/Close
- ✔ Wavy Line
- ✔ Spiral
- ✔ Roll
- ✔ Build Up
- ✔ Other

Each of these transitions includes several options from which you can choose. For example, if you choose Other, you can choose from the following options:

- ✔ Vertical Lines
- ✔ Horizontal Lines
- ✔ Vertical Checkerboard
- ✔ Horizontal Checkerboard
- ✔ Dissolve
- ✔ Automatic (random)

The following sections describe how to add, modify, and remove transitions.

Adding transitions

Probably the best way to understand how transitions work is by adding them to a presentation you've created. The following steps show how to add them:

1. **Open a presentation that includes several pages.**

2. **Choose Presentation⇨Page Transition.**

   The Page Transition dialog box appears. (See Figure 16-1.)

3. **Choose a transition from the Effect drop-down list.**

   My example uses the Fly In effect.

4. **Choose an option from the Option drop-down list.**

   My example uses the Fly In from Top Left option.

5. **Choose a setting for how fast the transition should work from the Speed drop-down list.**

   My example uses the Medium setting.

Figure 16-1: Use the Page Transition dialog box to set up transitions between pages.

6. Choose the Manual option.

This enables you to advance each page manually by pressing Enter or clicking the mouse button.

7. Click the Apply to All button.

This applies the same transition to every page.

8. Click the Preview button.

A small preview window appears. You can view your transition settings in this window before exiting the Page Transition dialog box.

9. Click the Play button next to the Preview button.

The preview window advances to the next page of your presentation.

10. Click Close.

The presentation window appears.

11. Choose File⇨Save to save your transition settings with your presentation.

To create a presentation that plays automatically — that is, each page advances after a specific amount of time without interaction from you — use the Automatic After setting. This is on the Page Transition dialog box. (See Figure 16-2.) Choose Automatic After and then enter a value in the time field. The example shown in Figure 16-2 has each page displaying for 25 seconds before the next appears. You can click the Apply to All button to have this setting take effect for all pages. Or if the setting should be for only the current page, click Apply. If you click Apply, you'll need to set times for all other pages in your presentation. Click Close.

Figure 16-2:
Set the Automatic After setting to use the auto-play features of Lotus Symphony Presentations.

Page Transition	
Transition Effect	
Effect:	Fly In
Option:	Fly In From Top Left
Speed	
Medium	
Page Advance	
○ Manual	
● Automatic after	00:00:25
☐ Automatically Preview	Apply Apply to All
Preview ▶	Close

You should test your animations by running the presentation in Screen Show mode. To do this, press F5 or choose Presentation⇨Play Screen Show. Use the following commands for navigating the slide show:

✔ Press Enter or click your mouse to advance to the next page.

✔ Press the Backspace key to return to the previous page.

✔ Press Esc to end the presentation and return to the Lotus Symphony Presentations main window.

To apply the same transition to multiple pages, but not to all of them, you can use this technique:

1. **Choose View⇨Page⇨Page Sorter View.**

2. **Hold down the Ctrl button and select the pages you want to add the transition to.**

   A black border appears around the selected pages.

3. **Choose Presentation⇨Page Transition.**

   The Page Transition dialog box appears.

4. **Choose the page transition settings for the selected pages.**

5. **Click the Apply button.**

   The page transition settings are applied to the currently selected pages only.

6. **Click the Close button.**

   The Page Sorter View window appears. (See Figure 16-3.) Notice that a small playback icon appears below each of the pages to which you added the transition.

You can click the playback icon below a page to see a preview of the transition.

Modifying transitions

After you build transitions into your presentation, you may want to modify them. You might, for instance, want to change the transition effect you have set for them, or change the auto-play setting to manual.

To modify transitions, do the following:

1. **Choose Presentation⇨Page Transition.**

   The Page Transition dialog box appears.

2. **Choose a different effect from the Effect drop-down list.**

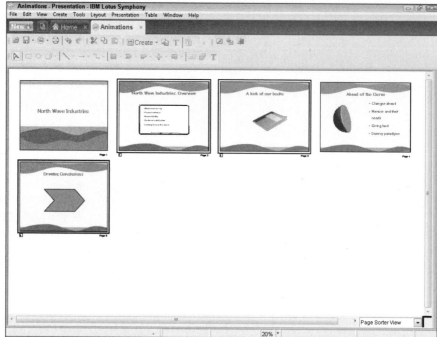

Figure 16-3:
Pages with
page
transitions
display a
playback
icon
beneath
their
thumbnail
images.

3. **Choose a different item from the Option drop-down list.**

4. **Click Apply to apply the modification to the current page only, or Apply to All to add the changes to all the pages.**

5. **Click Close.**

6. **Choose File⇨Save.**

   Lotus Symphony Presentations saves your changes to the presentation file.

 To apply the same transition to multiple pages, but not to all of them, you can use this technique. Choose View⇨Page⇨Page Sorter View. Hold down the Ctrl button on the mouse and click the pages you want to select. Now you can apply the same transition just to the pages you selected.

Removing transitions

If you no longer need page transitions, you can remove them. To do this, use the following steps:

1. **Choose Presentation⇨Page Transition.**

   The Page Transition dialog box appears.

2. **Choose No Effect from the Effect drop-down list.**

3. **Click Apply to All.**

    The page transitions are removed for each page in your presentation.

4. **Click Close.**

5. **Choose File⇨Save.**

    Lotus Symphony Presentations saves your new changes to the presentation file.

Inserting Image Animations

Image animations are custom-made animations you can create using sets of images you want to animate. Not only can you animate images, but you also can animate text and drawing objects.

Creating an image animation

You use the animation editor provided by Lotus Symphony Presentations to specify the animation settings. Each object selected in the animation is a static frame that becomes animated as all the objects are cycled through. For example, you can put together an image animation that cycles through a group of product images you insert in your pages. Or if your company has multiple divisions, you can create an image animation with each division's logo or building graphic.

You can't edit an image animation's individual frames. For that reason, make sure the objects you want to use in an animation are as error-free as possible before you begin the creation process. To modify the animation, you have to create a new animation.

To create an image animation, do the following:

1. **Open a presentation.**

2. **Display a page that includes several objects you want to use in your image animation.**

    Figure 16-4 shows a page with several objects selected that I'll use for my image animation.

3. **Select all the objects you want in your animation.**

To select all objects on a page, you can place the mouse to the top left of the group of images and drag the mouse to the bottom right. This "lassos" all the objects and displays selection handles around each of the images. Those images are now all selected.

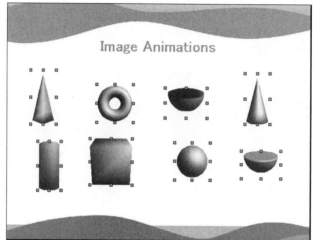

Figure 16-4:
A page with several objects for an image animation.

4. Choose Create➪Image Animation.

The Animation dialog box appears. See Figure 16-5.

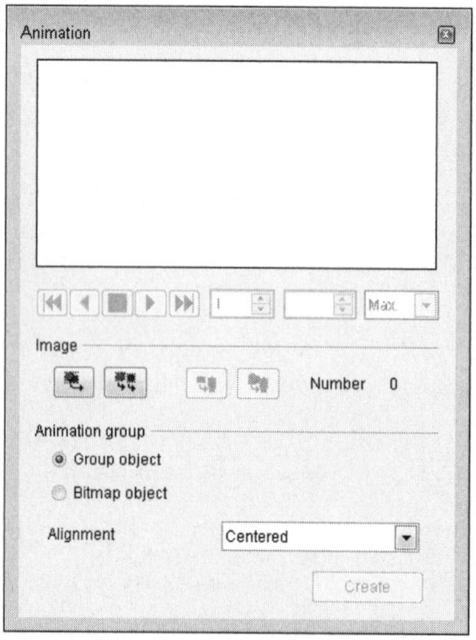

Figure 16-5:
The Image Animation dialog box.

5. **Click the Apply Object button, which is the first button under the Image label.**

   This adds all the selected objects to the frame window (at the top of the dialog box). The selection appears as one frame of the animation. Figure 16-6 shows how this looks.

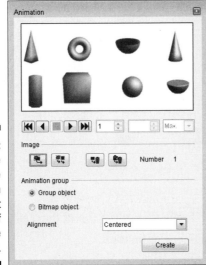

Figure 16-6:
Using the
entire
selection
as the first
frame of
the image
animation.

6. **Click the Apply Objects Individually button, which is the second button under the Image label.**

   This adds each of the selected objects as an individual frame. You can see only the last object, as shown in Figure 16-7, but the others are part of the animation as well. At this point, the animation:

   - Displays all eight of the 3D objects selected, in one frame.
   - Displays each of the 3D objects separately in its own frame.

7. **Click the Apply Object button again.**

   This adds the entire group of objects again, but this time as the final frame of the animation (10). At this point, the animation:

   - Displays all eight of the 3D objects in one frame at the beginning of the animation.
   - Displays each of the 3D objects separately in its own frame.
   - Displays all eight of the 3D objects in one frame at the end of the animation.

8. **Click Bitmap Object.**

Figure 16-7:
You can see
the layer
on which
the object
appears in
the anima-
tion by
looking in
the Image
Number
field.

9. **Click the Play button.**

The animation plays in the frame area at the top of the dialog box.

10. **Click Create to create the image animation.**

The animation appears on the current page.

11. **Click the Close button on the Animation dialog box.**

The Animation dialog box closes. Because it's difficult to discern the differences between the selected images for the animation and my new image animation, I've copied the new image animation to a blank page. It shows on Figure 16-8.

To play the animation, click off the image animation. The animation plays until you click it again.

When you play a slide show that includes an image animation on a page, use the Tab key to toggle on and off the animation. Press Tab once to turn off the animation; press Tab again to turn on the animation.

Modifying image animation objects

When you have the Animation dialog box open while creating an image, you can add new images to it by clicking the presentation page and selecting that image. After you close the Image Animation dialog box, however, you have to re-create the image animation if you decide to make changes to it.

Figure 16-8:
The new
image
animation
appears on
the current
page.

The following are some changes you might want to make:

✔ Add objects.

✔ Remove objects.

✔ Modify the object display duration.

✔ Change the number of *loops* (the number of times the animation repeats itself) the animation performs before stopping. The default is Max, which loops continuously.

✔ Change the alignment position.

To modify an image animation, do the following:

1. **Select the image animation you want to modify.**

2. **Choose Create⇨Image Animation.**

   The Animation dialog box appears..

3. **Click Apply Objects Individually.**

   This reloads the selected image animation so you can modify it.

4. **Select the objects you want to add to the image animation.**

   You may need to click the page tabs to display a different page and select the object you want to add. In my example, I want to add the book graphic to my image animation. I have to click the Page 3 tab and then select the book graphic. Figure 16-9 shows the selected book graphic behind the Animation dialog box, and then shows the Apply Object button on the Animation dialog box activated.

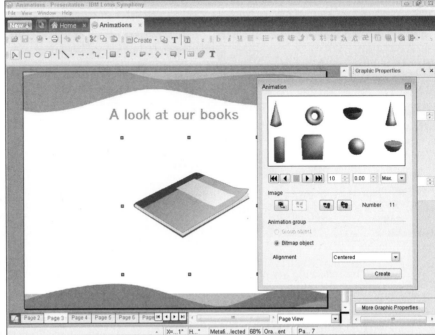

Figure 16-9:
You can
add a new
image to a
previously
created
image
animation.

5. **Click the Apply Objects button.**

   Lotus Symphony Presentations adds the newly selected object to the animation. It now becomes the last object in the loop.

6. **Click Create.**

   The animation is re-created using the object you just added.

7. **Click the Close button to close the Animation dialog box.**

The downside to re-creating the image animation is that you now have two image animations that are similar. To resolve this, display the page with the previously created animation and delete it. (See the next section.)

While you have the Animation dialog box open for your modifications, you also can remove an image from the animation. Do this by using the Image Number field and indicating the image number you want to remove. When it displays, click the Delete Current Image button. That image is removed from the image animation.

Removing image animations

When you no longer need an image animation object in your presentation, you can remove it. To remove an image animation, display the page on which the animation appears. Select the image animation, which pauses it, and then press Delete. Lotus Symphony Presentations deletes the image animation from your presentation.

Chapter 17

Creating Web Pages

. . . .

In This Chapter

▶ Styling documents for the Web

▶ Converting presentations to Web pages

▶ Using the Model Designer

▶ Publishing your Web pages to intranets or Web servers

. . . .

*I*t seems like just about everyone has her own Web site, blog, or other type of online presence. If you're one of the few left who doesn't have a Web page — or you aren't sure how to create a Web page for yourself — you should read this chapter. You find out how you can use Lotus Symphony Presentations to create and edit Web pages.

With Lotus Symphony Presentations, you can create Web pages that include text, graphics, tables, and hyperlinks. This chapter leads you through creating basic Web pages using these features. After you find out about creating and modifying Web pages, you're given some information on publishing your Web pages to a Web site or to an intranet site within your business or organization.

Lotus Symphony Presentations also includes a tool called the Model Designer. This tool enables you to work on XForms, which are XML-based Web forms that you use to collect information for applications, data repositories, and other forms. I show you some of the basics of working with Model Designer in this chapter.

Designing Documents for the Web

When you create Web pages, you save the document in a format that almost every computer can view, regardless of the type of computer or operating system. You use the HTML format to save your Web page in when you are ready to publish it to the Web. But as you create your Web pages, you save them in regular Lotus Symphony Presentations (actually the Open Document Presentation) format of `.odp`. You can use the Export feature in Lotus Symphony Presentations to export the file as an `.html` file, which prepares it for the Web.

HTML

Web pages use a coding language called the HyperText Markup Language, or HTML. The following shows an example of a line of code written in HTML:

```
<a href= http://www.wiley.
    com/WileyCDA/>Wiley</a>
```

This code tells a Web browser to display the text Wiley on the page and make it so that a user can click the text to go to the hyperlink shown in the brackets. There are many HTML codes you can add to pages. To find out more about HTML codes and how to use them, visit the W3C.org Web site at www.w3c.org/html.

Several different applications support the HTML standard for displaying documents known as Web pages. These applications include the following:

✔ Microsoft Internet Explorer

✔ Mozilla Firefox

✔ Safari (Apple only)

✔ Opera

✔ Lotus Symphony Web Processor

Figure 17-1 shows an example of a Web page you can create in Lotus Symphony Presentations. In Figure 17-2, you see how the Lotus Symphony Presentations file displays as a Web page in Microsoft Internet Explorer 7.

Figure 17-1: You can create a document that you export to a Web page in Lotus Symphony Presentations.

Figure 17-2:
The same document shown in Figure 17-1 displayed in a Web browser.

If you don't want to export your file to HTML, but you still want it published to the Web, you have a few options for doing so. The most obvious way includes saving the file as an Adobe Reader (.pdf) file. You also can save each page of your presentation as an image file in JPG format. (These are called *jpeg* files.) Most computers can read either of these file types. For reading PDF files, users can download the Adobe Reader application from www.adobe.com for free. Most Web browsers and image applications support PDF files.

When you export your Lotus Symphony Presentations presentation, Lotus Symphony saves each page of your presentation as a separate image file (in .jpg or .gif format) and then creates an HTML page that displays that page so that you can view it in a Web browser. In the section, "Converting Lotus Symphony Presentations files to Web pages," later in this chapter, you're shown how to export presentations into HTML files.

Using appropriate styles for Web pages

As you build the presentation files that you eventually want to use as a Web page, think about the features — such as the text styles — you want to appear on that page when you export it as a Web page. When you create Web pages from Lotus Symphony Presentations, you should get familiar with text styles and use them to highlight certain areas on your pages. For example, you can use the Title style to create page titles and headlines that stand out from regular body text (or Outline text in the standard Lotus Symphony Presentations template). By using the standard Lotus Symphony Presentations template, you can become familiar with the styles that look best on your exported Web pages.

To show the Style List in Lotus Symphony Presentations, choose Layout⇨Style List or press F11. Select an item on your presentation page, such as a headline or bulleted text item, and look at the style used by that item. The style shows up as highlighted in the Style List.

Figure 17-3 shows some of the standard Lotus Symphony Presentations styles you might use in presentations that you export as HTML pages.

Presentation style-Title style

Graphic style-Heading 2

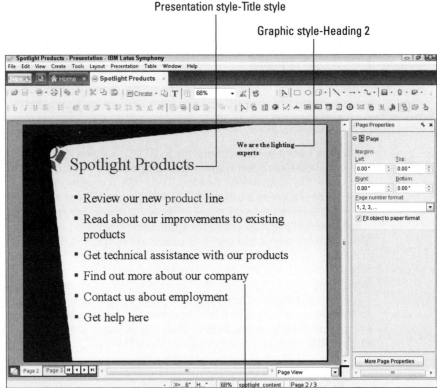

Figure 17-3:
A Lotus
Symphony
Presen-
tations page
with the
names of
styles.

Presentation styles-Outline 1

To apply a style, use the following steps:

1. **Open a presentation you want to format as a Web page.**

2. **Press F11 to open the Style List.**

3. **Select the text you want to format.**

4. **Select the style you want to use in the Style List.**

   Figure 17-4 shows selecting a new style (Heading 1) for the selected text in the table.

5. **Click Apply.**

   The selected style formats the text you selected in the presentation.

You really can't go wrong with the styles you choose when setting up presentations for exporting to HTML. Because the presentation pages become graphics files for the final Web page (in the form of .jpg or .gif format), just make sure that the styles you pick are consistent across the presentation (use the same heading style for your page titles, for instance) and that the text formats in a large enough font size to be read easily. As a general rule, text smaller than eight points can be difficult to read.

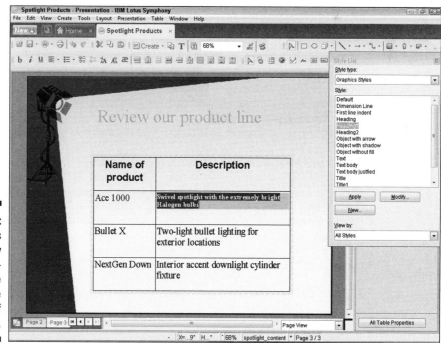

Figure 17-4:
A Lotus Symphony Presentations page with the names of styles.

Adding hyperlinks to pages

The hyperlink is probably the key feature of Web pages. Hyperlinks allow Web page authors to link one document to another document or to another place in the same document (called *bookmarks* or *targets*). Web page readers then use the hyperlinks to navigate to those documents or targets.

Hyperlinks use the form http://*site_address.site_domain*. For example, the hyperlink for the Wiley Products Web site is `http://www.wiley.com/WileyCDA/`. When you create hyperlinks in your presentation files, ensure you have the correct Web site addresses (also called *URLs*) or the links won't work properly. A good way to ensure you have the correct address is to navigate to that site using a Web browser, select the entire address in the Address bar of the browser (such as in Microsoft Internet Explorer), press Ctrl+C to copy the address to the Windows Clipboard, and then paste the address using Ctrl+V. You'll paste the address into the Target box as instructed in Step 4 of the steps that appear later in this section.

In general, Web browsers display hyperlinks as blue underlined text. With Lotus Symphony Presentations, you can add hyperlinks to your pages in two formats:

- ✔ **Text:** Displays in blue text without any underlining or other special formatting.
- ✔ **Button:** Displays a hyperlink button you can move around on the page to allow users to click on for the hyperlinked resource.

Hyperlinks in Lotus Symphony Presentations pages work a little differently than standard Web page documents you can create with other HTML editors (such as Microsoft Expressions or Adobe Creative Suite 3). When you export a Lotus Symphony Presentations file to HTML, the pages become image files. Everything on a page becomes part of the image — text, graphics, headings, tables, and hyperlinks. The hyperlink on the image isn't live; that is, you can't click it to navigate to that link. Instead, when you set up your hyperlink, you specify a Frame setting (such as _parent) which instructs Lotus Symphony Presentations to add that hyperlink to a text version of the content of the page that appears inside a text-only frame of your Web page. Read "Converting Lotus Symphony Presentations files to Web pages," later in this chapter, for more information.

To add a hyperlink to a page in Lotus Symphony Presentations, do the following:

1. **Open the presentation page on which you want to add a hyperlink.**

2. **Highlight the word or phrase you want to use as the hyperlink text.**

3. **Choose Create⇨Hyperlink.**

   The Hyperlink dialog box (see Figure 17-5) appears.

Figure 17-5:
Use the
Hyperlink
dialog
box to set
hyperlink
properties.

[Hyperlink dialog box showing:
Internet / Document tabs on left
Hyperlink type — Internet selected
Target: http://www.wiley.com/WileyCDA/
Further settings
Frame: _blank   Form: Text
Text: Bullet X
Name:
Description:
Remove Link   Apply   Close   Help   Back]

4. **Enter the address of the link in the Target box.**

5. **Select a Web page frame in which you want the link to appear using the Frame drop-down list.**

6. **Select Text from the Form drop-down list.**

7. **Click Apply to create the link.**

8. **Click Close.**

   The Hyperlink dialog box closes and the text you selected in Step 2 shows as a hyperlink.

You can test the hyperlink while viewing the Lotus Symphony Presentations page. To do this, make sure you have a connection to the Internet. Next, click the hyperlinked item on the page. Lotus Symphony opens the Web Browser tab and displays the page in the browser window. If the address is wrong, a different page appears or you get an error message stating that the page cannot be displayed.

Creating tables for Web pages

Many standard Web pages use tables to help align information on the page. Unlike true Web pages that are designed in HTML code, your Lotus Symphony Presentations files can be designed using standard Presentations objects and layout tools (including tables) to place text and other objects precisely where you want them. You don't have to use tables to get items arranged properly. The final presentation page, when exported as a Web page, will be a graphics file. You can, however, use tables in your Lotus Symphony Presentations files (see Figure 17-6) to help align information for your Web pages. You can read about adding tables to your pages in Chapter 13.

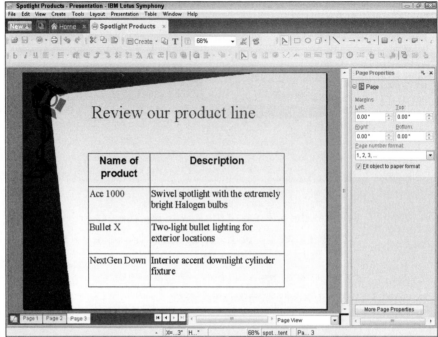

Adding graphics for Web pages

Graphics add a special touch to any Web page. You probably should consider adding them to your Lotus Symphony Presentations files that eventually are exported as Web pages. For example, you can add your company
logo as a graphic, insert pictures of your family, or provide snapshots of
products and similar images. To learn more about adding graphics to your
Lotus Symphony Presentations files, read Chapter 15.

Saving files for the Web

After you finish your presentation and before you export your presentation
as an HTML file (see the next section), first save your file as a normal Open
Document Presentation (.odp) file. This enables you to modify your presentation later if

- ✔ You don't like the way the exported Web page looks
- ✔ You discover an error on one of the pages
- ✔ You find out that a hyperlink on the pages needs to change
- ✔ You want to remove a page from the Web page

You can remove a page from the finished Web page by using other Web-page authoring tools, such as Microsoft Expressions or Windows Notepad, without bringing up the presentation again in Lotus Symphony Presentations. However, you'll need to learn some basic HTML coding. So until you get familiar with HTML codes, you may find it easier and less time consuming to make the edits to the original Presentations file and then re-export the file as HTML.

To save your presentation file to Open Document Presentation format, choose File➪Save, enter a name in the Save As dialog box, and click Save.

Converting Lotus Symphony Presentations files to Web pages

When you're ready to save your Lotus Symphony Presentations files as Web pages, you use the Export to HTML tool. This tool provides different options for the final page so that it's ready for Web publishing.

The following steps show how to use Export to HTML, but Table 17-1 describes each of the options you can choose during the process.

Table 17-1	Export to HTML Settings
Option	*Description*
Publication Type	Specifies HTML as the export file format.
Standard HTML Format	Exports the files using standard HTML formatting tags and specifications.
Standard HTML with Frames	Exports the files using standard HTML formatting tags and specifications with frames. The Web page that you're exporting becomes the page that displays as the main frame page. Lotus Symphony Presentations adds a frame page to the left side of the frame that displays a table of contents of your document.
Automatic	Exports the HTML page as an HTML presentation that automatically displays each page in a timed format.
Create Title Page	Exports a title page for your document.
Show Notes	Creates HTML pages of your presentation notes.
Monitor Resolution	Specifies the resolution of your new Web page, including Low, Medium, or High.

(continued)

Table 17-1 *(continued)*

Option	Description
Save Graphic As	Specifies if the pages in your Web pages are to be saved as JPEG or GIF format.
Quality	Specifies a value (you can use between 1 and 100) of the quality for the new Web page.
Restore Defaults	Sets the HTML Export dialog box settings to their defaults.

1. **Open a document you want to save as a Web page.**

2. **Choose File➪Export.**

   The Export dialog box appears. (See Figure 17-7.)

3. **Choose Hypertext Markup Language (HTML) from the File Format drop-down list.**

4. **Type a name for your new Web pages.**

   By default, Lotus Symphony Presentations uses the filename you used when you saved the file as an Open Document Presentations file. However, you should remove any spaces from the name. This makes the Web page adhere to normal HTML naming conventions.

   To make finding your exported pages easier later, you should create new folders in which to place each exported presentation. During the export process, each of your presentation pages creates several pages, so a three-page presentation will create more than 20 new files.

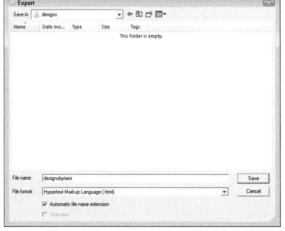

Figure 17-7:
The Export dialog box provides an option for saving your presentations as HTML files.

5. Click Save.

The HTML Export dialog box appears, as shown in Figure 17-8. Table 17-1 describes the options available on this dialog box. For now, keep the default settings. You can repeat Steps 1–5 later and choose different options for your Web pages, if you want to discover how each option changes the final version of your Web page.

6. Click Save.

Lotus Symphony exports your presentation as an exported HTML file.

When the export process finishes, you're returned to the Lotus Symphony Presentations window. You can now view your exported Web page.

I've been calling the exported presentation a *Web page*. In reality, as you read in the previous Tip, the export process actually creates a number of different Web pages. Sometimes Lotus Symphony uses the term *publication* to refer to this set of pages created.

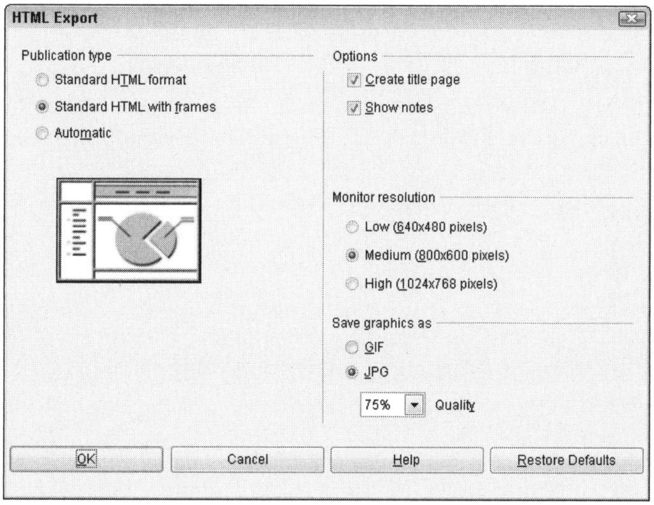

Figure 17-8:
The HTML Export dialog box provides several options for exporting your Web pages.

> **HTML Export**
>
> Publication type
> ○ Standard HTML format
> ● Standard HTML with frames
> ○ Automatic
>
> Options
> ☑ Create title page
> ☑ Show notes
>
> Monitor resolution
> ○ Low (640x480 pixels)
> ● Medium (800x600 pixels)
> ○ High (1024x768 pixels)
>
> Save graphics as
> ○ GIF
> ● JPG
> 75% ▼ Quality
>
> OK   Cancel   Help   Restore Defaults

Displaying your Web pages

After you export your presentation as an HTML file, you can display the Web pages in a Web browser. To do this, you must find the main HTML file that you saved to your disk during the export process. This file uses the name you put in the File Name field of the Export dialog box. (Refer to Figure 17-7.) In my example, I named it designsbytami. After the export, the filename becomes designsbytami.html and appears with the other files for that exported presentation.

Many files are created during the export process for a short three-page presentation. To display your presentation as a Web page (or a publication), double-click the main HTML page. In my case, I double-click the designs bytami.html file.

Figure 17-9 shows the beginning page of the Web publication.

Click the Click Here to Start link to begin navigating. Each part of the publication appears in frames. (See Figure 17-10.) A table of contents that lists each page appears on the left side of the window. Each presentation page (slide) appears in the middle frame on the right under the top navigation links. Since I selected the option for showing notes, those would appear (if I added them to my presentation) in the lower-right frame.

Click the With Contents link to display text from each page underneath its heading name in the table of contents frame on the left. Figure 17-11 shows how the text from the middle page appears. Click the Without Contents link to collapse the content under the table of contents pages.

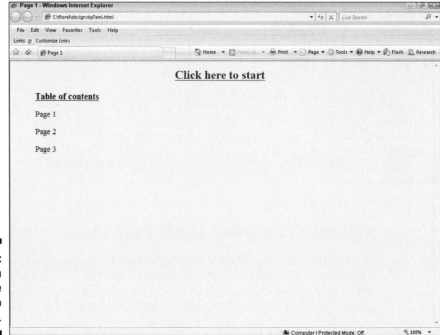

Figure 17-9:
The main page of the new Web publication.

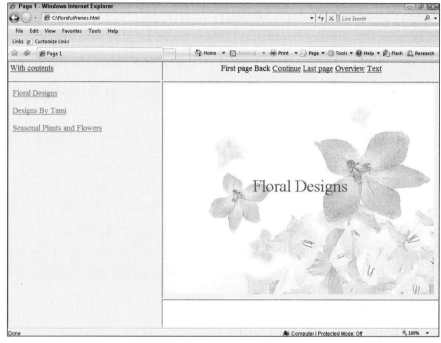

Figure 17-10:
Display
the frame
structure by
clicking the
Click Here
to Start link.

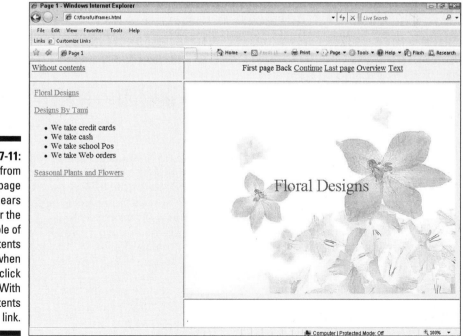

Figure 17-11:
Text from
each page
appears
under the
table of
contents
when
you click
the With
Contents
link.

To navigate through each page, use the links along the top of the page or click the page name in the table of contents frame. For example, you can click the Designs By Tami link on the left frame to display its page.

The Text link in the top-right frame displays on the text and notes of each page. For example, when I click the Text link, the first page of the publication appears. This page has only a title and no notes. To see the graphics again, click the Graphics link.

Use the following links for additional navigation:

- **First Page** displays the publication's first page.
- **Back** displays the previously displayed page.
- **Continue** displays the next page in the publication.
- **Last Page** displays the final page of the publication.
- **Overview** displays the table of contents of the publication.
- **Text/Graphics** displays only text for each page or the graphics for each page.

Publishing Your Web Pages

After you export your Lotus Symphony Presentations file to HTML, you can publish the files to the Web or intranet location. When you do this, you make the pages available to other users who have access to the Web or your intranet.

Publishing your Web pages to an intranet site

Many companies and organizations set up internal sites (also called *intranets*) on their networks for employees and authorized customers to connect to via the Internet. These internal sites provide access to Web resources, local area network files, and similar content. In some companies, employees are allowed to publish personal, departmental, or project Web pages for internal users to access. For your exported Lotus Symphony Presentations files, you can publish them to intranet sites for training, documentation, or information purposes.

When you publish the exported Web pages, be sure to copy all the files in the publication set over to the intranet folder area.

Ask your network administrator where you should copy the files for your publication. Each organization and network setup is different. Also, you probably will be required to enter a username and password to gain access to your network before you can copy your files to it.

In addition to copying the pages, make sure you have a link to the main page of the publication. In my example, I would add a link on my company's home page to the `designbytami.html` file. This way, users can click that link to get to my publication. Without that link, no one would be able to find my pages.

Publishing your Web pages to a Web server

Publishing the exported Web pages to a Web server includes the same concerns covered in the preceding section. In fact, when you publish pages to an intranet, you're essentially publishing them to a Web server. (Or you're posting the pages for someone else to physically move them to a Web server.)

A *Web server* is a computer (or multiple computers) that runs a special type of software (Web server software) for hosting Web pages and managing users who connect to those pages. Examples of Web server software include Microsoft Internet Information Services (IIS), Apache, and Google GWS.

If you don't have an Internet Web server to which to publish your pages, you can set one up or acquire access to a server to post your Web pages. If you decide to set up your own Web server, you're looking at a lot of cost and time to manage the server.

Most users just starting out will, on the other hand, use Web server services. These are called *Web hosting services.* Some Web hosting services provide some hosting for free (usually by requiring ads to appear on your pages), while others are strictly fee-based.

The following list names a few of these types of services:

- ✔ AccuWeb Hosting at `www.findmyhosting.com/gohost.asp?host=6748&plan=21653`

- ✔ ANR Host at `www.findmyhosting.com/gohost.asp?host=8099&plan=24790`

- ✔ Quality Host Online at `www.findmyhosting.com/gohost.asp?host=5393&plan=22344`

- ✔ 1&1 Internet at `www.1and1.com`

Chapter 18

Presenting a Screen Show

. . . .

In This Chapter

▶ Finalizing your presentation

▶ Coordinating the presentation with your speech

▶ Presenting and navigating a slide show

. . . .

*F*inally, the day comes when you have to show your presentation to the rest of the world. Or at least to a small group of your friends or colleagues. When your Lotus Symphony Presentations screen show is ready, use this chapter to help guide you into preparing for the show as well as figuring out what you should do during the presentation.

Some of the best screen shows can be ruined by minor problems that creep up when you least expect them to — during the actual presentation. Minimize problems by preparing for them and eliminating as many potential problems before you get on stage. For example, you may prefer to run your screen show as an automated presentation. (Pages display automatically after a predetermined amount of time.) If so, take the time to practice your full presentation, including all of your talking points, to ensure that your timing for each page is exact. You don't want your timing off so much that you're stuck waiting for a page to display — or speeding up your talking points to catch up to pages that are displaying too quickly.

Preparing Your Show for Presentation

Your show is finished. All the pages are set up the way you like them. You've added graphics, but not so many of them that they distract viewers from your main points. And you have the smoothest transitions between slides that you've ever seen.

What are you waiting for then? On with the show!

Before you press F9 to start the show, take a few moments to go over some of the following final touches to your presentation.

- ✔ Proofread your pages.
- ✔ Establish overall timings of your show.
- ✔ Establish pacing between pages.
- ✔ See where you may need accompanying notes.

Let's look at ways to prepare your show for a presentation in front of an audience.

Putting the final wraps on a show

How do you know when your presentation is finished? I can't tell you that definitively, but I can offer some things to look for when your presentation might be ready for an audience.

- ✔ You have at least one page completed. A blank show is about as entertaining as it sounds.
- ✔ You run out of things to say.
- ✔ You have enough pages to fill the allotted time. This may be as good a reason as any other to stop work on your show.
- ✔ Your planned topic is sufficiently covered for your planned audience and the presentation fits within the allotted time frame.

The last item is probably the most correct choice. Only you will know when your presentation is really finished.

Knowing what things to look for when finished

The bottom line to any presentation is how well your message is received by your audience. To achieve this end, your presentation should look polished and be as error-free as possible.

Here's a list of things to do every time you finish a presentation and before you hit the Play Screen Show command. If you do everything on this list, you can be sure your presentation will be as polished and error-free as you can make it:

✔ **Run the spell check.** Do this each time you modify a presentation, regardless of how small the changes are. You don't know how many times little errors creep into your pages, in particular those where a letter is inadvertently deleted from a word adjacent to the word or phrase you're editing.

✔ **Remove blank pages.** It's easy to add new pages to your presentations — so easy that you may accidentally insert two pages when you want only one. Use the Page Sorter View (choose View⇨Page⇨Page Sorter View) to look for any blank pages that have crept into your presentation. Figure 18-1 shows a presentation in Page Sorter view, providing you with a quick view of any blank pages.

✔ **Check footers for proper information.** Make sure the page footer includes the information you want your audience to see on each page. Examples of good footers include page numbers, your Web site address, the name of the presentation, or your company's logo.

✔ **Make hard copies for the audience.** After your presentation is finished, create handouts for the audience using the Handouts option on the Print Options dialog box, which is shown in Figure 18-2. To do this, choose File⇨Print⇨Option. Click the Handouts option and then click OK. Click OK to start the print feature.

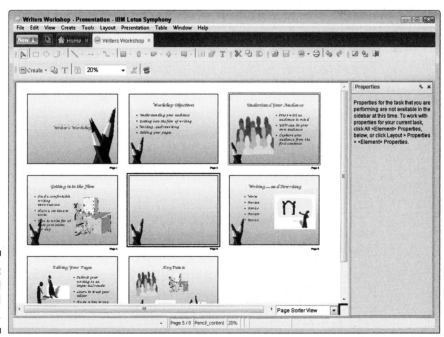

Figure 18-1:
Remove all unwanted blank pages.

✔ **Check for text flowing off the page.** When a text box includes too much information, the extra text flows off the bottom of the page. That text doesn't appear on your page when you play your screen show. Examine each page in Page view, looking for text boxes that fall below the page. Resize the text box, reduce the amount of text in the box, or move some of the text to another slide to fix the problem.

✔ **Ensure objects don't hide other objects.** Often a graphic, text box, or chart lies on top of another object, obscuring the view of that object. Look at each page carefully and resize, move, or delete any objects that are causing problems like this.

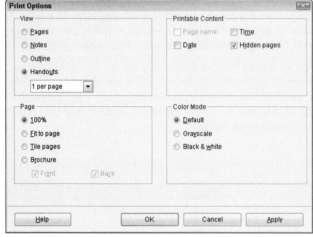

Figure 18-2: Create handouts of your presentation using the Handouts print option.

Not only do you have to double-check your pages for problems prior to beginning your presentation, but you also should check the hardware resources you plan to use. You don't want to spend countless hours preparing a presentation only to have a hardware glitch ruin the big show. Prepare for possible catastrophes by knowing what hardware you need for the presentation, where you need to show the presentation, and how you copy your presentation file to the presentation computer.

You may want to arrive at the presentation venue early to check and set up your presentation. The hardware resources to check include the following:

✔ **Computer:** In many cases, you need a computer on which to store your presentation and then direct it to a projector for display. Some projectors have built-in flash memory areas on which you can store your presentation. Traditionally, though, most presentation environments use a computer linked to a projector. If this is the case for your presentation, ensure the computer works, has a copy of IBM Lotus Symphony installed, and can communicate with the projector.

✔ **Projector and screen:** Digital projectors take input from a computer, media card, or wireless connection and display your presentation on a large screen or wall. Depending on the venue where you plan to show your presentation (a conference room, meeting room, or other place), you may or may not need to provide the projector. Check to ensure the projector has the following: proper VGA cables for connecting the projector to the computer, remote control device (if applicable for that projector), power cord, and working head lamp (the bulb that shines your pages on the screen). Also, know how to lower the screen if it's not already lowered.

✔ **Storage:** Prior to leaving for the presentation venue, you may want to create multiple copies of your presentation. This way, if one copy of the presentation becomes corrupted or lost, you can revert to a duplicate copy. Also, copying the presentation to a flash drive and rewriteable CD or DVD disc ensures you have your presentation on different media types. This is in case the presentation computer has only one way to copy the presentation onto the system. Don't assume that all computers have USB ports or CD/DVD drives, or that you'll have permission to access these drives.

✔ **Light switch locations:** Know where light switches for the venue are located and how they work. Are the lights timed? Do you need a key to turn off the lights? Get these answers prior to starting your show. You don't want to be stuck showing your presentation in a bright room.

If you plan to use a laptop for the presentation, charge the battery before the presentation or connect the AC adapter to a wall outlet. Presentations can last awhile, so don't get caught with a dead or dying battery during your presentation.

Rehearsing Your Timings

IBM Lotus Symphony allows you to rehearse timings for presentations you play back automatically. This enables you to set the amount of time a page displays before it automatically changes to the next page. This is handy if you want your presentation to flow from one page to the next without any interaction from you.

The rehearse timings feature also provides a tool for practicing your presentation. If you plan to advance pages manually during your presentation but you'd like to know how long you spend on each page as well as how much time your entire show lasts, turn on the rehearse timings feature, practice your presentation, and record your timings. Timings for each page appear in the Object Bar the next time you preview your presentation in the Page Sorter view.

REMEMBER

You don't have to use the rehearse timings feature if you don't plan to play back your show using the automatic play back feature.

To rehearse page timings, perform the following steps:

1. **Open the presentation in Lotus Symphony.**

2. **Choose View⇨Page⇨Page Sorter View.**

   Figure 18-3 shows the presentation in Page Sorter view.

3. **Click the Rehearse Timings button from the Context Sensitive toolbar.**

   Figure 18-4 shows the screen show starting with the Rehearse timer in the upper-left corner of the screen.

4. **Rehearse what you plan to say for the first page.**

   Don't be shy here. Say the words out loud in the tone and speed you plan to use during the presentation.

5. **Click the mouse button once.**

   The next page displays. Rehearse what you plan to say for this page.

6. **Continue rehearsing through the entire show.**

   When you reach the last page and click the mouse button, the show stops and returns to the Page Sorter view window.

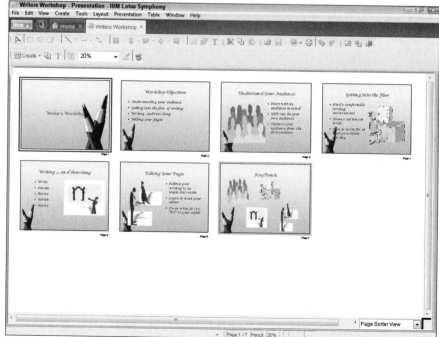

Figure 18-3:
Use the Rehearse Timings toolbar from the Page Sorter view.

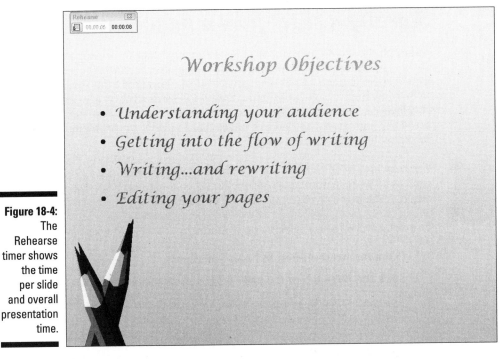

Figure 18-4:
The
Rehearse
timer shows
the time
per slide
and overall
presentation
time.

You can view the timings for each page by looking in the Object Bar. This
tells the amount of time you plan to spend on each slide.

When you plan to do a presentation in which you advance each page manually, you may want to write the timings for each page onto the Notes view of
the page. You then can print the Note for each page for reference during your
presentation.

Playing a Screen Show

After you have your presentation ready, you can play it back. Lotus
Symphony provides you with a couple of different ways to start your presentation. You can choose to show it from the beginning of the show or launch it
from a specific page. The following sections describe the two methods.

In addition, while showing a presentation, you have a few options to play
around with. For example, you can zoom into a page while showing it or use
the pen to mark up a page during a presentation.

Finally, when you finish the presentation you need a way to end it. I show you
how to do that in the "Ending a Show" section.

Starting a show from a page

Although the most common, or at least the most *logical,* way to start a screen show is to launch it from the beginning page, you can start a screen show from a specific page within your presentation. You might, for example, need to preview how a page looks in its completed form while you're editing it. Displaying it in slide view gives you that answer, but you may not want to scroll through an entire range of pages just to see it. No problem. Just play the show from the current page.

You may also need to jump out of a show while you're giving a presentation, such as to work in another program. You then can jump back into the presentation at the point at which you left off by using the method shown here.

To start a show from a specific page, perform the following steps:

1. **Open the presentation in Lotus Symphony.**

2. **Click the page tab of the page from which you want to start the show.**

    Figure 18-5 shows a page selected in the Lotus Symphony Presentations editor.

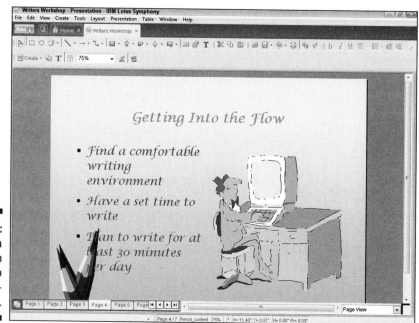

Figure 18-5:
Selecting a page from which to start a presentation.

3. **Choose Presentation➪Play from Current Page.**

   The screen show starts, with the current page showing. Figure 18-6 shows the selected page as the starting point for showing the screen show.

4. **Click the left mouse button to advance to the next page.**

   You also can press the Enter key on the keyboard to go to the next page.

Another way to start a presentation from the current page is to press the Shift+F5 shortcut key.

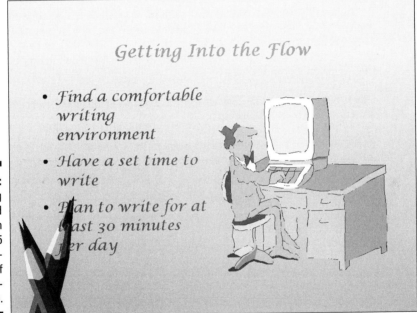

Figure 18-6: Showing the selected page from Figure 18-5 as the starting point of the presentation.

Getting Into the Flow

- *Find a comfortable writing environment*
- *Have a set time to write*
- *Plan to write for at least 30 minutes per day*

Starting a show from the start

After you finish working on your screen show, you're ready to show it as a presentation. The most logical way to do this is to start from the first page and progress one page at a time until you come to the last page; then you end it.

The following shows how to start a show from the first page:

1. **Open the presentation in Lotus Symphony.**

2. **Choose Presentation⇨Play Screen Show.**

Figure 18-7 shows a presentation starting from the first page.

Zooming while you give a show

Let's say a page in your presentation has information that displays smaller on-screen than what you'd like. Some charts, lists, graphics, and small details fall into this category. If this happens in your presentations, you can resize the information using Lotus Symphony editing tasks from Chapters 14 and 15.

But let's say you don't realize how difficult it really is to see something in your presentation until you're playing back your show, or you just can't make the item larger without jeopardizing the intent of the page or reworking your entire presentation. If you find yourself in these situations, simply use the Presentation Zoom feature.

The Presentation Zoom feature enables you to enlarge the current page while your screen show is running.

Zooming doesn't affect the actual page or its content. Instead, it applies a magnifying glass effect so your page appears larger on the projector screen.

Writer's Workshop

Figure 18-7:
Starting a presentation from the first page.

To use the Presentation Zoom feature, do the following:

1. **Open the presentation in Lotus Symphony.**

2. **Choose Presentation⇨Play Screen Show to start the presentation.**

3. **Click the left mouse button to advance to a page you want to zoom on.**

4. **Press the plus sign (+) on the numeric keypad.**

   The screen show page enlarges.

5. **Press the minus sign (–) on the numeric keypad to zoom out.**

6. **Press the multiplication sign (*) on the numeric keypad to return the page to its original size.**

Ending a show

As you give a show, you'll run into two times when you may need to stop a show. The most common — and obvious — time is when you advance to the end of the last page and naturally need to end the show. The other time is when you're in the show on a page other than the last one. For example, you may be on page 3 of a 15-page show and decide to end the show.

Lotus Presentations provides a quick way to end a show. The following shows how:

1. **Open the presentation in Lotus Symphony.**

2. **Choose Presentation⇨Play Screen Show to start the presentation.**

3. **Press Esc to end the show.**

   The presentation ends and you return to the Lotus Symphony editing window.

Navigating During a Presentation

The whole purpose of creating a Lotus Symphony Presentations slide show is to present it to some form of audience. The audience may be a live audience in an auditorium, board room, training environment, or high school gymnasium. Your audience could also be one that is virtual — that is, one that you don't necessarily present to in a face-to-face setting. Rather, it could be across a Web environment, saved to a user's desktop and played back during a time convenient for that user, or a help desk presentation used for helping users understand a difficult technical experience.

During the presentation, you (or anyone else running the slide show, for that matter) need to know how to navigate the show. The following sections discuss the different ways to get from page to page during a presentation.

Moving around with the mouse

The most common way to navigate during a presentation is with the mouse. It provides a quick way to go from one page to the next, while also enabling you the capabilities to back up to a previous page, write or draw free-hand on a page, or point to an on-screen item.

Table 18-1 shows the mouse controls you can use to navigate during a presentation.

To change the pointer from an arrow to a pen pointer, choose Presentation⇨Screen Show Settings⇨Screen Show. Select the Mouse Pointer as Pen option. Click OK.

Table 18-1	Mouse Techniques for Navigating During a Presentation
Action	*Result*
Left-click	Advances to the next page.
Right-click	Displays the previous page.
Left-click and hold	Enables you to use the pen function to write notes, underline, or perform similar free-hand actions on your page.

When you come to the end of the presentation, left-click one more time to close the presentation window and return to the editing window. This ends the presentation.

Moving around with the keyboard

If you're close enough to the computer when giving your presentation, consider using the keyboard to help navigate through the slide show. The keyboard provides additional control shortcuts that a mouse or remote control cannot provide. For example, with the keyboard, you can press the Home key to jump quickly from any page back to the first page of your presentation. Another helpful key is the Esc key. It allows you to quickly terminate the show and return to the editing window.

Table 18-2 lists the keyboard shortcuts you can use during presentations.

Table 18-2	Keyboard Shortcuts for Navigating During a Presentation
Keyboard Shortcut	*Result*
Enter	Advances to the next page.
Spacebar	Advances to the next page or next animation effect.
Right Arrow	Advances to the next page without activating an animation effect.
Page Down	Advances to the next page.
Backspace	Displays the previous page.
Page Up	Displays the previous page.
Home	Returns to the first page of the presentation.
End	Displays the last page of the presentation.
Type a number and press Enter	Displays the page number you enter.
Esc	Ends the presentation and displays the Lotus Symphony editing window.

Navigating with remote controls

A handy way to navigate during a presentation is to use a remote control device that synchronizes with a digital projector using infrared technology. The remote control allows you the flexibility of running the presentation while not standing next to the computer on which the presentation is saved. With many of these remote controls, you have different features. For example, you can advance forward in a presentation, move backward during a slide show, or stop a show. In addition, some remote controls include laser pointers that enable you to point at items on-screen from a distance. To use these remote controls, your projector must support a remote control device and you must have the ability to hook up the computer to the projector. A special cable, for example, runs from the projector to the computer to enable the remote control to function as a mouse device.

Part V
The Part of Tens

The 5th Wave   By Rich Tennant

"Needlepoint my foot! These are Documents fonts. What I can't figure out is how you got the pillow cases into your printer."

In this part . . .

From the title of this part, you probably expect something with a little bit of class and dignity. You're right.

What book in the *For Dummies* series is truly complete without The Part of Tens? Here, you'll find lots of this author's raw opinions: my best reasons for using Lotus Symphony and my top ten places to find support.

Chapter 19

Ten Reasons to Use
IBM Lotus Symphony

● ●

*I*f you read this entire book on Lotus Symphony, you have a good idea of
why you would want to use it for your primary Office suite. The following are ten reasons why I think it's a good idea to use Lotus Symphony. You
may have different reasons than I do, but I bet at least one of the reasons is
because of its price.

It's Free

What more do you want? In the time it takes you to download the program
(and yes, the time it takes is kind of long), you can get a full-fledged professional Office-type application suite, and it costs you nothing. You can even
walk away and fill up your coffee mug, talk to your cubicle neighbor, and grab
another scone while you download Lotus Symphony. Likewise, when updates
become available, IBM states that those are free as well. No long-term con-
tracts or commitments to buy anything — now or in the future.

It Includes an Easy-to-Use
Word Processor

Almost every computer user needs a word processor. With Lotus Symphony
Documents, you get a powerful, yet easy-to-use word processor to help you
create, edit, view, and print documents. You also can download templates to
help you get started creating documents, such as memos, business letters,
resumes, and similar documents.

Some of the features that make it a great word processor include

> ✔ **A table editor for creating and editing tables:** With the Freehand
> Table command, you can draw a table in your document by creating
> a rectangle of the outside border, and then drawing vertical lines for
> each column and horizontal lines for your rows.

✔ **Calculation functions:** For tables that include data on which you want to perform analytical functions, you can use the Formula Input Line to add calculations to your documents.

✔ **Instant Corrections:** Use this feature to automatically correct typos, replace words, or insert common symbols. For example, you can type (C), and Lotus Symphony changes what you typed automatically to the copyright symbol (©).

It Supports Open Source Files and a Wide Range of Others

Lotus Symphony is designed to create and support Open Document Format (ODF) files. Lotus Symphony also provides support for a number of different file formats that users encounter daily. Some of these formats may seem obscure to you, such as the Lotus WordPro (.lwp) file format. However, word processing users who have been around for awhile may remember one of the all-time great, early Windows word processors — *Ami Pro*. Lotus purchased this application, renamed it Lotus WordPro, and now Lotus Symphony Documents supports that file type.

It Supports Microsoft Office Files

In the preceding section, I mention that Lotus Symphony supports a wide range of files. The majority of users who have Office suites on their computers have Microsoft Office installed, so it's important to note that Lotus Symphony can handle the majority of files created by the Microsoft Office applications.

Lotus Symphony doesn't technically support the Microsoft Office 2007 Open XML format (for example the .docx format that Microsoft Office Word 2007 creates). You can, however, save files within Microsoft Office applications to supporting formats (such as .doc in Microsoft Office Word 2007) and then import those files into Lotus Symphony.

You Can Use It to Create Powerful Business Analysis Spreadsheets

Spreadsheets are one of the most important files found in a business. They're used for basic list making, database reporting, business analysis, and more. I even know users who like to use spreadsheets for creating memos!

Lotus Symphony Spreadsheets can do all those things — you should just use Lotus Symphony Documents to write your memos — plus other features. When analyzing business data, these features are quite helpful:

- ✔ **What-if calculations:** Create different outcomes based on input you enter in your calculations, such as loan payments based on different pay rates, periods, and interest.

- ✔ **Charts:** Provide at-a-glance summaries of data in colorful and *dynamic* (the chart changes when the data behind the chart changes) charts.

- ✔ **DataPilot tables:** A DataPilot table is the OpenOffice version of a Microsoft Excel Pivot Table. These tables permit you to manipulate data in different ways to see outputs. For example, you may have a table showing inventory of shirts sold in the U.S. market. With DataPilot tables, you can rearrange this data so that you can see other outputs, such as which region sold the most T-shirts, which region had the best-selling dress shirts, and so on.

It Provides Powerful Collaboration Features to Work in Lotus Domino Environments

Lotus Domino provides an enterprise-wide environment for multiple users to collaborate. With Lotus Symphony plug-ins, users can extend their Symphony environments to work with various Lotus Domino features. For example, plug-ins are available for letting users create and share Lotus Symphony Documents files with other users in a shared environment. These shared files can be edited by multiple users and posted on a shared network area for all users to see.

It Supports Open Document Format (ODF)

The OpenDocument Format (ODF) specification enables Lotus Symphony to provide users with applications that support many different formats for exchanging information. Businesses and organizations don't have to worry about proprietary file formats not being supported by other businesses or organizations. As long as each site uses an ODF-compliant application, the file format is readable.

It Has a Developer's Toolkit

With the Lotus Symphony Developer toolkit, users can extend the application by programming their own features and capabilities. For example, users may need additional toolbars created for specific actions they perform during their everyday business days. Or a company may want data brought in from a custom database table so users can merge that data into spreadsheets or documents. With the Lotus Symphony Developer toolkit, you can set up these types of solutions.

It Has a Built-In Web Browser

The Web Browser portion of Lotus Symphony displays many of the Web pages that Microsoft Internet Explorer (IE) 5.5 and above supports. Many users will probably continue using IE as their main Web browser, but the Lotus Symphony Web Browser is handy when you want to connect to the IBM Lotus Symphony Web pages for support, training, and updated files.

The Lotus Symphony Web Browser is handy but don't look for it to replace your other Web browsers, such as IE, Opera, or Mozilla Firefox. Why? Some reasons are that you can't save bookmarks to Web pages in a bookmarks (or Favorites) list and Lotus Symphony has limitations on its security features, such as pop-up blocking.

Despite Its Cost, It's Feature-Rich

Yes, I said it before (several times, in fact), but it's important to note that even though the price is right, so are the features you get with it. Some businesses and organizations may shy away from Lotus Symphony because it *is* free, but they shouldn't. Instead, they should at least put together a pilot team to investigate Lotus Symphony's features and conversion tools. Even if they decide in the future that Lotus Symphony isn't right for their needs, the worst that can happen is that their files will be supported by many different applications (such as OpenOffice.org), which isn't exactly a bad thing. Plus, many of those applications are free as well.

Chapter 20

Ten Places to Look for Support for Lotus Symphony

S ooner or later you'll need some help with something in Lotus Symphony. You may need help with an installation problem, help with setting up a DataPilot table in Lotus Symphony Spreadsheets, or help with how to work with animation features in a Lotus Symphony Presentations file.

Conversely, you may become experienced in certain parts of Lotus Symphony, which leads you to want to help out other users.

During these times, look at the Web sites I list here to help you better understand Lotus Symphony or to communicate help to others.

Lotus Symphony Home Page

```
http://symphony.lotus.com/software/lotus/symphony/home.jspa
```

The Lotus Symphony Home Page site is the IBM home page for Lotus Symphony on the Web. From this page, you can link to a number of different resources located on the IBM site to help you work with Lotus Symphony.

Lotus Symphony Support Forums

```
http://symphony.lotus.com/software/lotus/symphony/index.jspa?search_type=forum
```

The Support Forums page displays links to the support forum pages available for Lotus Symphony. Not only can you navigate to other pages (some are listed in the following sections), but you can also see a synopsis of the most popular topics on the site.

Lotus Symphony Forum: Have a Question

```
http://symphony.lotus.com/software/lotus/symphony/supportForum.jspa?search_
                type=forum&forumID=41
```

Have a question about Lotus Symphony? If so, hit this site, ask your question, and look for an answer. Answers are available from IBM Lotus Symphony product personnel as well as other users who post answers to common questions.

The Have a Question site also allows you to submit answers to questions. To do this, click the Reply to This Topic link on the left side of the page.

Lotus Symphony Forum: General Feedback

```
http://symphony.lotus.com/software/lotus/symphony/supportForum.jspa?search_
                type=forum&forumID=5
```

When you want to leave a message about Lotus Symphony and that message doesn't fall into the categories listed on the Support Forums page, leave it on the General Feedback site. Here you may find information about features other users are requesting, links to other support-type Web sites, and more.

Lotus Symphony Documents Forum: Issues and Troubleshooting

```
http://symphony.lotus.com/software/lotus/symphony/supportForum.jspa?search_
                type=forum&forumID=3
```

For many users, the Issue and Troubleshooting page is the *meat and potatoes* part of the Lotus Symphony Support Forum Web site. In this area, you find information on solving common and not-so-common problems with Lotus Symphony Documents. Topics include

- ✔ Problems with installation and downloading
- ✔ Issues with starting Lotus Symphony Documents
- ✔ Questions about formatting Lotus Symphony Documents

- ✔ Problems with tables
- ✔ Concerns with references and indexes in your documents

Lotus Symphony Presentations Forum: Issues and Troubleshooting

```
http://symphony.lotus.com/software/lotus/symphony/supportForum.jspa?search_
            type=forum&forumID=7
```

Here's another important site for troubleshooting problems, but this site's devoted to Lotus Symphony Presentations. Topics, such as the following are discussed:

- ✔ Concerns with converting Microsoft PowerPoint presentations into Lotus Symphony Presentations
- ✔ Questions with setting up timing and animation effects
- ✔ Problems with outputting shows to PDF format
- ✔ Questions about setting up bulleted lists in tables

Lotus Symphony Spreadsheets Forum: Issues and Troubleshooting

```
http://symphony.lotus.com/software/lotus/symphony/supportForum.jspa?search_
            type=forum&forumID=11
```

When you experience problems or have questions about Lotus Symphony Spreadsheets, visit the Lotus Symphony Spreadsheets Forum: Issues and Troubleshooting site. Here you can find out about

- ✔ Lotus Symphony Spreadsheets functions
- ✔ Chart defaults and color schemes
- ✔ DataPilot tables
- ✔ Quick Calculation problems
- ✔ Database functions

Lotus Symphony Buzz

```
http://symphony.lotus.com/software/lotus/symphony/buzz.jspa
```

For up-to-date information about Lotus Symphony, visit the Lotus Symphony Buzz site. You can find out information about updates to the software, awards that Lotus Symphony has won, and other Symphony buzz.

Lotus Symphony Help

```
http://symphony.lotus.com/software/lotus/symphony/jumpToHelp.jspa
```

The focus of the Help page is to provide you with links to pages associated with the different Lotus Symphony applications. You can find links to the following for Lotus Symphony Documents, Lotus Symphony Presentations, and Lotus Symphony Spreadsheets:

✔ **FAQs:** Frequently Asked Questions about the Lotus Symphony programs.

✔ **Demos:** Includes demonstration files for each of the Lotus Symphony applications. On the Demos for Lotus Symphony Documents, for example, you can download and view a demo for creating a table of contents.

✔ **Tutorials:** Need some step-by-step guidance about a feature? Read this book, or you can see if a tutorial for your problem exists at this site.

✔ **Technotes:** Provides technical information about the Lotus Symphony applications.

✔ **Toolbar Reference Card:** Shows a visual representation of the toolbars found on the Lotus Symphony applications and a description of each toolbar button. The card also compares the Lotus Symphony applications to the Microsoft Office applications (such as Microsoft Word).

✔ **Keyboard Reference Card:** Shows a keyboard-equivalent reference for how to transition from Microsoft Office applications (such as Microsoft Excel) to Lotus Symphony applications.

Lotus Symphony For Dummies Author Site

```
http://tidrow.bravehost.com/
```

This site is maintained by me, the author of this book. You can find information about the book, *IBM Lotus Symphony For Dummies,* as well as up-to-date information about Lotus Symphony. Be sure to visit this site and fill out my guestbook.

Part VI
Appendixes

"I wrote my entire cookbook in Lotus Symphony. The other programs I saw just didn't look fresh."

In this part . . .

Sometimes you'll see the word spelled as appendices. I find it troubling when you take a word like appendix and give it two irregular plural forms. It reminds me of the type of information I cover here, from installing Lotus Symphony, to listing Symphony functions, to finally telling you what's on the CD-ROM. Wait. That's three irregular computer subject forms.

Appendix A

Installing IBM Lotus Symphony

In This Appendix

▶ Understanding system requirements

▶ Acquiring the IBM Lotus Symphony install program

▶ Installing Lotus Symphony

*B*efore you can start using IBM Lotus Symphony, you have to install it on your local computer. Lotus Symphony runs as a single program. Lotus Symphony Documents, Lotus Symphony Spreadsheets, Lotus Symphony Presentations, and the Symphony Web Browser are all installed when you install Lotus Symphony. You don't have to worry about selecting different options to ensure each of these applications is installed. They're installed automatically for you.

Conversely, you can't pick-and-choose only the applications you want on your system. For instance, if you plan to install just the Lotus Symphony Documents portion of the suite, forget about it. It's all or nothing.

In this appendix, you find out the system requirements for installing Lotus Symphony, how to acquire Symphony, and which steps are required for installing Symphony.

Understanding System Requirements for IBM Lotus Symphony

In most cases, if your computer currently runs a suite of applications, such as a recent version of Microsoft Office (Office 2003 or Office 2007, for example), your computer will probably have the requisite hardware to install Lotus Symphony. But to be sure that your system can install and run Lotus Symphony, review the list of system requirements.

If your system doesn't meet these basic requirements, you need to upgrade it so that it meets these requirements.

✔ **Operating system:** Microsoft Windows XP or Microsoft Windows Vista. You must have Administrator rights to install software.

✔ **Memory:** 512 MB of Random Access Memory (RAM). For better results, you may want to have over 1GB of RAM on your system.

✔ **Free hard drive space:** 750 MB.

✔ **Internet Web browser:** Internet Explorer 5.5 or higher, Mozilla Firefox, or Opera. You need a Web browser to connect to and download the Lotus Symphony Installer program.

✔ **E-mail address:** Required for signing in to download Lotus Symphony Installer.

✔ **Internet connection:** A high-speed Internet connection is recommended in order to download the IBM Lotus Symphony Install program.

The Lotus Symphony install routine doesn't support systems that have the Microsoft Windows XP or Microsoft Vista 64-bit platforms running on an AMD 64 CPU.

Do you currently have Microsoft Office installed on your computer? If so, you may want to keep it on your system. You may run across some times when a document you want to open doesn't convert perfectly in Lotus Symphony. For example, some objects in Microsoft Office PowerPoint don't open flawlessly in Lotus Symphony Presentations. You may want to keep PowerPoint on your system to view and edit those presentations until you can re-create them in Lotus Symphony Presentations.

Acquiring a Copy of the IBM Lotus Symphony Install Program

You can download a copy of Lotus Symphony to install on your computer by visiting the IBM Lotus Symphony Download Web site. From this Web site, you can download the software to your computer and then run the install routine.

The install program is a single file and is approximately 190 MB. If you have a dial-up connection to the Internet, you may want to forego the download because it may take several hours to download it from that connection. Instead, you may want to ask a friend or colleague who has a high-speed connection (such as a cable or DSL connection) to download the install program for you. Your helper can then save the file to a removable media device for you to copy the file to your local computer.

To download IBM Lotus Symphony, use the following steps:

1. **Open a Web browser, such as Internet Explorer, and connect to `www.ibm.com/software/lotus/symphony`, as shown in Figure A-1.**

2. **Click the Download button.**

   The IBM Software Downloads search Web page appears, with the IBM Lotus Symphony displaying.

3. **Click the IBM Lotus Symphony link under the Search Results heading. (Make sure you click the one that specifies Windows under the Operating System column.)**

   The download page for Lotus Symphony appears.

4. **Select English from the Language drop-down list.**

5. **Click the Continue link at the bottom of the page.**

   The Sign In page appears.

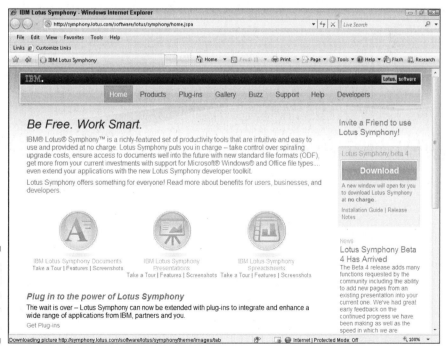

Figure A-1:
The IBM
Lotus
Symphony
Web site.

6. **If you have an IBM ID, click the Sign In link. This leads you to a log-on page, at which you can log on using your IBM ID credentials. For the following steps, however, I assume you just want to download the Lotus Symphony Installer and don't have an IBM ID. To follow along, click the Proceed without an IBM ID link.**

The contact information Web page appears, as shown in Figure A-2.

7. **Fill out the sign in information.**

You must sign in with your first and last names, e-mail address, and country.

8. **Scroll to the bottom of the page and click I Agree.**

9. **Click the I Confirm link.**

The next download page appears.

10. **Scroll to the bottom of the page.**

Two tabs appear: one for downloading using the Download Director, and the other for using HTTP.

The Download Director is a separate application that helps you download the Lotus Symphony Installer. The Download Using HTTP option enables you to download a single file using standard Web page download techniques.

Figure A-2:
You must sign in to access the download page.

11. **Click the Download Using HTTP tab to display that tab's option.**

12. **Click the Download Now link.**

    The File Download dialog box appears.

13. **Click Save.**

    The Save As dialog box appears, as shown in Figure A-3.

14. **Select a drive and folder on your computer where you would like to store the `IBM_Lotus_Symphony_w32.exe` file.**

    Be sure to remember where you saved the file to make it easier to locate for the steps described in the following section, "Installing Lotus Symphony."

15. **Click the Save button.**

    The status of the download appears.

    The Estimated time left figure is an approximate time calculated by Windows to give you a rough idea of how long the download will take to finish.

After the download process completes, continue to the next section, which shows you just how easy it is to install Lotus Symphony.

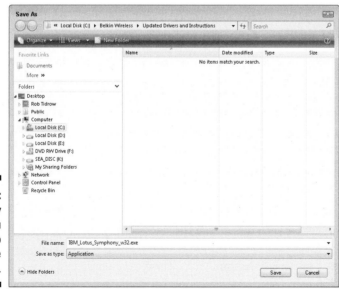

Figure A-3:
Specify where you want to save the install file.

Deleting beta files

Were you one of the many thousands of users who participated in the IBM Lotus Symphony Beta program? If you were, you should uninstall any copies of the beta software currently residing on your computer. The reason for doing this is to ensure that the most current release of Lotus Symphony installs completely onto your computer. Often beta programs leave behind files and configuration settings that aren't used by the release copy of the software. To remove any beta programs of Lotus Symphony, open the Control Panel (choose Start⇨Control Panel) and then start the Programs and Features applet (in Windows Vista) or the Add or Remove Programs applet (in Windows XP). Locate the IBM Lotus Symphony item and click Uninstall/Change (in Vista) or Remove (in XP). Work through the steps to remove the beta software.

Installing Lotus Symphony

The file you use to install Lotus Symphony on your computer is called `IBM_Lotus_Symphony_w32.exe`. As described in the preceding section, "Acquiring a Copy of the IBM Lotus Symphony Install Program," the file is downloaded to your computer and stored in a folder someplace on your system.

The following steps lead you through installing Lotus Symphony on your computer.

1. **Locate the `IBM_Lotus_Symphony_w32.exe` file on your computer and double-click it.**

   The files stored in the `IBM_Lotus_Symphony_w32.exe` file are extracted and stored temporarily on your computer.

2. **Click the Next button when the Installation Wizard for IBM Lotus Symphony screen appears (see Figure A-4).**

3. **Click the I Accept the Terms in the License Agreement button on the Software License Agreement window and then click Next.**

4. **Click Next on the next wizard screen to keep the default location.**

   The next screen includes the install location and amount of space required for the installation.

5. **Click the Install button.**

   As the Lotus Symphony Installer program runs, an information screen appears with a progress bar displaying the status of the installation.

6. **When the last wizard screen appears after the setup process finishes, click Finish.**

The IBM Lotus Symphony program appears. If you aren't ready to begin working in Lotus Symphony, choose File⇨Exit. Otherwise, turn to Chapter 1 to find out more about Lotus Symphony and its applications.

Figure A-4:
The
Installation
Wizard for
IBM Lotus
Symphony
helps
you work
through the
installation
process.

Appendix B

Function Reference

In This Appendix

▶ Operator Reference

▶ Function Reference

This appendix gives you handy quick references for operators and functions. I think you'll find them useful!

Lotus Symphony Operator Reference

Lotus Symphony includes operators that specify calculation types being performed on items in a formula. For example, the + operator enables you to combine two values or expressions. Two types of operators are available:

- **Comparison operators** enable you to compare two values or expressions and return TRUE or FALSE.
- **Arithmetic operators** enable you to perform some type of arithmetic operation on two values in a formula. The results return as numeric values.

The available operators are as follows:

- AND **(comparison):** Combines two values or expressions in a formula.
- + **(arithmetic):** Combines two expressions or values in a formula.
- Eqv **(comparison):** Calculates the equivalence of two expressions.
- Imp **(comparison):** Performs a logical implication on two expressions.
- − **(arithmetic):** Subtracts two expressions or values in a formula.
- / **(arithmetic):** Divides two expressions or values in a formula.
- Mod **(comparison):** Gives you a return of the integer remainder of a division calculation.
- * **(arithmetic):** Multiplies two expressions or values in a formula.

- ✔ ^ **(arithmetic):** Raises a value to a specific power.

- ✔ Not **(comparison):** Negates an expression by inverting the values.

- ✔ Or **(comparison):** Performs a logical OR disjunction on two expressions.

- ✔ Xor **(comparison):** Performs a logical Exclusive-Or combination of two expressions.

Lotus Symphony Function Reference

The following list describes the functions available in Lotus Symphony. Functions are prebuilt formulas that perform some type of operation or calculation and then return a value. For example, the Sqr function returns the square of a number.

Abs: Shows the absolute value of a numeric expression.

Array: Returns a Variant with a data field.

Asc: Evaluates a string expression and returns the first character as an ASCII (American Standard Code for Information Interchange) value.

Atn: This is a trigonometric function. It returns the arctangent of a numeric expression.

Blue: Returns the color blue.

CBool: Converts a numeric expression or string comparison to a Boolean expression.

CByte: Converts a numeric or string expression to a Byte type.

CDateFromIso: Use this function when a string includes a date in ISO format to return the internal date.

CDateToIso: When the DateSerial or DateValue functions are used, you can get the date in ISO format from a serial date number.

CDate: Converts a string or numeric expression to a date value.

CDbl: Converts a string or numeric expression to a double type.

CInt: Converts a numeric or string expression into an integer.

Universal Network Objects

Uno is the Universal Network Objects specification of OpenOffice.org. It is the main component model for OpenOffice.org application (such as Lotus Symphony) that enables interoperability (kind of like a "go-between" interpreter) between different programming languages (such as C++ and Java). Users can create add-ons or other objects (such as dialog boxes) using the UNO specifications. Look at `http://udk.openoffice.org/` for more information.

CLng: Converts a numeric or string expression into a long integer.

CSng: Converts a numeric or string expression into a `Single` data type.

CStr: Converts a numeric expression to a string expression.

Choose: Use this function when you need to return a selected value from a list of arguments.

Chr: Returns the character that corresponds to a specified character code.

Cos: Calculates the cosine of an angle.

CreateUnoDialog: This function, when evaluated during Basic runtime, can create a Basic Uno object that represents an Uno dialog control.

CreateUnoListener: Creates an instance of an Uno listener.

CreateUnoService: Using the `ProcessServiceManager`, this function instantiates an Uno service.

CreateUnoStruct: Creates an instance of an Uno structure type.

DateSerial: Returns a date value for a day, month, or year you specify.

DateValue: Returns a number from a date string or calculates the difference between two dates.

Day: Used with DateSerial or DateValue to return a value that represents the day of the month.

DimArray: Returns a variant array.

`EqualUnoObjects`: If two basic Uno objects represent the same instance of an Uno object, this function returns True.

`Erl`: Finds the location (represented as the line number) of an error during execution of your program.

`Err`: Returns an error code of an error during execution of your program.

`Error`: Returns an error code's error message.

`Exp`: Returns the base of the natural logarithm (e = 2.718282) raised to a power.

`FindObject`: Addresses an object at run-time as a string parameter.

`FindPropertyObject`: Addresses objects at run-time as a string parameter.

`Fix`: Returns an integer of a number that included fractional parts.

`Format`: Converts a number to a string. Based on formatting instructions you provide, the function can then format the string.

`GetProcessServiceManager`: Use this function (required to instantiate a service using `CreateInstanceWithArguments`) to return the central Uno `ServiceManager`, `ProcessServiceManager`.

`GetSolarVersion`: Shows the version number of Lotus Symphony.

`GetSystemTicks`: Returns the number of system ticks by the operating system.

`Green`: Returns the color green.

`HasUnoInterfaces`: Tests for Uno interface support.

`Hex`: Shows a number's hexadecimal value.

`Hour`: Converts a time value into an hour value when used with the `TimeSerial` or the `TimeValue` functions.

`InStr`: Shows the string position when that string is placed within another string.

`InputBox`: Provides a prompt in a dialog box for user input.

`Int`: Returns an integer based on a number.

`IsArray`: Determines whether a variable is a data field in an array.

`IsDate`: Evaluates whether a string value can be converted to a date variable.

`IsEmpty`: Evaluates whether a variant variable contains nothing (also known as "empty").

`IsMissing`: Evaluates whether a function is called.

`IsNull`: Evaluates a Variant to find out whether it includes a null value.

`IsNumeric`: Evaluates an expression and returns True if the expression can be converted to a number. It returns False if it can't.

`IsObject`: Evaluates to see whether an object variable is an OLE object.

`IsUnoStruct`: Returns True if an object is an Uno struct.

`LBound`: Returns an array's lower boundary.

`LCase`: Converts uppercase letters to lowercase letters in a string.

`LTrim`: Deletes all spaces at the beginning of a string expression.

`Left`: Use this function in a string expression to return the number of leftmost characters that you specify.

`Len`: Returns the number of bytes to store a variable or how many characters are in a string.

`Log`: Use this function for a number to return its natural logarithm.

`Minute`: Use this function with the `TimeSerial` function or the `TimeValue` function to return the minute of the hour of a serial time value.

`Month`: Returns the month when used with the `DateSerial` or the `DateValue` functions.

`MsgBox`: Displays a dialog box that returns a value and shows a message.

`Now`: Returns the system date and time as a date value.

`Oct`: Returns a number's octal value.

`QBColor`: Use this function for the RGB color code.

`RGB`: Returns the integer value for a red, green, and blue color.

`RTrim`: Removes any spaces at the end of a string.

`Red`: Returns the color red.

`Right`: Returns *n* number of characters to the right in a string value.

`Rnd`: Returns a random number (an integer) between 0 and 1.

`Second`: Returns the seconds as an integer value generated by the `TimeSerial` or `TimeValue` functions.

`Sgn`: To indicate that a number passed to a function is positive, zero, or negative, this function returns an integer value between –1 and 1.

`Sin`: Returns the sine of an angle.

`Space`: Returns a string of spaces.

`Sqr`: Calculates the square root of a number.

`Square Root` **calculation function:** Calculates square roots.

`StrComp`: Returns an integer based on a comparison of two strings.

`Str`: Converts a numeric value into a string.

`String`: Creates a string. It creates a string from a character entered or from the first character of a string passed to the function.

`Switch`: Returns a value from a list of arguments.

`Tan`: Returns the radians of an angle's tangent.

`TimeSerial`: Returns a numeric value of a specified hour, minute, and second expression.

`TimeValue`: Calculates a time value from the specified hour, minute, and second values in a string.

`Timer`: Use this function (after declaring a variable to call it) to return the number of seconds since midnight.

`Trim`: Deletes all spaces from the beginning and ending of a string expression.

TwipsPerPixelX: Returns a count of the twips representing pixel width.

TwipsPerPixelY: Returns the height of a pixel in twips.

TypeName **and** VarType: Use TypeName for a string variable and VarType for a numeric value.

UBound: Returns an array's upper boundary value.

UCase: Converts a string's lowercase characters into uppercase ones.

Val: Converts a string into a numeric expression.

WeekDay: When a date number is created using the DateSerial or the DateValue function, the WeekDay function returns the number corresponding to the weekday.

Year: Returns the year from a serial date number created by the DateSerial or the DateValue function.

Appendix C

About the CD

In This Appendix

▶ System requirements

▶ Using the CD with Windows, Linux, and Mac

▶ Checking out what you can find on the CD

▶ Troubleshooting

*T*he CD that comes with this book includes several items. For starters, it includes the full version of IBM Lotus Symphony, which you can install from the CD and begin using as you work this book. The CD also contains, a plug-in application and clip art files you can use with your IBM Lotus Symphony installation to create word processing documents, spreadsheets, and presentations. Finally, you'll find some of the sample files I used during the writing of this book.

System Requirements

Make sure that your computer meets the minimum system requirements shown in the following list. If your computer doesn't match up to most of these requirements, you may have problems using the software and files on the CD. For the latest and greatest information, please refer to the ReadMe file located at the root of the CD-ROM.

✔ A PC running Microsoft Windows XP or Windows Vista

✔ A CD-ROM drive

If you need more information on the basics, check out these books published by Wiley Publishing, Inc.: *PCs For Dummies* by Dan Gookin; *Macs For Dummies* by Edward C. Baig; *iMacs For Dummies* by Mark L. Chambers; *Windows XP For Dummies* and *Windows Vista For Dummies,* both by Andy Rathbone.

Using the CD

To install the items from the CD to your hard drive, follow these steps.

1. **Insert the CD into your computer's CD-ROM drive.**

   The license agreement appears.

   Note for Windows users: The interface won't launch if you have auto-run disabled. In that case, choose Start⇨Run. (For Windows Vista, choose Start⇨All Programs⇨Accessories⇨Run.) In the dialog box that appears, type *D:\Start.exe*. (Replace *D* with the proper letter if your CD drive uses a different letter. If you don't know the letter, see how your CD drive is listed under My Computer.) Click OK.

2. **Read through the license agreement and then click the Accept button if you want to use the CD.**

   The CD interface appears. The interface allows you to browse the contents and install the programs with just a click of a button (or two).

What You'll Find on the CD

The following sections are arranged by category and provide a summary of the software and other goodies you can find on the CD. If you need help with installing the items provided on the CD, refer to the installation instructions in the preceding section.

For each program listed, I provide the program platform (Windows) plus the type of software. The programs fall into one of the following categories:

- ✔ **Shareware programs** are fully functional, free, trial versions of copyrighted programs. If you like particular programs, register with their authors for a nominal fee and receive licenses, enhanced versions, and technical support.

- ✔ **Freeware programs** are free, copyrighted games, applications, and utilities. You can copy them to as many computers as you like — for free — but they offer no technical support.

- ✔ **GNU software** is governed by its own license, which is included inside the folder of the GNU software. There are no restrictions on distribution of GNU software. See the GNU license at the root of the CD for more details.

- ✔ **Trial, demo, or evaluation versions** of software are usually limited either by time or functionality (such as not letting you save a project after you create it).

IBM Lotus Symphony.exe

This file includes the entire IBM Lotus Symphony release product. You can install IBM Lotus Symphony on your computer and use it free of charge. If you want to stay current with the product updates, be sure to visit the IBM Lotus Symphony Web site. The sites you should visit are included in Chapter 21.

Forum Support Plug-In For IBM Lotus Symphony

Open Source full version

The Forum Support Plug-In for IBM Lotus Symphony provides a plug-in that lets you quickly and easily connect to and participate in online support forums for IBM Lotus Symphony. It is provided on this CD-ROM to give you an opportunity to review the types of plug-ins available and types of plug-ins that can be created for IBM Lotus Symphony.

Clip Art

Samples provided for free

Bundled with the IBM Lotus Symphony for Dummies CD-ROM is a collection of clip art images from ClipArt.com. The ClipArt.com Web site is a business devoted to providing a number of different types of images (clip art, 3D clip art, photos, and more) for users to use in their documents, Web sites, presentations, and other types of files. You can subscribe to the service by visiting www.clipart.com. These images included on this CD, however, are provided free of charge to encourage you to use them and see the wonderful benefits of downloading addition images from ClipArt.com (there is a fee for additional images you download).

Sample Book Files

Samples provided for free

I've also included some of the sample files you can find in the book. I throw these on the CD to help you get a running start on some of the examples I discuss in this book, so that you don't have to worry too much about creating your own data sources to follow along.

Troubleshooting

I tried my best to compile programs that work on most computers with the minimum system requirements. Alas, your computer may differ, and some programs may not work properly for some reason.

The two likeliest problems are that you don't have enough memory (RAM) for the programs you want to use, or you have other programs running that are affecting installation or running of a program. If you get an error message such as Not enough memory or Setup cannot continue, try one or more of the following suggestions and then try using the software again:

- ✔ **Turn off any antivirus software running on your computer.** Installation programs sometimes mimic virus activity and may make your computer incorrectly believe that it's being infected by a virus.

- ✔ **Close all running programs.** The more programs you have running, the less memory is available to other programs. Installation programs typically update files and programs, so if you keep other programs running, installation may not work properly.

- ✔ **Have your local computer store add more RAM to your computer.** This is, admittedly, a drastic and somewhat expensive step. However, adding more memory can really help the speed of your computer and allow more programs to run at the same time.

Customer Care

If you have trouble with the CD-ROM, please call Wiley Product Technical Support at 800-762-2974. Outside the United States, call 317-572-3993. You can also contact Wiley Product Technical Support at http://support.wiley. com. Wiley Publishing will provide technical support only for installation and other general quality control items. For technical support on the applications themselves, consult the program's vendor or author.

To place additional orders or to request information about other Wiley products, please call 877-762-2974.

Index

• *Symbols and Numerics* •

+ (addition) operator, 214
& (concatenation) operator, 214
/ (division) operator, 214
=> (equal to or greater than)
    operator, 215
=< (equal to or less than) operator, 215
= (equals) operator, 214
> (greater than) operator, 215
< (less than) operator, 215
* (multiplication) operator, 214
– (subtraction) operator, 214
1&1 Internet Web site, 311
2D (two dimensional) charts, 189
3D Quickshape drawing object, 280
3D (three dimensional) charts, 189

•*A*•

Abs function, 348
absolute references
  basic description of, 165
  formula example, 168, 213
  relative reference differences, 166
  special characters, 168
  values of, 169–170
  when to use, 169
accent marks, 85
ACCRINT function, 220
AccuWeb Hosting Web site, 311
addition (+) operator, 214
Adobe Reader program, 63
alignment, captions, 113
All Toolbars toolbar, 20
American Standard Code for Information
    Interchange (ASCII), 163
Anchor command (Layout menu), 101
anchoring, 102

anchors, footnotes, 118
AND operator, 347
animations
  build up effects, 284
  checkerboard effects, 285
  cross-fading effects, 284
  dissolve effects, 285
  fade effects, 284
  fly-in effects, 284
  horizontal line effects, 285
  image, 289–293
  open/close effects, 284
  overuse of, 284
  in presentations, 283–287
  roll effects, 284
  spiral effects, 284
  uncover effects, 284
  vertical line effects, 285
  wavy line effects, 284
APIs (Application Programming
    Interfaces), 31
applications
  about this book, 1
  COMM, 12
  DOC, 12
  FORM, 12
  GRAPH, 12
  OpenProj, 29
  SHEET, 12
  spreadsheet, 205–209
ARABI function, 220
area charts, 189
Arial font, 80
arithmetic operators, 347
Arrange tool, 277
Array function, 348
arrow keys (keyboard navigation), 71
Arrows drawing object, 280
Asc function, 348

ASCII (American Standard Code for Information Interchange), 163
Atn function, 348
author Web site, 336
automatic transition advancement, 286

• *B* •

background colors
  Master Page design, 270
  presentations, 263–265
  tables, 110
  of text, 84
Background Fill command (Layout menu), 264
backgrounds
  bitmaps, 264–265
  cross-hatching, 264
  gradients, 264
  spreadsheet, 199–200
Baig, Edward C. (*Macs For Dummies*), 355
bar charts, 189
basic computer experience, about this book, 2
Basic Shapes drawing objects, 280
bibliographic references, 117–118
bitmaps, 264–265
blank documents, 56
blank pages, Instant Layout feature, 241
Block Arrows drawing object, 280
Blue function, 348
boilerplate text, spreadsheets, 149
bold text, 2, 84
Bookman font, 80
Bookmark Document button (help system), 41
bookmarks, 302
Bookmarks button (help system), 41
borders
  chart, 196, 200–201
  table, 110
brightness, graphic, 203–204
browsers
  discussed, 302
  ease of use, 332
  system requirements, 340
build up effects, 284

bulleted lists
  color in, 88
  creating, 87
  editing, 88–89
  formatting text in, 243
  in presentations, 242–243
  symbols used in, 88–89
  tabs, 242
buttons
  Bookmark Document (help system toolbar), 41
  Bookmarks (help system toolbar), 41
  Close, 23
  Contents (help system toolbar), 41
  Create a New Document, 54
  Create a New Presentation, 16
  Go Back (help system toolbar), 40
  Go Forward (help system toolbar), 40
  Home (help system toolbar), 40
  Links (help system toolbar), 41
  Maximize (help system toolbar), 40–41
  Print Page (help system toolbar), 41
  Print Preview, 177–179
  Refresh/Show Current Topics (help system toolbar), 40
  Search Results (help system toolbar), 41
  Show All Topics (help system toolbar), 40
  Show in Table of Contents (help systems toolbar), 41
  Start, 10
  Web page, 302
Buzz forum, 336

• *C* •

calculations
  date, 215–216
  filtering, 216–218
  formulas, 211–214
  operators, 214–215
  Solve Equations tool, 218–220
  time, 215–216
Calibri font, 80
callouts, 82

Callouts drawing object, 280
captions
  alignment, 113
  creation, 111–112
  deleting, 113
  description example, 112
  editing, 112
  graphics for, 111–113
  over text entry benefits, 111
  placement, 112
  for tables, 111–113
  text properties, 113
CBool function, 348
CByte function, 348
CD (*IBM Lotus Symphony For Dummies*)
  Clip Art items, 357
  customer care, 358
  forum support, 357
  installing items from, 356
  programs found on, 356
  release products, 357
  sample book files, 357
  system requirements information, 355
  technical support, 358
CDate function, 348
CDateFromIso function, 348
CDateToIso function, 348
CDbl function, 348
CD-R, distributing spreadsheet
    applications using, 207
cells, spreadsheet
  brief description of, 150–151
  multiple, selecting data in, 159
  naming scheme, 150
Chambers, Mark L. (*iMacs For
    Dummies*), 355
chapter format, cross-references, 115
Chart Setup wizard, 190–191
charts
  area, 189
  bar, 189
  basic description of, 187
  borders around, 196
  changing type of, 197–198
  column, 189

creation, 190–191
deleting, 193
editing, 192–196
Instant Layout feature, 241–242
label formatting, 195–196
line, 189
moving, 193
naming, 191
pie, 189
previewing, 191
radar, 189
resizing, 192–193
in spreadsheets, 187–191
standards column and row example,
    188
stock, 189
styles, 197–198
titles, 191, 195–196
3D (three dimensional), 189
2D (two dimensional), 189
updating data in, 194
usage guidelines, 189–190
x-axis, 189, 191
XY, 189
y-axis, 189, 191
checkerboard effects, 285
Choose function, 349
Chr function, 349
CInt function, 348
citations, 119
Clip Art
  adding to documents, 67–68
  Web site, 275, 278
  where to find, 357
ClipartConnection Web site, 278
CLng function, 349
Close button, 23
Close Preview button (Print Preview
    feature), 178–179
closing
  IBM Lotus Symphony, 23
  presentations, 258
  Search pane, 45
collaboration, 30, 331

colors
  in bulleted lists, 88
  font, 84
  graphic, 203–204
column charts, 189
columns
  DataPilot tables, 225
  spreadsheet, 151
COMM application, 12
comparison operators, 347
complex documents, 105–106
compressing text, 85
computer preparation for Lotus
    Symphony, 32
concatenation (&) operator, 214
Connectors drawing object, 280
Contents button (help system), 41
context menus, 237
conversion, to Lotus Symphony, 33–36
Copy command (Edit menu), 154,
    163–164
copying
  data into spreadsheets, 154
  text in documents, 68
Corel WordPerfect Office suite, 28
corrections, 69, 252–253. *See also* spell
    checking
Cos function, 349
COUNT function, 220
Courier font, 80
Create a New Document button, 54
Create a New Presentation button, 16
Create Master Page tool, 271
Create Table command (Table
    menu), 107
CreateUnoDialog function, 349
CreateUnoListener function, 349
CreateUnoService function, 349
CreateUnoStruct function, 349
cropping, 205
cross-fading effects, 284
cross-hatching, 263–264
cross-references
  chapter format, 115
  creation, 114–116

deleting, 116
field-shadings, 116
page format, 115
placement, 115
target name, 115
updating, 116
CSng function, 349
CStr function, 349
Ctrl+End key (keyboard navigation), 71
Ctrl+Home key (keyboard navigation), 71

• **D** •

DataPilot tables
  columns, 225
  editing, 227
  filtering data, 226–227
  outputting data, 227–228
  rows, 225
  setting up, 224–226
date
  calculations, 215–216
  Date fields, inserting in documents, 117
DATE function, 220
DateSerial function, 349
DateValue function, 349
Day function, 349
deleting
  captions, 113
  charts, 193
  cross-references, 116
  graphics from documents, 102
  graphics from presentations, 277–278
  image animations, 295
  images from image animations, 294
  presentation pages, 267, 269
  text in documents, 68
  text in endnotes, 123
  transitions, 288–289
demos, support, 336
Developer Toolkit
  basic description of, 30
  downloading, 31
  ease of use, 332
DimArray function, 349

display quality, presentations, 248
dissolve effects, 285
distribution, spreadsheet applications, 206–207
division (/) operator, 214
DOC application, 12
.doc (Word document)
  brief description of, 130
  conversion items, 131–132
  converting, 133–134
  importing, 132–133
  saving files to, 133
document types
  brief description of, 129
  .doc (Word document), 130–134
  files, 130–131
  importing, 131
  .lwp, 130
  OASIS, 130
  ODT files, 130
  .rtf, 130
  .sxw, 130, 134
documents. *See also* tables
  adding Clip Art to, 67–68
  adding graphics to, 67–68
  adding paragraphs to, 66–67
  applying styles to, 92–93
  blank, 56
  brief description of, 53
  complex, 105–106
  conversion for Lotus Symphony, 33–36
  copying text in, 68
  Create a new Document button, 54
  creating, using existing document, 60–61
  creating, using templates, 56–59
  creating from scratch, 56
  cross-references, 114–116
  Date fields, 117
  deleting graphics in, 102
  deleting text in, 68
  editing text in, 68–69
  fields, 116–117
  footnotes, 117–121

indexes, 126–128
Insert Corrections feature, 69
margin settings, 66
moving within, 70–71
navigating within, 70–71
New Document tab, 54
outputting, 73–76
overwriting text in, 69
Page numbers, 117
positioning graphics in, 100–102
previewing, 73–74
printing, 75
resizing graphics in, 99–100
rulers in, 72–73
saving, 61–65, 76
saving as templates, 96
spell checking, 69–70
starting, 54–55
templates, 95–99
Time fields, 117
TOC (table of contents), 123–126
types, 55
typing new text in, 66–67
zoom settings in, 72
Documents window features, 14–15
DOLLAR function, 220
downloading
  Developer Toolkit, 31
  IBM Lotus Symphony, 341–343
  templates, 57, 96
drawing objects
  creating, 280–281
  defined, 262
  list of, 280
  in presentations, 280–281
  resizing, 281
DVD-R, distributing spreadsheet applications using, 207

• E •

Edit menu commands
  Copy, 154, 163–164
  Paste, 154, 164

editing
  bulleted lists, 88–89
  captions, 112
  charts, 192–196
  DataPilot tables, 227
  endnotes, 123
  footnotes, 119–120
  formulas, 214
  functions, 223–224
  image animations, 293–294
  Master Page design, 268–270
  numbered lists, 90
  styles, 95
  tables, 109–110
  text in documents, 68–69
  transitions, 287–288
effects, text, 85. *See also* animations
Ellipse Quickshape drawing object, 280
e-mail
  starting spreadsheets from, 144
  system requirements, 32, 340
emphasis marks, 85
End key (keyboard navigation), 71
ending screen shows, 323
endnotes
  adding text to, 122
  creation, 122–123
  deleting text in, 123
  editing, 123
  formatting, 123
  styles, 123
Enter key (keyboard navigation), 71
equal to or greater than (=>)
    operator, 215
equal to or less than (=<) operator, 215
equals (=) operator, 214
EqualUnoObjects function, 350
equations. *See* calculations; formulas;
    functions
Eqv operator, 347
Erl function, 350
Err function, 350
Error function, 350
exception rulers, Instant Correction
    replacement, 253

Exit command (File menu), 23
exiting. *See* closing
Exp function, 350
Export command (File menu), 64, 306
exporting
  DataPilot data, 227–228
  documents, 73–76
Extrusion drawing object, 280
Eyedropper tool, 278–279

• F •

fade effects, 284
FAQs (Frequently Asked Questions), 336
feedback, 48–49
fields, inserting in documents, 116–117
field-shadings, cross-references, 116
file formats. *See also* document types
  ODF (Open Document Format), 23, 26,
    62–63
  PDF (Portable Document Format), 29,
    63–64
  RTF (Rich Text Formatting), 65
  TXT (Text file), 65
  WSX (Word Processing Document), 65
File menu commands
  Exit, 23
  Export, 64, 306
  New, 55, 57
  Open, 34, 60
  Preferences, 22
  Print, 75
  Print Preview, 74
  Save, 63, 288–289
  Save As, 61, 65, 96, 267
  Template Organizer, 99
fill tools, spreadsheets, 153–154
filtering
  calculations, 216–218
  DataPilot table data, 226–227
FindObject function, 350
FindPropertyObject function, 350
First Page button (Print Preview
    feature), 177
Fix function, 350

flash drives, distributing spreadsheet applications using, 207
Flow Charts drawing object, 280
fly-in effects, 284
fonts
  changing, 81
  color, 84
  common types, 80
  effective use of, 81
  glyphs, 79
  Install New Font command, 80
  installing new, 80
  kerning, 81
  size, 82–83
  styles, 84
  typeface, 79–82
Fontwork drawing object, 280
footers, 183
footnotes
  anchors, 118
  brief description of, 117
  creation, 118–119
  editing, 119–120
  formatting, 120–121
  inserting additional text in, 120
  number formats in, 119
  paragraph styles, 121
  styles, 120–121
  symbols in, 119
FORM application, 12
Format function, 350
formats. *See* document types; file formats
formatting. *See also* styles
  basic description of, 77
  endnotes, 123
  footnotes, 120–121
  subscripts, 102–103
  superscripts, 102–104
  text, 78–79
formulas
  absolute references example, 168, 213
  basic calculation example, 212
  basic description of, 211
  cell references, 213

editing, 214
entering in spreadsheets, 213
how to use, 212
named ranges in, 173–174
relative reference example, 166–167, 213
spreadsheet, 211–215
SUM function, 212
forums, 333–335
freeware programs, 356
Frequently Asked Questions (FAQs), 336
functions
  Abs, 348
  ACCRINT, 220
  ARABI, 220
  Array, 348
  Asc, 348
  Atn, 348
  basic description, 211
  Blue, 348
  CBool, 348
  CByte, 348
  CDate, 348
  CDateFromIso, 348
  CDateToIso, 348
  CDbl, 348
  Choose, 349
  Chr, 349
  CInt, 348
  CLng, 349
  Cos, 349
  COUNT, 220
  CreateUnoDialog, 349
  CreateUnoService, 349
  CSng, 349
  CStr, 349
  DATE, 220
  DateSerial, 349
  DateValue, 349
  Day, 349
  DimArray, 349
  DOLLAR, 220
  editing, 223–224
  EqualUnoObjects, 350
  Erl, 350

functions *(continued)*
Err, 350
Error, 350
Exp, 350
FindObject, 350
FindPropertyObject, 350
Fix, 350
Format, 350
GetProcessServiceManager, 350
GetSolarVersion, 350
Green, 350
HasUnoInterfaces, 350
Hex, 350
Hour, 350
InputBox, 350
InStr, 350
Int, 350
IPMT, 220
IsArray, 351
IsDate, 351
IsEmpty, 351
IsMissing, 351
IsNull, 351
IsNumeric, 351
IsObject, 351
IsUnoStruct, 351
LBound, 351
LCase, 351
Left, 351
LEN, 220
Len, 351
Log, 351
LOOKUP, 221
LTrim, 351
Minute, 351
Month, 351
MsgBox, 351
nested, 224
NOW, 216
Now, 351
Oct, 351
parameters, 221
PI, 221
QBColor, 351
Red, 352

REPT, 221
RGB, 352
Right, 352
Rnd, 352
RTrim, 352
Second, 352
selecting, 221–223
Sgn, 352
Sin, 352
Space, 352
spreadsheet, 220–224
Sqr, 352
Square Root, 352
Str, 352
StrComp, 352
String, 352
SUM, 212, 221
Switch, 352
T, 221
Tan, 352
Timer, 352
TimeSerial, 352
TimeValue, 352
Trim, 352
TwipsPerPixelX, 353
TwipsPerPixelY, 353
TypeName, 353
UBound, 353
UCase, 353
Val, 353
WeekDay, 353
Year, 353
Futura font, 80

• G •

Gallery tab, 47
General Feedback forum, 334
GetProcessServiceManager
    function, 350
GetSolarVersion function, 350
GetSystemTicks function, 350
glyphs, 79
GNU software, 356
Go Back button (help system toolbar), 40

Go Forward button (help system toolbar), 40
Google Docs suite
  brief description of, 130
  IBM Lotus Symphony comparisons/ differences, 28
Gookin, Dan (*PCs For Dummies*), 355
gradients, 264
GRAPH application, 12
graphics
  adding to documents, 67–68
  adding to presentations, 275–276
  adding to spreadsheets, 199–205
  adding to Web pages, 304
  anchoring, 102
  brightness, 203–204
  captions for, 111–113
  colors, 203–204
  cropping, 205
  deleting from documents, 102
  deleting from presentations, 277–278
  in documents, resizing, 99–100
  Eyedropper tool, 278–279
  in logos, 275
  moving, 203
  moving within presentations, 276–277
  positioning in documents, 100–102
  in presentations, 273–277
  ready-to-add, 202
  resizing, 203
  resizing in presentations, 277
  rotating, 203
  sparing use of, 275
  themes, 274
  viewing, 202
  when to use, 274–275
  where to find, 275, 278
graphs. *See* charts
Green function, 350
Guide when Moving tool, 250
Guideline Grid tool
  presentations, 249–250
  turning off, 250
  turning on and setting, 249–250

• *H* •

handouts, presentation, 315
hard copies, presentations, 315
hard disk space, system requirements, 32
HasUnoInterfaces function, 350
Have a Question forum, 334
headers, 183
headings, 124. *See also* styles
height and width settings, presentations, 261
help system
  Bookmark Document button, 41
  Bookmarks button, 41
  brief description of, 37
  Contents button, 41
  contents of help topics, 38–39
  Go Back button, 40
  Go Forward button, 40
  Help Feedback link, 48–49
  Help page, 336
  Home button, 40
  Links button, 41
  links to other documents, 40
  Maximize button, 40–41
  navigating between help documents, 40
  Nothing Found label, 42
  online resources for, 46–47
  opening Help window, 38
  Print Page button, 41
  Product Feedback link, 48–49
  Refresh/Show Current Topic button, 40
  running searches for help documents, 42–44
  Search Results button, 41
  Show All Topics button, 40
  Show in Table of Contents button, 41
  specific application, 41–42
  subtopics, 39
  switching between help and Lotus Symphony window, 38
Hex function, 350
Home button (help system toolbar), 40
Home key (keyboard navigation), 71

home page (IBM Lotus Symphony)
 brief description of, 10
 support, 333
Home tab, 13
horizontal line effects, 285
horizontal placement of rulers, 73
horizontal rotation, 203
hosting services, Web, 311
Hour function, 350
HTML (Hypertext Markup Language), 298–299
hyperlinks, 302–303

• *I* •

IBM Word Processing Document (.sxw), 130, 134
icons, about this book, 4
iMacs For Dummies (Chambers), 355
image animations
 creation, 289–292
 deleting, 295
 deleting images from, 294
 editing, 293–294
 objects, 292–294
 playing, 292
images. *See* graphics
Imp operator, 347
Import Data feature, 154–156
importing
 data into spreadsheets, 163–164
 .doc (Word documents), 132–133
 document types, 131
 templates, 147–148
indentation settings, 94
indexes
 creation, 128
 effective, 126–127
 entries, setting up, 127–128
 main entries, 127
 professional indexers, 126
Infopops, 37
InputBox function, 350
Insert Corrections feature, 69

insertion point, 66
installation
 install program, acquiring copy of, 340–341
 Lotus Symphony, 344–345
Instant Corrections replacement
 brief description of, 69
 exception rulers, 252–253
Instant Layout feature, 240–242
InStr function, 350
Int function, 350
Internet
 connections, 32, 340
 help resources, 46–47
interoperability benefits, 29
intranets, 310–311
IPMT function, 220
IsArray function, 351
IsDate function, 351
IsEmpty function, 351
IsMissing function, 351
IsNull function, 351
IsNumeric function, 351
IsObject function, 351
Issues and Troubleshooting forums, 334–335
IsUnoStruct function, 351
italicized text, 84
italics, about this book, 2

• *J* •

JPG format, 299

• *K* •

kerning, 81
keyboards
 document navigation, 71
 presentation navigation, 237–238
 reference card, 336
 screen show navigation, 324–325
 spreadsheet navigation, 157–158
KOffice program, 130

• L •

label formatting, charts, 195–196

LAN (local area network), 76

language settings, text, 85

Last Page button (Print Preview feature), 178

Layout menu commands
  Anchor, 101
  Background Fill, 264
  Style List, 93, 300

LBound function, 351

LCase function, 351

Left function, 351

Len function, 220, 351

licensing agreement, Lotus Symphony installation, 344

line charts, 189

Lines drawing object, 280

Links button (help system toolbar), 41

lists
  bulleted, 87–89, 242–243
  numbered, 89–90, 243

local area network (LAN), 76

Log function, 351

logos
  graphics, 275
  in Master Page design, 270

long-term data presentation, 27

LOOKUP function, 221

loops, transitions, 293

Lotus Quickr connector plug-in, 30

LTrim function, 351

.lwp (Lotus WordPro) document type, 130, 134

• M •

macros
  Lotus Symphony benefits, 29
  naming, 208–209
  recording, 208
  running, 209
  saving, 209
  in spreadsheets, 208–209

Macs For Dummies (Baig), 355

main entries, indexes, 127

main window (IBM Lotus Symphony), 11–12

margin settings
  documents, 66
  presentations, 261–263

Master Page design
  background color, 270
  Create Master Page tool, 271
  editing, 268–270
  logos in, 270
  saving as different format, 268
  viewing, 268

Maximize button (help system toolbar), 40–41

memory, system requirements, 31, 340

menu bar
  Documents window, 15
  main window, 12
  Presentations window, 17
  Spreadsheets window, 18
  Web Browser window, 20

menus, context, 237

Microsoft Office suite
  file types, Lotus Symphony supported, 34
  IBM Lotus Symphony comparisons/ differences, 28

Microsoft Word, 64–65

Microsoft Works suite, 28

Minute function, 351

misspellings, 252–253. *See also* spell checking

mistakes, Instant Correction replacement, 252–253

Mod operator, 347

monospaced font, about this book, 2

Month function, 351

mouse
  document navigation, 70–71
  presentation navigation, 236–237
  screen show navigation, 324
  spreadsheet navigation, 157

moving
  charts, 193
  within documents, 70–71
  graphics, 203
  graphics in presentations, 276–277
  presentation pages, 266–267
  within presentations, 236–239
  within spreadsheets, using keyboard,
    157–158
  within spreadsheets, using mouse, 157
  toolbars, 21–22
MsgBox function, 351
multiplication (*) operator, 214

• N •

named ranges, 173–174
named references, 170
naming
  charts, 191
  macros, 208–209
  ranges, 171–172
  spreadsheet items, 150
  tables, 108
navigation
  within documents, 70–71
  within presentations, 236–239
  during screen shows, 323–325
nested functions, 224
New command (File menu), 55, 57
New Document tab, 54
Next Page button (Print Preview feature),
    177, 179
Not operator, 348
Notes View, viewing presentations, 247
Now function, 216, 351
number formats, in footnotes, 119
numbered lists
  creating, 89–90
  editing, 90
  formatting text in, 243
  numbered styles, 90
  in presentations, 243
numbers, selecting in spreadsheets,
    158–159

• O •

OASIS (Organization for the
    Advancement of Structured
    Information Standards), 26, 130
objects, image animation, 292–294
Oct function, 351
ODF (Open Document Format)
  advantages of, 23
  brief history of, 26
  Lotus Symphony support, 331
  saving documents as, 62–63
  saving spreadsheets in, 160–161
  specification, 27
ODT document type, 130
1&1 Internet Web site, 311
online resources, 46–47
Open command (File menu), 34, 60
Open Document Format. *See* ODF
open source files, 330
open/close effects, 284
opening files saved in other spreadsheet
    formats, 161–163
OpenOffice.org suite
  brief description of, 130
  IBM Lotus Symphony comparisons/
    differences, 28
  Web site, 29
OpenProj application, 29
operands, 214
operating system requirements, 31, 340
operators
  arithmetic, 347
  comparison, 347
  list of, 347–348
  spreadsheet, 214–215
optional parameters, 221
Or operator, 348
Organization for the Advancement of
    Structured Information Standards
    (OASIS), 26, 130
organization, about this book, 2–4
Outline View, viewing presentations,
    245–246
outlining options, TOC, 125

outputting
  DataPilot data, 227–228
  documents, 73–76
overwriting text in documents, 69

• P •

Page Down key (keyboard
    navigation), 71
page format
  cross-references, 115
  presentations, 260–262
page numbers
  inserting in documents, 117
  presentations, 262
page orientation and landscape options,
    presentations, 260
page setup options, printing
    spreadsheets, 182–184
Page Sorter View, viewing presentations,
    245–246
Page tabs (Presentation window), 17
Page Up key (keyboard navigation), 71
Page View, viewing presentations, 245
pagebreaks, viewing and removing
    unwanted, 180–181
pages, adding to presentations, 240–242
paragraphs
  adding to documents, 66
  spacing between, 67
  styles, footnotes, 121
parameters, function, 221
Paste command (Edit menu), 154, 164
paths, 15
PCs For Dummies (Gookin), 355
PDF (Portable Document Format)
  Adobe Reader program, 63
  brief description of, 29
  reading documents saved as, 63
  saving documents as, 63–64
photographs. *See* graphics
PI function, 221
pictures. *See* graphics
pie charts, 189
playback

image animations, 292
  screen shows, 319–323
plug-ins
  Lotus Quickr connector, 30
  Lotus Symphony benefits, 29
Portable Document Format (PDF)
  Adobe Reader program, 63
  brief description of, 29
  reading documents saved as, 63
  saving documents as, 63–64
portable hard drives, distributing
    spreadsheet applications using, 207
positioning graphics in documents,
    100–102
Preferences command (File menu), 22
presentations. *See also* screen shows
  adding graphics to, 275–276
  adding tables to, 253–255
  animations in, 283–287
  background colors, 263–265
  blank pages, removing, 315
  bulleted lists in, 242–243
  checking hardware resources for,
      316–317
  closing, 258
  creating from existing presentation, 233
  creating from templates, 233–236
  deleting graphics from, 277–278
  deleting pages from, 267, 269
  display quality, 248
  drawing objects, 262, 280–281
  editing tables in, 255–256
  file conversions, 233
  final touches, 313–315
  graphics in, 273–277
  Guide when Moving tool, 250
  Guideline Grid tool, 249–250
  hard copies as handouts, 315
  height and width settings, 261
  image animations, 289–293
  inserting text in, 239–240
  Instant Corrections replacement,
      252–253
  Instant Layout feature, 240–242
  jumping to specific page, 238–239

presentations *(continued)*
  margin settings, 261–263
  Master Page design, 268–271
  moving graphics within, 276–277
  moving pages within, 266–267
  moving tables in, 257
  moving within, 236–239
  multiple copies of, 317
  navigation within, 236–239
  new page additions, 240–242
  Notes View, 247
  numbered lists in, 243
  order of pages, changing, 267, 269
  Outline View, 245–246
  page format settings, 260–262
  page numbering, 262
  page orientation and landscape
    options, 260
  page properties description, 259–260
  Page Sorter View, 245–246
  Page View, 245
  practicing, 284
  Presentation Zoom feature, 322–323
  projector and screens for, 317
  proofreading, 314
  Rehearse Timings feature, 317–319
  resizing graphics in, 277
  reviewing, 314–315
  rulers for, turning on, 251
  saving, 257–258
  saving as Web page, 304–305
  screen shows, playing, 319–323
  snap lines, 251–252
  Spell Checker tool, 252
  spell checking, 315
  starting new, 231–232
  switching between views, 247
  table commands, 255–256
  text reflow in, 316
  text styles, 244–245
  text, adding to cells, 255
  thumbnail views, 266
  tools for, 248–252
  transitions, 284–288

troubleshooting, 335
  viewing, 245–248
  zoom options, 247–248
Presentations window features, 16–17
previewing
  charts, 191
  documents, 73–74
  transitions, 286
Previous Page button (Print Preview
    feature), 177
Print button (Print Preview feature), 178
Print command (File menu), 75
Print Page button (help system), 41
Print Preview feature
  Close Preview button, 178–179
  First Page button, 177
  Last Page button, 178
  Next Page button, 177, 179
  Previous Page button, 177
  Print button, 178
  Print Preview Options button, 178
  printing documents, 73–74
  printing spreadsheets, 176–179
  Zoom In button, 178
  Zoom Out button, 178
Print Preview Options button (Print
    Preview feature), 178
print ranges, 172–173
printing
  documents, 75
  Print Preview feature, 73–74, 176–179
printing spreadsheets
  basic description, 175
  entire spreadsheets, 179–180
  headers and footers, 183
  landscape and portrait options, 182
  in other formats, 181
  page setup options, 182–184
  pagebreaks, viewing and removing
    unwanted, 180–181
  previewing for print, 176–179
  print options, setting up, 182–185
  printer settings, 185
Product Feedback link, 48–49

Products tab, 47
projectors, for presentations, 317
proofreading presentations, 314
publishing Web pages, 310–311

• *Q* •

QBColor function, 351
quotation marks, 253

• *R* •

radar charts, 189
RAM (random access memory), 31, 340
ranges
  basic description of, 170
  named, 173–174
  naming, 171–172
  print, 172–173
Rathbone, Andy
  Windows Vista For Dummies, 355
  Windows XP For Dummies, 355
RCP (Rich Client Platform), 12
read-only templates, 97
recording macros, 208
Rectangle Quickshape drawing
    object, 280
Red function, 352
Refresh/Show Current Topics button
    (help system toolbar), 40
Rehearse Timings feature, 317–319
relative references
  absolute reference differences, 166
  basic description of, 165
  formula example, 166–167
remote controls, screen show
    navigation, 325
removing. *See* deleting
REPT function, 221
resizing
  charts, 192–193
  drawing objects, 281
  graphics in documents, 99–100
  graphics in presentations, 277
  graphics in spreadsheets, 203

resources. *See* support
RGB function, 352
Rich Client Platform (RCP), 12
Rich Text Formatting (RTF), 65, 130
Right function, 352
Rnd function, 352
roll effects, 284
rotating
  graphics, 203
  horizontally, 203
  text, 85
  vertically, 203
rows
  DataPilot tables, 225
  spreadsheet, 151
RTF (Rich Text Formatting), 65, 130
RTrim function, 352
Ruler command (View menu), 73
rulers
  brief description of, 15, 72
  horizontal placement, 73
  turning on/off, 73, 251
  vertical placement, 72–73
running macros, 209

• *S* •

Save As command (File menu), 61, 65,
    96, 267
Save command (File menu), 63, 288–289
saving
  files for Web pages, 304–305
  files to Word document, 133
  macros, 209
  Master Page design as different
    format, 268
  presentations, 257–258
  spreadsheets, 160–161
  templates, 95–97
  templates in Template Organizer
    tool, 99
  transitions, 286

saving documents
  file format options, 61
  in Open Document format, 62–63
  in PDF format, 63–64
  for reuse, 76
  as template files, 61, 96
  in Word and other formats, 64–65
scale width, text, 85
Screen Show mode, transitions, 287
screen shows. *See also* presentations
  ending, 323
  navigation during, 323–325
  playing, 319–323
  starting from first page, 321–322
  starting from specific page, 320–321
  zooming during, 322–323
screens, for presentations, 317
scroll bars (Documents window), 15
Search pane, 45
Search Results button (help system), 41
searches, running for help documents,
    42–44
Second function, 352
sections, TOC, 124
servers, Web, 311
Sgn function, 352
shareware programs, 356
SHEET application, 12
Shift+End key (keyboard navigation), 71
Shift+Home key (keyboard
    navigation), 71
shortcuts, to IBM Lotus Symphony, 10
Show All Topics button (help system
    toolbar), 40
Show in Table of Contents button (help
    system toolbar), 41
sidebar
  Documents window, 15
  Presentations window, 17
  Spreadsheets window, 19
Sign In page, 341–342
Sin function, 352

sites. *See* Web sites
size, font, 82–83
slideshows. *See* presentations; screen
    shows
snap lines, 251–252
Solve Equations tool, 218–220
Space function, 352
spacing
  between paragraphs, 67
  between text, 85
special characters, absolute
    references, 168
specification, ODF, 27
speed settings, transitions, 285
Spell Checker tool, 252
spell checking
  how to replace words, 70
  Instant Correction replacements, 69,
    252–253
  presentations, 315
  red squiggly line indicator, 69
  Spell Check tool, 69–70
spiral effects, 284
spreadsheets
  absolute references, 165, 168–170
  applications, 205–209
  backgrounds, 199–200
  basic description of, 141
  boilerplate text, 149
  border colors and sizes, 200–201
  cells, 150–151
  changing data types in, 152
  charts in, 187–191
  columns, 150–151
  converting data in, 134–137
  copying data into, 154
  creating from existing spreadsheets,
    148–149
  creating from scratch, 145
  creating from templates, 145–148
  DataPilot tables, 224–226
  ease of use, 330–331

embedding data from other documents, 154–156

entering content in, 150–154

fill tools, 153–154

formulas, 211–215

functions, 220–224

graphics, 199–205

headers and footers, 183

Import Data feature, 154–156

importing data from word processing files, 163–164

importing data into, 154–156

landscape and portrait print options, 182

macros, 208–209

manually entering data, 151

moving within, using keyboard, 157–158

moving within, using mouse, 157

naming conventions, 150

navigation within, 156–158

new blank spreadsheet example, 142

opening files saved in other formats, 161–163

operators, 214–215

in other formats, printing, 181

page setup options, 182–184

pagebreaks, viewing and removing unwanted, 180–181

previewing for print, 176–179

print options, setting up, 182–185

printer settings, 185

printing entire, 179–180

ranges, 170–174

relative references, 165–167

repeating data in, 152–154

rows, 150–151

saving, 160–161

selecting all data, 159–160

selecting data in multiple cells, 159

selecting words or numbers in cells, 158–159

starting new, 142–144

troubleshooting, 335

Spreadsheets window features, 17–19

Sqr function, 352

Square Root function, 352

Starfish Software company, 26

Stars and Symbols drawing object, 280

Start button, 10

starting

  documents, 54–55

  IBM Lotus Symphony, basic description, 9–11

  IBM Lotus Symphony, when Windows starts, 22–23

  presentations, 231–232

  screen shows from specific page, 320–321

  spreadsheets, 142–144

  Template Organizer tool, 97

status bar

  Documents window, 15

  main window, 12

  Presentations window, 17

  Spreadsheets window, 19

  Web Browser window, 20

Stock Art Web site, 278

stock charts, 189

Str function, 352

StrComp function, 352

stretching text, 85

strikethrough text, 84

String function, 352

Style List command (Layout menu), 93, 300

styles. *See also* formatting

  advantages of, 92

  applying to documents, 92–93

  brief description of, 90–91

  chart, 197–198

  creating new, 93–95

  editing, 95

  endnote, 123

  font, 84

  footnote, 120–121

styles *(continued)*
  indentation settings, 94
  paragraph settings, 94
  text, 244–245
  TOC (table of contents), 125
  Web page, 299–301
subscripts, 102–103
subtraction (–) operator, 214
SUM function, 212, 221
superscripts, 102–104
support
  author Web site, 336
  demos, 336
  FAQs, 336
  forums, 333–335
  General Feedback forum, 334
  Have a Question forum, 334
  home page, 333
  Issues and Troubleshooting, 334–335
  keyboard reference card, 336
  Lotus Symphony benefits, 29
  technotes, 336
  toolbar reference card, 336
  tutorials, 336
  Wiley Product Technical Support Web
    site, 358
Support tab, 47
Switch function, 352
.sxw (IBM Word Processing Document),
    130, 134
symbols
  bulleted list, 88–89
  in footnotes, 119
Symbols and Stars drawing object, 280
system requirements
  brief description of, 339
  e-mail address, 32, 340
  hard disk space, 32, 340
  Internet connection, 32, 340
  memory, 31, 340
  operating system, 31, 340
  Web browser, 340

• *T* •

T function, 221
Table menu commands, 107
table of contents (TOC)
  creation, 124–125
  headings and sections, 124
  how to read, 126
  initial setup, 123–125
  outlining options, 125
  styles, 125
  updating, 125–126
tables. *See also* documents
  adding to presentations, 253–255
  adding to Web pages, 303
  background color, 110
  borders, 110
  brief description of, 106
  captions, 111–113
  DataPilot, 224–228
  design considerations, 107
  editing, 109–110
  initial setup, 107–109
  Instant Layout feature, 241
  moving within presentations, 257
  naming, 108
  presentation, 253–257
tabs
  bulleted lists, 242
  Documents window, 15
  Gallery, 47
  Home, 13
  main menu, 12
  New Document, 54
  Page, 17
  Presentations window, 17
  Products, 47
  Spreadsheets window, 18
  Support, 47
  Web Browser window, 20
  Worksheet, 19
Tan function, 352

targets, Web page, 302

technical support, 358

technotes, 336

Template Organizer tool

  brief description of, 57–59

  importing templates using, 147–148

  opening templates in, 235

  saving templates in, 99

  selecting templates in, 98

  starting, 97

templates

  for calculators, 145–146

  common list of, 96

  creating documents using, 56–59

  creating presentations from, 233–236

  creating spreadsheets from, 145–148

  downloading, 57, 96

  examples of, 56–57

  for grade school books, 146

  importing, 147–148

  for invoices, 145

  Lotus Symphony benefits, 29

  pre-build document settings, 95

  for purchase orders, 146

  read-only, 97

  saving, 95–97

  saving documents as, 96

  saving in Template Organizer tool, 99

  selecting, 98

  styles, 90–91

  template files, saving documents as, 61

  Template Organizer tool, 57–59

  uses for, 146–147

text

  accent marks, 85

  adding to documents, 66–67

  adding to endnotes, 122

  adding to presentations, 239–240

  background color, 84

  bold, 2, 84

  in bulleted lists, 243

  compressing, 85

  deleting from endnotes, 123

  in documents, copying, 68

  in documents, deleting, 68

  in documents, editing, 68–69

  effects, 85

  emphasis marks, 85

  font size, 82–83

  font styles, 79–82

  formatting, 78–79

  Insert Corrections feature, 69

  insertion point, 66

  italicized, 84

  language settings, 85

  in numbered lists, 243

  overwriting, 69

  properties, 84–86

  rotating, 85

  scale width, 85

  spacing between, 85

  stretching, 85

  strikethrough, 84

  style options, 85

  subscripts, 102–103

  superscripts, 102–104

  underlined, 84

  wrap options, 101

Text file format (TXT), 65, 130

themes, graphics, 274

ThinkFree Desktop suite, 28

three dimensional (3D) charts, 189

three dimensional (3D) Quickshape

  drawing object, 280

thumbnail views, 266

time calculations, 215–216

Time fields, inserting in documents, 117

Timer function, 352

Times New Roman font, 80, 82

TimeSerial function, 352

TimeValue function, 352

title bar

  Documents window, 15

  Presentations window, 16

  Spreadsheets window, 18

  Web Browser window, 20

titles
  chart, 191, 195–196
  Instant Layout feature, 241–242
TOC (table of contents)
  creation, 124–125
  headings and section, 124
  how to read, 126
  initial setup, 123–125
  outlining options, 125
  styles, 125
  updating, 125–126
Toolbar command (View menu), 21
toolbar reference card, 336
toolbars
  All Toolbars, 20
  basic description of, 20
  Documents window, 15
  moving, 21–22
  Presentations window, 17
  Spreadsheets window, 18
  turning on/off, 21
  Web Browser window, 20
  Zoom, 72
tools
  Arrange, 277
  Create Master Page, 271
  Eyedropper, 278–279
  Guide when Moving, 250
  Guideline Grid, 249–250
  Solve Equation, 218–221
  Spell Checker, 252
  Template Organizer, 57–59, 97–99,
    147–148, 235
Tools menu commands, 116, 126
transitions
  adding, 285–287
  applying to multiple pages, 287–288
  automatic advancement, 286
  build up effects, 284
  checkerboard effects, 285
  cross-fading effects, 284
  deleting, 288–289

  dissolve effects, 285
  editing, 287–288
  fade effects, 284
  fly-in effects, 284
  horizontal line effects, 285
  loops, 293
  open/close effects, 284
  previewing, 286
  random effects, 285
  roll effects, 284
  saving, 286
  Screen Show mode, 287
  speed settings, 285
  spiral effects, 284
  testing, 287
  uncover effects, 284
  vertical line effects, 285
  wavy line effects, 284
trial, demo and evaluation versions, 356
Trim function, 352
troubleshooting, 358
Troubleshooting forums, 334–335
turning on/off
  Guideline tool, 249–250
  rulers, 73, 251
  snap lines, 251–252
  toolbars, 21
tutorials, 336
TwipsPerPixelX function, 353
TwipsPerPixelY function, 353
two dimensional (2D) charts, 189
TXT (Text file format), 65, 130
typeface, font, 79–82
TypeName function, 353

UBound function, 353
UCase function, 353
uncover effects, 284
underlined text, 84

Uniform Resource Locators (URLs), 20, 302
Universal Network Objects, 349
Update command (Tools menu), 116, 126
updating
  chart data, 194
  cross-references, 116
  TOC (table of contents), 125–126
URLs (Uniform Resource Locators), 20, 302
user interface description, 11

• *V* •

vertical line effects, 285
vertical placement of rulers, 72–73
vertical rotation, 203
View menu commands
  Ruler, 73
  Toolbar, 21
viewing
  Master Page design, 268
  presentations, 245–248
Vintage Stock Art Web site, 278

• *W* •

wavy line effects, 284
Web Browser window, 19–20
Web hosting services, 311
Web pages
  adding graphics to, 304
  adding tables to, 303
  basic description of, 297
  bookmarks, 302
  browsers, 302
  buttons, 302
  displaying, 307–310
  HTML (Hypertext Markup Language), 298–299
  hyperlinks, 302–303
  page example, 298

publishing, 310–311
  saving files for, 304–305
  styles, 299–301
  targets, 302
  URLs, 302
Web servers, 311
Web sites
  AccuWeb, 311
  author, 336
  Clip Art, 275, 278
  ClipartConnection, 278
  OASIS, 130
  1&1 Internet, 311
  OpenOffice.org, 29
  Stock Art, 278
  Vintage Stock Art, 278
  Wiley Product Technical Support, 358
  W3C, 298
Weekday function, 353
width and height settings, presentations, 261
Wiley Product Technical Support Web site, 358
Windows Vista For Dummies (Rathbone), 355
Windows XP For Dummies (Rathbone), 355
Wingdings, 80
Word document (.doc)
  conversion items, 131–132
  converting, 133–134
  importing, 132–133
  saving files to, 133
Word Processing Document (WSX), 65
word processors
  defined, 14
  ease of use, 329–330
Word (Microsoft), 64–65
words, selecting in spreadsheets, 158–159
Worksheet tab (Spreadsheets window), 19

wrapped text, 101
WSX (Word Processing Document), 65
W3C Web site, 298

• X •

x-axis, chart data, 189, 191
Xor operator, 348
XY charts, 189

• Y •

y-axis, chart data, 189, 191
Year function, 353

• Z •

Zoho Office suite, 28, 130
zooming
    within documents, 72
    Presentation Zoom feature, 322–323
    during screen shows, 322–323
    settings, changing, 72
    viewing presentations, 247–248
    Zoom In button (Print Preview
        feature), 178
    Zoom Out button (Print Preview
        feature), 178
    Zoom toolbar, 72

Notes

Notes

Notes

Notes

BUSINESS, CAREERS & PERSONAL FINANCE

0-7645-9847-3

0-7645-2431-3

Also available:
- Business Plans Kit For Dummies
  0-7645-9794-9
- Economics For Dummies
  0-7645-5726-2
- Grant Writing For Dummies
  0-7645-8416-2
- Home Buying For Dummies
  0-7645-5331-3
- Managing For Dummies
  0-7645-1771-6
- Marketing For Dummies
  0-7645-5600-2

- Personal Finance For Dummies
  0-7645-2590-5*
- Resumes For Dummies
  0-7645-5471-9
- Selling For Dummies
  0-7645-5363-1
- Six Sigma For Dummies
  0-7645-6798-5
- Small Business Kit For Dummies
  0-7645-5984-2
- Starting an eBay Business For Dummies
  0-7645-6924-4
- Your Dream Career For Dummies
  0-7645-9795-7

HOME & BUSINESS COMPUTER BASICS

0-470-05432-8

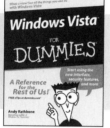

0-471-75421-8

Also available:
- Cleaning Windows Vista For Dummies
  0-471-78293-9
- Excel 2007 For Dummies
  0-470-03737-7
- Mac OS X Tiger For Dummies
  0-7645-7675-5
- MacBook For Dummies
  0-470-04859-X
- Macs For Dummies
  0-470-04849-2
- Office 2007 For Dummies
  0-470-00923-3

- Outlook 2007 For Dummies
  0-470-03830-6
- PCs For Dummies
  0-7645-8958-X
- Salesforce.com For Dummies
  0-470-04893-X
- Upgrading & Fixing Laptops For Dummies
  0-7645-8959-8
- Word 2007 For Dummies
  0-470-03658-3
- Quicken 2007 For Dummies
  0-470-04600-7

FOOD, HOME, GARDEN, HOBBIES, MUSIC & PETS

0-7645-8404-9

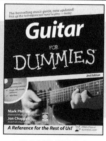

0-7645-9904-6

Also available:
- Candy Making For Dummies
  0-7645-9734-5
- Card Games For Dummies
  0-7645-9910-0
- Crocheting For Dummies
  0-7645-4151-X
- Dog Training For Dummies
  0-7645-8418-9
- Healthy Carb Cookbook For Dummies
  0-7645-8476-6
- Home Maintenance For Dummies
  0-7645-5215-5

- Horses For Dummies
  0-7645-9797-3
- Jewelry Making & Beading For Dummies
  0-7645-2571-9
- Orchids For Dummies
  0-7645-6759-4
- Puppies For Dummies
  0-7645-5255-4
- Rock Guitar For Dummies
  0-7645-5356-9
- Sewing For Dummies
  0-7645-6847-7
- Singing For Dummies
  0-7645-2475-5

INTERNET & DIGITAL MEDIA

0-470-04529-9

0-470-04894-8

Also available:
- Blogging For Dummies
  0-471-77084-1
- Digital Photography For Dummies
  0-7645-9802-3
- Digital Photography All-in-One Desk Reference For Dummies
  0-470-03743-1
- Digital SLR Cameras and Photography For Dummies
  0-7645-9803-1
- eBay Business All-in-One Desk Reference For Dummies
  0-7645-8438-3
- HDTV For Dummies
  0-470-09673-X

- Home Entertainment PCs For Dummies
  0-470-05523-5
- MySpace For Dummies
  0-470-09529-6
- Search Engine Optimization For Dummies
  0-471-97998-8
- Skype For Dummies
  0-470-04891-3
- The Internet For Dummies
  0-7645-8996-2
- Wiring Your Digital Home For Dummies
  0-471-91830-X

* Separate Canadian edition also available
* Separate U.K. edition also available

Available wherever books are sold. For more information or to order direct: U.S. customers visit www.dummies.com or call 1-877-762-2974.
U.K. customers visit www.wileyeurope.com or call 0800 243407. Canadian customers visit www.wiley.ca or call 1-800-567-4797.

SPORTS, FITNESS, PARENTING, RELIGION & SPIRITUALITY

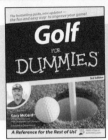

0-471-76871-5

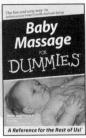

0-7645-7841-3

Also available:
- Catholicism For Dummies
  0-7645-5391-7
- Exercise Balls For Dummies
  0-7645-5623-1
- Fitness For Dummies
  0-7645-7851-0
- Football For Dummies
  0-7645-3936-1
- Judaism For Dummies
  0-7645-5299-6
- Potty Training For Dummies
  0-7645-5417-4
- Buddhism For Dummies
  0-7645-5359-3

- Pregnancy For Dummies
  0-7645-4483-7 †
- Ten Minute Tone-Ups For Dummies
  0-7645-7207-5
- NASCAR For Dummies
  0-7645-7681-X
- Religion For Dummies
  0-7645-5264-3
- Soccer For Dummies
  0-7645-5229-5
- Women in the Bible For Dummies
  0-7645-8475-8

TRAVEL

0-7645-7749-2

0-7645-6945-7

Also available:
- Alaska For Dummies
  0-7645-7746-8
- Cruise Vacations For Dummies
  0-7645-6941-4
- England For Dummies
  0-7645-4276-1
- Europe For Dummies
  0-7645-7529-5
- Germany For Dummies
  0-7645-7823-5
- Hawaii For Dummies
  0-7645-7402-7

- Italy For Dummies
  0-7645-7386-1
- Las Vegas For Dummies
  0-7645-7382-9
- London For Dummies
  0-7645-4277-X
- Paris For Dummies
  0-7645-7630-5
- RV Vacations For Dummies
  0-7645-4442-X
- Walt Disney World & Orlando
  For Dummies
  0-7645-9660-8

GRAPHICS, DESIGN & WEB DEVELOPMENT

0-7645-8815-X

0-7645-9571-7

Also available:
- 3D Game Animation For Dummies
  0-7645-8789-7
- AutoCAD 2006 For Dummies
  0-7645-8925-3
- Building a Web Site For Dummies
  0-7645-7144-3
- Creating Web Pages For Dummies
  0-470-08030-2
- Creating Web Pages All-in-One Desk
  Reference For Dummies
  0-7645-4345-8
- Dreamweaver 8 For Dummies
  0-7645-9649-7

- InDesign CS2 For Dummies
  0-7645-9572-5
- Macromedia Flash 8 For Dummies
  0-7645-9691-8
- Photoshop CS2 and Digital
  Photography For Dummies
  0-7645-9580-6
- Photoshop Elements 4 For Dummies
  0-471-77483-9
- Syndicating Web Sites with RSS Feeds
  For Dummies
  0-7645-8848-6
- Yahoo! SiteBuilder For Dummies
  0-7645-9800-7

NETWORKING, SECURITY, PROGRAMMING & DATABASES

0-7645-7728-X

0-471-74940-0

Also available:
- Access 2007 For Dummies
  0-470-04612-0
- ASP.NET 2 For Dummies
  0-7645-7907-X
- C# 2005 For Dummies
  0-7645-9704-3
- Hacking For Dummies
  0-470-05235-X
- Hacking Wireless Networks
  For Dummies
  0-7645-9730-2
- Java For Dummies
  0-470-08716-1

- Microsoft SQL Server 2005 For Dummies
  0-7645-7755-7
- Networking All-in-One Desk Reference
  For Dummies
  0-7645-9939-9
- Preventing Identity Theft For Dummies
  0-7645-7336-5
- Telecom For Dummies
  0-471-77085-X
- Visual Studio 2005 All-in-One Desk
  Reference For Dummies
  0-7645-9775-2
- XML For Dummies
  0-7645-8845-1

EALTH & SELF-HELP

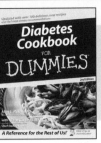

0-7645-8450-2

0-7645-4149-8

Also available:

Bipolar Disorder For Dummies
0-7645-8451-0

Chemotherapy and Radiation
For Dummies
0-7645-7832-4

Controlling Cholesterol For Dummies
0-7645-5440-9

Diabetes For Dummies
0-7645-6820-5* †

Divorce For Dummies
0-7645-8417-0 †

Fibromyalgia For Dummies
0-7645-5441-7

Low-Calorie Dieting For Dummies
0-7645-9905-4

Meditation For Dummies
0-471-77774-9

Osteoporosis For Dummies
0-7645-7621-6

Overcoming Anxiety For Dummies
0-7645-5447-6

Reiki For Dummies
0-7645-9907-0

Stress Management For Dummies
0-7645-5144-2

DUCATION, HISTORY, REFERENCE & TEST PREPARATION

0-7645-8381-6

0-7645-9554-7

Also available:

The ACT For Dummies
0-7645-9652-7

Algebra For Dummies
0-7645-5325-9

Algebra Workbook For Dummies
0-7645-8467-7

Astronomy For Dummies
0-7645-8465-0

Calculus For Dummies
0-7645-2498-4

Chemistry For Dummies
0-7645-5430-1

Forensics For Dummies
0-7645-5580-4

Freemasons For Dummies
0-7645-9796-5

French For Dummies
0-7645-5193-0

Geometry For Dummies
0-7645-5324-0

Organic Chemistry I For Dummies
0-7645-6902-3

The SAT I For Dummies
0-7645-7193-1

Spanish For Dummies
0-7645-5194-9

Statistics For Dummies
0-7645-5423-9

Get smart @ dummies.com®

- **Find a full list of Dummies titles**
- **Look into loads of FREE on-site articles**
- **Sign up for FREE eTips e-mailed to you weekly**
- **See what other products carry the Dummies name**
- **Shop directly from the Dummies bookstore**
- **Enter to win new prizes every month!**

Separate Canadian edition also available
Separate U.K. edition also available

ailable wherever books are sold. For more information or to order direct: U.S. customers visit www.dummies.com or call 1-877-762-2974.
K. customers visit www.wileyeurope.com or call 0800 243407. Canadian customers visit www.wiley.ca or call 1-800-567-4797.